Interest Groups
in American Society

L. Harmon Zeigler
G. Wayne Peak

University of Oregon

second edition

Interest Groups
in American Society

Prentice-Hall, Inc., Englewood Cliffs, New Jersey

ISBN: 0-13-469270-5
Library of Congress Catalog Card No.: 75-37142
Printed in the United States of America
10 9 8 7 6 5 4 3 2

Prentice-Hall International, Inc., *London*
Prentice-Hall of Canada, Ltd., *Toronto*
Prentice-Hall of Australia, Pty. Ltd., *Sydney*
Prentice-Hall of India Private Limited, *New Delhi*
Prentice-Hall of Japan, Inc., *Tokyo*

Contents

Interest Groups
in American Society

one

The Group
as a
Political Concept

The literature of political science abounds in terms that denote an aggregate of individuals—interest group, social or political movement, voluntary association, class, pressure group, organized interest, party, and so on. Some of these terms are used almost interchangeably; others have a very specific and unique meaning. If the student of politics is not to be overcome by the bewildering array of terms and if he is to understand precisely what is the subject of *Interest Groups in American Society*, we must explicitly define our concepts and reduce them to a more manageable number.

An *interest*, as we shall use the term, is a desire for, or concern over, either an abstract or a material political object.[1] According to our definition, then, persons who want the government to deliver mail twice instead of once a day, those

1

who want lower taxes, and those who want equal freedom for all men all have political interests. The objects of desire differ, to be sure— some desire a service, some an economic policy, and some an abstract value; nevertheless, each can be characterized as political. We shall refer to such objects as political *goods*, for they are either material or abstract things which people value.

When consensus does not exist over the acquisition of a particular political good, conflict occurs and the acquisition of that good becomes an *issue*. *Interest groups* are associations of individuals who share a desire for a contested political good. In the most general sense an interest group can be defined as a goal-seeking social aggregate. Such a definition, however, is too general for our purposes, because it would include all forms of organized human activity. Since our concern is with things political, a first step toward restricting the concept would be to include within our definition only those social aggregates which have political goals. Such an aggregate, however, could as well be a party or a government as an interest group. To exclude the notion of government as interest group we shall stipulate that to qualify as an interest group, a social aggregate must have as its goal some political objective which its members are incapable of obtaining by virtue of any formal political positions they may hold— either individually or collectively. Such a definition does not preclude interest groups from existing within the structure of government or from being composed of governmental officials; it merely states that such aggregates cannot satisfy their demands internally but must resort to externally-directed action for their goal fulfillment. This type of group will be discussed in more detail in later chapters.

We must also distinguish between political parties and interest groups, for both seek political goals; however, the natures of those goals differ markedly. The primary function of parties is seeking and gaining public office—filling an institutional political *role*. Interest groups, on the other hand, have as their primary function providing a political good or goods for their members. They may support candidates for public office, but they do so only as a tactic in their goal-seeking activity. Candidate support is incidental to the acquisition of political goods. To exclude parties from our definition, we shall assert that an interest group is a social aggregate which seeks political goods that it is incapable of providing for itself.

There remains only one additional qualification—that of organization. Implicit in the notion of goal-directed activity by a social aggregate is the idea of coordination, which in turn implies organization. As Peter Blau has observed,

An organization comes into existence when explicit procedures are established to coordinate the activities of a group in the interest of achieving specific objectives. The collective efforts of men may become formally organized either because all of them have some common interests or because a subgroup has furnished inducements to the rest to work in behalf of its interest.[2]

Consequently, the definition of "interest group" at which we have arrived and behind which we will stand is *an organized social aggregate which seeks political goods that it is incapable of providing for itself.* An alternative formulation of this definition is a collection of individuals who seek, through coordinated activity, to influence the political system without attempting to place group members in formal government offices.

It is important not to confuse the concepts of group interest and organized association. The former is a shared desire for a particular political good or set of political goods. Organization, on the other hand, is a manifestation of social technology; it is a means by which individuals coordinate their energies and resources toward accomplishing a common objective.

Pressure politics takes many forms and uses many varying types of techniques. Underlying these patterns, however, there is a basic common denominator of organization. The existence of an organization indicates that a collection of individuals have undergone a perceptive process sufficiently intense to stimulate a frequent rate of interaction. A very important distinction must be made between a goal-seeking aggregate and a mere collection of individuals who happen to have, through no conscious act, something "in common." For instance, it may be said that the individuals who happen to be waiting in line to be admitted to a theatre are a group in the physical sense of the word. The same may be said for a number of other types of similarities. Truman refers to this classification of individuals as "categoric groups." By this he means that there are endless varieties of categories to which every person might belong, such as alcoholics, people who make over $10,000 a year, and so on.[3] The goal-seeking group, however, is distinguished from the categoric group on the basis of interaction among its members. The interaction process is vital. The members of the goal-seeking aggregate may be observed to interact with one another in certain recurring patterns. Organization occurs when these patterns of interaction have become sufficiently formalized to justify the insurance of stability by institutionalization. Organization, then, represents a stage—a rather advanced stage—in the degree of interaction.

In the competition among interests, the existence of highly organized pressure groups is a factor of crucial importance. Organization represents a concentration of resources toward the realization of political influence. Organized structures of power can wield a predominant force when confronted by diffuse, unorganized interests. Therefore, if one could equalize all other factors it could be said that interests supported by organizations have a better chance of success than interests which do not enjoy the participation of organizations.

Although we have defined interest groups so that they encompass both the concept of interest and that of organization, these concepts must remain analytically distinct. Our ultimate objective is to understand as fully as possible the functioning of interest groups in the American political system. To do so we must recognize that the degree and type of a group's organization has as much bearing on its resulting political behavior as does the particular interest which binds its members together. The interplay between these two underlying facts of group life creates the wide diversity we observe in interest group activity.

In view of the variety of terms used to denote what we have defined as an interest group, we are compelled now to designate those which are encompassed by our particular usage. It is sufficient at this point merely to agree with Henry Ehrmann that "once it is determined that only those organizations which have a stake in the political process belong to the interest group universe, the term may be used interchangeably with 'pressure groups,' 'organized interests,' 'lobbies,' 'political groups,' or 'power groups.' "[4] To this list of synonyms we would add only "voluntary associations."

The historical existence of interest groups in America can be traced back even beyond its earliest years as a nation. A hasty perusal of *Federalists* No. 9 and No. 10 reveals clearly that the Founding Fathers recognized their existence. In fact, Charles A. Beard and subsequent political historians have argued that the Founding Fathers themselves constituted what might be called an interest group.[5] In 1835, Alexis de Tocqueville, commenting on his observations during an earlier trip to the United States, wrote:

> In no country in the world has the principle of association been more successfully used, or applied to a greater multitude of objects, than in America. Besides the permanent associations, which are established by law, under the names of townships, cities, and counties, a vast number of others are formed and maintained by the agency of private individuals.[6]

Given this long tradition of group activity, one would expect students of politics to have recognized it and to have studied group phenomena for many years. Surprisingly, only in relatively recent years has political science "discovered" the group.

THE INSTITUTIONAL BIAS OF NINETEENTH CENTURY POLITICAL RESEARCH

"Like all literature, writings on politics follow fashion," writes Heinz Eulau.[7] This remark should not be taken to mean that political scientists are frivolous in research design but rather to indicate that the study of politics is a constantly expanding discipline. E. Pendleton Herring has written that "political science as a subject of systematic inquiry started with Aristotle...."[8] There is little reason to dispute this claim. However, the purpose of this book is to explore an aspect of politics that has only recently become the object of professional inquiry. Although there may be some justification for Earl Latham's tracing of group theory to the writings of the English philosophical pluralists (Figgis, Maitland, G. D. H. Cole, and Harold Laski), there is a substantial consensus that the study of interest groups was given its first major emphasis with the appearance of Arthur Bentley's *The Process of Government* in 1908.[9] *The Process of Government*, as the title implies, described politics as a system whereby interest groups achieve a favorable allocation of social resources through the institutions of government. This means that the formal institutions of government, considered apart from the system of social pressures in which they function, are of slight significance. Bentley's book came at a period in the history of American political science in which research was heavily oriented toward the study of legally constituted structures. A relatively new discipline in colleges and universities, political science depended heavily on European jurisprudence as its intellectual cornerstone. The fundamental characteristic of political science at this time was its preoccupation with law. This meant that the legal aspects of political relations, particularly those legal aspects embodied in formal constitutions, served as an adequate guide to the realities of politics. By concerning themselves exclusively with governmental institutions—those organizations legally designated to perform specified tasks for the society—political scientists looked only to those who had formal authority. The basic problem of discovering the actual centers of power was not explored. As David Easton rightly declares, "Most tended to act as though the study of the distribution of power as delineated in the constitution constituted the core of political research."[10]

The state as the core of political science

A brief survey of some of the writings of this period will serve to illustrate their institutional bias. Theodore Woolsey's *Political Science or the State* considered the problem of showing how juristic concepts of "right" give meaning to institutions as manifested in formal constitutions. This discussion of philosophical rights is narrowly legalistic in that it shows no concern with underlying patterns of activity which operate through the institutions. Nor is there any interest in the people who helped to form the institutions. Government is thus portrayed as a purely mechanical device, almost as though it had a will of its own. Underlying this approach is the utilitarian concept of law as expressed by Jeremy Bentham. Woolsey, like Bentham, assumed that people are rational creatures. Therefore, all that is necessary to achieve political change is to issue laws formally establishing new relations and men will automatically adjust.[11] Law presumably exists in a sphere beyond the control of man.

The utilitarian preoccupation with law, as typified by Woolsey, was combined with reliance on the writings of German historians to produce the basic unit of research: the state. It was generally agreed that political science achieved the status of a unique academic discipline by means of its concern with the complex of institutions placed under the heading of "the phenomena of the state." At the first public meeting of the American Political Science Association in 1904, Professor Frank J. Goodnow outlined the nature of the field as "that science that treats of the organization known as the state."[12] This indicated that political research had merely extended its concern for law to a consideration of the source of law for a particular society. However, the same lack of awareness of patterns of activity underlying law became characteristic of the study of the state. One may rightly ask: What is this institution known as the state? There was no ready-made answer to this question. One writer records 145 separate definitions.[13] Woolsey defined the state as "the body or community which thus by permanent law, through its organs administers justice within certain limits of territory...."[14] However, there was no real agreement. Some writers, such as W. W. Willoughby, went so far as to embody the state with a juristic personality, with a life independent of the society over which it presumably exercised authority.[15] Political scientists wrote about the state as though the activities of people were of no importance. For instance, Goodnow classifies the legitimate fields of political inquiry into: (1) the expression of state will, (2) the content of state will as expressed, and (3) the execution of state will.

Hence the state was separated from its social context and studied in isolation. Political science limited itself to the study of the formal organization of the organs of state. This institutional approach was essentially static. The resulting method was almost exclusively descriptive and classificatory. The crucial problems were formal ones: bicameral government versus unicameral government, and the advantages of the American cabinet system versus the British parliamentary system.

The limitations of this narrow institutionalism are readily apparent. Consider, for example, a legal approach to democracy. From the purely legal standpoint, once a nation has representative government it has democracy. However, it can be verified empirically that such is not the case. Germany, for example, did not become a democracy after World War I although the accouterments of popular government, such as political parties and elections, were present. In other words, the description of a legal distribution of power cannot inquire into the problem of the degree to which the political behavior of the people in a particular society actually conforms to the legal prescription.[16] A legal description of American government would presumably lead one to the conclusion that the electoral college is a fundamental decision-making unit, while a study of the social patterns underlying the formal constitution would produce a contrary conclusion. To summarize, we paraphrase George E. G. Catlin, who suggested that the exponents of the legal approach assumed that the state is a clock in which we can take for granted the hand that winds it up and confine ourselves to a study of mechanism.[17]

The reaction against legalism

This type of research was not destined to remain long in the vanguard. Indeed, there was a revulsion from the extremities of the legal approach as early as 1885, when Woodrow Wilson published *Congressional Government*.[18] Other political scientists such as A. Lawrence Lowell and James Bryce exhibited a strong belief that political studies must have a relevance to the actualities of practical politics.[19] Noteworthy as these efforts were, they were still confined to formal institutions. Wilson described the representative branch of government in "realistic" terms while Bryce and Lowell were concerned with the activities of political parties. Bryce regarded the political party as the "great moving force" of politics, and did much in helping to bring about an empirical revolution in political research. Still, inquiry into the process of government as part of a more general social system was lacking. No one had yet sought to explain the importance of nongovernmental organizations such as organized interest groups; nor had the influence of environmental factors like social class, regional identification, and ethnic group loyalties been taken into account. Finally, although there was a growing interest in empirical research, the dominant trends of political science in the nineteenth century were clearly institutional and legal.

ARTHUR BENTLEY AND CONFLICT THEORY

Such was the nature of political knowledge when Bentley wrote. It would not be entirely correct to say that *The Process of Government* was a refutation of legalism, for Bentley's intellectual development stems from an entirely different tradition. While political science was concentrating on the legal aspects of politics, sociology (the field in which Bentley took his formal training) was dominated by the implications of Social Darwinism. In its original form, Social Darwinism was a rather rudimentary effort to transfer the findings of Darwin from the biological to the social sphere. In their original formulations, the famous doctrines of "the survival of the fittest" and the "struggle for existence" were incorporated into highly normative laissez-faire social theories by Herbert Spencer and William Graham Sumner. However, more systematic studies of society produced a more refined derivative which has been labeled "conflict theory." Among the more significant conflict theorists were Ludwig Gumplowicz, Gustav Ratzenhofer, Rudolph Von Jhering, and Albion Small, with whom Bentley studied at the University of Chicago. While most of these writers are clearly dated and of little significance considered alone, they are important because of Bentley's heavy reliance on them. Later, when we undertake a critical evaluation of Bentley, it will add to our comprehension if we understand the academic antecedents of the group theory of politics.

Among the conflict theorists who influenced Bentley's thought, there were two distinct schools. One approach, exemplified by Gumplowicz and Von Jhering, minimized the importance of the autonomous individual. The other approach, of which Ratzenhofer and Small are typical, began with the opposite assumption that the fundamental unit in society is the individual. The core of Gumplowicz's system is the doctrine that social change is wholly the product of social groups, intergroup conflict being the social analogue of the biological struggle for existence. In this conflict, the group is the primary element; the individual is entirely a product of group interaction and not a causal force. He maintains that sociologists can never know the origin of society but must assume the existence of social groups to start the process.

What are the groups on which social change depends? The groups which Gumplowicz uses in his interpretation are concrete physical entities consisting of people who can be separated from other groups. Actually the Gumplowicz type of group is little more than a refinement of the Marxian class.[20] They are perhaps most aptly described as tribes, hordes, or racial groups.

While the orientation of Gumplowicz is toward the group as a whole, the concern of Ratzenhofer and Small is the individual, who as a single rational unit combines with other persons to form groups. According to Ratzenhofer, every individual is endowed with certain inner forces of a psychic character, which he called "interests." The social process is the result of interaction between persons with conflicting interests. Both Ratzenhofer and Small developed a category of innate individual interests. While the two categories of individual interests are not important for our purposes, we should keep in mind that for both men the social process depended on conflicts between each individual's perception of his well-being. The individual is a complex package of instincts, needs, or desires conditioned by racial, economic, or other factors. However, only through participation in groups which represent these interests can satisfaction be achieved. The social process is thus the interaction between individuals who pool their resources with others of similar attitudes. Building from this foundation Ratzenhofer states, "The social process is a continual formation of groups around interests and a continual exertion of reciprocal influences by means of group action."[21]

The individual and group as activity

Bentley's place in the development of conflict theory is that of a synthesizer or amalgamator of the two variant strains of thought. In an extensive preparatory statement, Bentley refutes the Ratzenhofer–Small position of interpreting the social process in terms of the feelings, ideas, or attitudes of participants in political events. The activities of groups, he argues, must be interpreted as a reaction to the pressures of other groups rather than as a result of individual interaction. According to Bentley, the psychological attitudes of the individual are not an appropriate unit of study because there is no way of establishing a causal relationship between these attitudes and the formation of public policy. To Bentley, any satisfactory explanatory system must identify causes. As we have seen, one of the most commonly advanced "causes" among the conflict theorists was the individual attitude. Carried to its most extreme statement, as for example by Franklin Giddings, the argument stated that there is a measurable correlation between "cultural advancement" and inherent psychological attributes, the character of the individual thus forming the character of the society.[22] Rather than undertaking the tracing of social movements to individual attitudes, Bentley urged that the student of politics focus his attention on activity. The individual person as a bearer of attitudes is not a satisfactory unit of study; the appropriate unit is the activity of the individual. As stated by Charles B. Hagan, a leading interpreter of Bentley, "The individual is his activity."[23]

If the individual is his activity, it follows that the groups which interact in the political process can also be known only through activity. This means that Bentley's group is not at all similar to the Small model. Rather than a social aggregate, the Bentleyan group is in reality no more than a mass of purposive activity. In identifying the "raw material" of government, Bentley succinctly emphasizes his concern for activity: "It is first, last and always activity, action, 'something doing,' the shunting by some men of other men's conduct along changed lines, the gathering of forces to overcome resistance to such alterations, or the dispersal of one grouping of forces by another grouping."[24] This clearly means that the individual, in a science of politics, is a fiction. On the other hand, the physical or reified group which characterized Gumplowicz's writings is equally insignificant. The Bentleyan group is no more than a cross section of activity.

The notion of a scientific study of the process of politics, if it is to be based solely upon the group, is perhaps best stated in Bentley's words:

> If we can get our social life stated in terms of activity and nothing else, we have not succeeded in measuring it, but we have at least reached a foundation upon which a coherent system of measurement can be built up. Our technique may be very poor at the start . . . but we shall cease to be blocked by the intervention of immeasurable elements, which claim to be themselves the real causes of all that is happening, and which by their spook-like arbitrariness make impossible any progress toward dependable knowledge.[25]

This passage suggests one of several possible critical evaluations of Bentley based on the obvious fact that his writings are dated by an uncompromising hostility to introspective psychology, which he regarded as an "immeasurable element."

It may be seen that Bentley, while relying on the theories of the sociological conflict school, abstracted only a negligible portion in its original form. To summarize Bentley's definition of the group, it may be stated that the group is a conceptual device through which to view the flow of political activity. It does designate a certain portion of the individuals of a society—a mass of men not cut off physically from other masses but distinguished by a common activity. This does not preclude the people who participate in one pattern of activity from taking part in many simultaneous group activities. *Group* and *activity* are equivalent terms. The same may be said for the concept of interest. Whereas Ratzenhofer had designated interest as the individual's perception of his environment, Bentley equates interest with group activity: "The group and the interest are not separate. There exists only the one thing, that is, so many men bound together in or along the path of a certain activity."[26]

Politics as group conflict

When compared to the legal approach to the study of government, Bentley's *Process of Government* provides a refreshing note of candor. In assessing the ultimate significance of the book, David Easton's comment that "Bentley stands as the watershed between the simple realism of Wilson and the more complex realism of the group approach . . ." provides an adequate guide.[27] It would be a mistake to adopt an uncritical acceptance of Bentley's own peculiar approach. However, it would be equally erroneous to dismiss it because of some of its obvious ambiguities. Consider, for example, Bentley's approach to the idea of political reality. He maintained that political scientists had allowed their discipline to die by confining it to a "formal study of the most external characteristics of governing institutions" and, at most, a study of the action of men organized into the structure of government. What is lacking is a description of a deeper level of activity understood as group behavior. Governmental institutions, rather than possessing an independent existence, are products of "lower-lying political groups." Therefore, the process of government consists of the conflict among groups for the control of the activity of governmental institutions. Whereas the legalistic approach divorced governmental organizations from social interaction, Bentley interpreted such institutions as the product of social conflict: "We shall have to take all these political groups, and get them stated with their meaning, with their value, with their representative quality. We shall have to get hold of political institutions, legislatures, courts, executive officers, and get them stated as groups, and in terms of groups."[28]

Bentley thus stated that all aspects of government, including the abstract notion of the state, are phenomena of groups pressing against one another. Pressure seems to be transmitted from one group to another in what Easton has described as a "hydraulic" theory of power. It should be noted that this hydraulic theory can exist only on the assumption of a political system, or series of interrelated units. While Bentley dismissed the existence of a social whole or common interest, he did not exclude the idea of a social system. The political process is equated with the "equilibration of interests, the balancing of groups." The balance of group pressures is the existing state of society. Since he defines society as a system of interacting groups, the tendency toward a "balancing" among competing group interests suggests that there is a natural relatedness among the various parts of the process.

Confusion and Agreement

Bentley's "attempt to fashion a tool," as he called his book, lay dormant for many years; many of its implications, and nearly all of its limitations, were left unanswered. However, inquiry into the nature and activities of political interest groups was proceeding independently of the Bentleyan frame of reference. In 1928, Peter Odegard's *Pressure Politics* appeared.[29] This was an exhaustive examination of the origin and activities of the Anti-Saloon League. The history of this organization is traced from its beginnings as an abstract and unorganized social movement to a highly cohesive national lobby. Full attention is given to its extremely complicated techniques and strategies of pressure, and the countergroups arrayed in opposition to the Anti-Saloon League form part of the description. While there should be an adequate recognition of the pioneering significance of Odegard's effort, it was essentially a descriptive study with little or no emphasis on theoretical problems.

In 1929, E. Pendleton Herring exhibited a concern for theorizing about the role of groups in the political process. In *Group Representation Before Congress*, Herring examined the activities of more than 100 formal pressure groups.[30] His classification of these groups and his systematic examination of the reasons for their origin appear to be highly viable, and they clearly influenced the work of later writers such as David Truman. More important, Herring viewed the rising significance of organized groups as an indication of a reconstitution of human relationships. Although apparently unfamiliar with Bentley, Herring offers the following concept of the individual:

"[the individual] is a mere cipher in a larger and emergent unit: the organized group."[31] While the reliance on organized activity is too narrow, Herring's dismissal of the individual certainly is within the Bentleyan scheme.

Finally, mention should be made of E. E. Schattschneider's *Politics, Pressures and the Tariff*.[32] In describing the activities of economic-oriented organizations during the tariff revision legislation of 1929–30, Schattschneider not only affords some penetrating insights into group tactics, but also presents a series of categories through which to organize various types of pressure group activity. As valuable as these contributions are, they did not provide much help toward developing an adequate conceptual framework for the study of interest groups. More explicitly, the role of the individual in relation to the group needed further exploration.

Psychological attributes and group norms

As we have seen, Bentley recognized the individual only through his activity, never as an autonomous, introspective unit. The study of politics is the study of activity; "there is nothing of the social that is not activity of men." Accordingly, motives, desires, perceptions, and any other individual mental state must be disregarded. This particular aspect of interest group theory has been severely criticized on many grounds. One of the most common grounds for criticism is that Bentley himself was unclear. He seemed unable to rid his theory of individual mental states irrespective of his passionate insistence on the primacy of group activity. For instance, he states on the one hand that ideas and motives "give us absolutely no help in interpreting the doings of social men" and on the other hand:

> The "ideas" and "feelings" as set apart concretely, serve to indicate the values of the activities which are our raw materials . . . and yet there is not a shred of all the activity which does not present itself as an affair of feeling and intelligence. It cannot be stated with these phases left out. . . . It can only be stated as purposive activity . . . as the doings of wanting-knowing men in masses.[33]

Perhaps the best way of understanding the role of the individual is to state that a person's psychological attributes become matters for inquiry when they are used as a means of orientation toward the political world in which he participates. "Ideas" and "feelings" serve to give the individual man his orientation in the social activity in which he is involved; they serve to define him as an individual.

Professor Vernon Van Dyke, after a careful evaluation of Bentley's position with respect to the individual, reaches this conclusion: ". . . he tried to drive them [feelings, faculties, ideas, and ideals] from the field of inquiry—only to find that he could not get along without them. It seems much more sensible to grant that feelings, faculties, ideas, and ideals may help to explain behavior."[34] Group theorists who followed Bentley have, in fact, taken this "more sensible" approach. This is certainly true of David Truman, whose *The Governmental Process* is an explicit effort to put the formulations of Bentley to practical use. Truman defines an interest group as "any group that, on the basis of one or more shared attitudes, makes certain claims upon other groups in the society for the establishment, maintenance, or enhancement of forms of behavior that are implied by the shared attitudes." The individual, rather than serving primarily as an intersection of activity (as in Bentley), becomes the bearer of attitudes that serve to define the goals of the group. To understand the group, we must understand the attitudes, or "common interests," of the individuals whose activity comprises the observable behavior of the group.

David Truman's approach

Truman repudiates the notion that an emphasis on groups means the invalidation of the individual. He explains that the study of interest groups does not involve mystical entities such as the "group mind," which has a personality or will of its own: "a group is real only in the sense that the interactions that are the group can be observed."[35] This does not substitute the group for the individual but only implies that "when men act in consistent patterns, it is reasonable to study these patterns and designate them in collective terms."[36] Therefore, it is necessary on some occasions to study particular individuals, using the methods of the psychologist. The study of groups and the study of individuals are two approaches to the same thing.

A further clarification of Truman's repudiation of the existence of a conflict between individual and group is afforded by his treatment of the phenomena known as overlapping group affiliations. The individual, according to this notion, is never wholly absorbed in any group to which he belongs. Any person characteristically belongs to many groups, ranging from the primary or face-to-face groups through religious and economic affiliations and formal associations. Each organization or association may play a part in the policy formation process, and the demands of the various groups may conflict. As a consequence of overlapping affiliations, not all members of any given organization support the stated goals of the organization in equal degrees of intensity. There are many illustrations of overlapping affiliations. Consider, for example, the case of labor unions whose leadership is Communist dominated but whose membership is largely Catholic. On the issue of Soviet–American relations, about which the union members were exposed to conflicting influences, the individuals exhibited a strong tendency to withdraw from the conflict by losing interest in the subject.[37]

Truman's treatment of the individual is clearly more reliable than the rather crude Marxian determinism of, for example, Gumplowicz. By treating groups as fluid patterns of interactions rather than as static objects, individual differences are readily incorporated within group theory. It should be made clear that, while interest groups arise as a result of interaction based on shared attitudes, the attitudes themselves are formed by the group identifications of individuals. As soon as a child is old enough to play with groups of other children, he meets group influences and standards. A boy cannot act too differently from his friends if he is to be accepted. Workers may agree on an acceptable speed of production and exert sufficient pressure on "rate busters" who deviate from the accepted norm that the standards of the group will prevail. Such groups deliberately intend to exert pressure for uniformity of attitudes among their members. This is also true of other more formal groups such as churches and political parties. Informal groups induce conformity without the conscious intention of doing so and without the individual's awareness that it is happening. This is generally the case with patterns of interaction which, even though they have not been institutionalized into a formalized structure, may exert significant influence on each member's attitudes by means of informal standards of behavior.

We should not leave Truman's treatment of the individual without noting that he marshaled strong scientific support for his position. In psychology, reaction against the Freudian assumption that the person can be understood apart from his culture is illustrated by modern psychoanalytic theory as typified by Karen Horney and Harry Stack Sullivan. The essential conclusions of this type of psychoanalytic theory are that the basic forms of knowledge are collectivities, not particulars, and that what Freud regarded as "innate" personality traits are in fact induced as a result of interpersonal influences. In the words of George Herbert Mead,

The behavior of an individual can be understood only in terms of the behavior of the whole social group of which he is a member, since his individual acts are involved in larger social acts which go beyond himself. . . . We are not . . . building up the behavior in terms of the behavior of the separate individuals comprising it; rather we are starting out with a given social whole of complex group activity, into which we analyze (as elements) the behavior of separate individuals composing it.[38]

To conclude this section, we have learned that group theory, in its more refined form, rejects the idea that there is "a politics of individuals that opposes a politics of groups." However, the assumption of a group-versus-individual scheme is not absent from political theory in opposition to the group theory. One of Bentley's critics, Robert MacIver, for example, asserts that the individual is never fully amalgamated by society and always preserves some measure of autonomy. A more realistic statement would be that a person never gives himself completely to any group with which he identifies, whether the group is a formally organized pressure group or a barely discernible category such as region or chronological age. Further, there is no individual attitude which is exclusively determined by any single group. Nevertheless, attitudes are products of groups; there is no autonomous man. Alfred de Grazia accurately reflects the methodological bias of the group theorists by offering this analysis of "nongroup" attitudes: "Are they not in the last analysis a personal, private and, in an absolute sense, unique combination of his group roles? For instance, may not one man be . . . an 'old-socialist-atheist-majoritarian' and another man a 'young-Christian-socialist-pluralist'; whereupon both share roles as socialists but never think and act socialist in the same way?"[39]

VARIATIONS ON A THEME: POLITICS AND POWER

The political scientists discussed so far have, with varying degrees of clarity, defined politics as a struggle among competing groups. Another group of writers accepts this definition implicitly but approaches the problem from another angle. Rather than concentrating on the actors in the struggle for power (individuals and groups), they focus attention on the "political act." The political act may be understood as the "act of control, or as the act of human or social control." The leading students of the act of control are George E. G. Catlin, Harold Lasswell, and, to a degree, the late American political scientist V. O. Key.

What is power? First and foremost, it is a relational complex and not a tangible object to be possessed. Power cannot exist in a vacuum, but consists essentially of a relationship of "superordination and subordination, of dominance and submission, of the governors and the governed." The popularity voiced statement that a particular group "has" power does not adequately picture the fundamentally relational basis of power. Hence, to say that "big business" or the "labor bosses" have the power is not correct until we realize that there must be some group in relation to which the "powerful" unit is dominant.

George E. G. Catlin's concept of power

The relational aspects of political power are succinctly put by the English political scientist George E. G. Catlin. He, like the group theorists, complained against the institutional bias of traditional political science. All through Catlin's writing we find him searching for a science of politics. That is to say, he was groping for a way to develop highly probable generalizations about political behavior, much the same way in which the physical scientist develops generalizations about the behavior of atoms, molecules, and other units of the physical world. The only conceivable way in which this can be accomplished, argues Catlin, is for political scientists to locate a phenomenon which occurs with a frequency sufficient to warrant observation over an extended period of time. If we study the institution known as the state we will not locate enough of them to develop generalizations. The same holds true for other institutions such as legislatures or even organized groups.

The only phenomenon which occurs frequently enough to provide a basis for generalization is the political act, the act of control: "It appears . . . well to define politics . . . as a study of the act of control. . . ."[40] In approaching a more specific definition, Catlin enlarges on the idea of the political act. He begins with the notion of the individual will, that is, with the desire of every individual to satisfy his wants: "The science of politics has two axioms: first, that each man desires to 'have his own way' in life; secondly that men cannot avoid living together."[41] It appears from this statement that Catlin's political act is actually resting on an individualistic basis, much like the earlier Hobbesian struggle for power. This is not entirely accurate, for there is much in Catlin that resembles the group theories of Ratzenhofer and Small. The individual is indeed the political unit, or more correctly, the individual will (as distinct from the physiological individual) is what political scientists must study. The individual does not live in a world where the will is automatically transferred into the position of control. Rather, each individual will, in seeking fulfillment, meets resistance from opposing desires. The clash of wills necessitates a system of political activity, or struggle. What is the basic unit in this struggle? Catlin is very explicit on this point: "The unit in the construction of the political structure must remain the active individual, assenting or dissenting, supporting or weakening that structure, centripetal or centrifugal to that system. The individual is autonomous if not uninfluenced."

What role does the group play in this structure? In criticizing the idea of the state as a unit of study, Catlin maintains that society is not a collection of individuals bound into any unique organization such as the state. Society is "an aggregate of individuals organized into various groups, sometimes contrary, sometimes mutually inclusive, sometimes overlapping." In other words, the individual is prior to the group and selects on a rational basis the groups through which he can most readily realize his will. It is an individualistic ego satisfaction mechanism which lies at the heart of the group formation process. Groups exist only to magnify the individual's ego: "The liberty of man lies in his power of selection of the social group which he will support as order-keeping authority, or of the group to which he will go for political goods which he may happen to esteem even higher than peace and order. It lies in his power to choose his political market."[42]

The assumption of the rational, autonomous individual places Catlin's theory of power at the fringe of group theory as illustrated by the Bentley–Truman approach. This approach, as we have learned, posits a rejection of the idea that individuals exist in some degree of isolation and then form into groups. For example, Truman attacks the Italian sociologist Gaetano Mosca's assertion that men have an "instinct" for banding together in groups, on the ground that the notion of instinct assumes a temporal priority of the individual over the group. Much the same type of argument is offered by Bentley in his refutation of the theories of Ratzenhofer and Small that are also built on the foundation of individual desires.

Harold Lasswell's emphasis on symbols

Much more compatible with the development of the theory of group conflict are the writings of Harold Lasswell. He agrees with Catlin's emphasis on power, but does not approach the phenomenon through the narrow device of the autonomous individual. In one of his earlier studies, *Psychopathology and Politics*, he exhibited a tendency to rely strongly on the introspective psychoanalytic techniques of Freud in explaining political behavior. However, in 1955, at the American Psychological Association meeting in San Francisco, Lasswell read a paper entitled "Psychopathology and Politics: Twenty-Five Years After" in which he revised many aspects of his earlier position. Lasswell drew attention to his earlier work: "It is not surprising to find that Freud continued to talk about 'man' versus 'society' rather than to recognize that it is always a case of 'man in society' versus (or with) 'man in society.' "[43]

"Man in society versus (or with) man in society" are the participants in the political process. However, Lasswell's more complete definition of politics does not take as its first premise the struggle for power as a result of individual wills (which seems to suggest that those who pursue power adopt power as an end in itself rather than as a means to an end). A more explicit statement of his concept of the political process is found in *World Politics and Personal Insecurity*:

> Political analysis is the study of the changes in the shape and composition of the value patterns of society. Representative values are safety, income, and deference. Since a few members of any community at any given time have the most of each value, a diagram of the pattern of distribution of any value resembles a pyramid. The few who get the most of any value are the *elite*; the rest are the rank and file. An elite preserves its ascendancy by manipulating symbols, controlling supplies, and applying violence. Less formally expressed, politics is the study of *who gets what, when, and how.*[44]

Since the distribution of values depends on the influence of the members of society, the study of politics is a "study of influence and the influential." In *Power and Society*, written in collaboration with Abraham Kaplan, a more comprehensive description of the relation of power to values is given: "The political act takes its origin in a situation in which the actor strives for the attainment of various values for which power is a necessary (and perhaps also sufficient) condition."[45]

Lasswell's framework is useful in understanding the operations of political pressure groups, for we can certainly substitute "group" for "actor" in the political formula defining the political act. Thus politics is a process through which competing patterns of activity (which may take the form of organized groups) seek to enforce forms of behavior consistent with their values. One should be quick to point out, however, that Lasswell did not use the term *group* as though it were the exclusive actor in the political act. His definition of a group is simply "an organized aggregate" whereas an interest group is "an interest organized for the satisfaction of the interest." The reliance on organizations as a requisite for the existence of a group is fundamentally different from the definition of either Bentley or Truman. However, Lasswell correctly noted that the political scientist should interest himself neither in individuals nor in groups as "social atoms" but rather in interaction among competitors for the achievement of goals.

A significant contribution by Lasswell, which has only recently come into extensive use, is his treatment of political symbols. None of the major group theorists deal extensively with problems of perception, but Lasswell has always addressed himself to cognitive processes and particularly to nonrational responses to emotionally powerful symbols. He wrote that "politics is the process by which the irrational bases of society are brought out into the open" and that "widespread and disturbing changes in the life-situation of many members of society" produce reactions that are stated largely in symbolic terms bearing only a limited relevance to actual needs: "The political symbol becomes laden with the residue of successive positive and negative identifications, and with the emotional charge of displaced private motives."[46] Lasswell further argues that political symbols, because of their emotional qualities and ambiguities of reference in relation to individual experience, are ideally suited to the satisfaction of group demands. However, Lasswell was not specific as to the conditions under which political symbols play a major role in the political process.

Murray Edelman, a political scientist whose writings are based on the concept of politics as a struggle among groups, has built on Lasswell's treatment of symbols. He argues that, although public policy may be understood as "the resultant of the interplay among groups," there are patterns of group activity whose essential characteristic is interest in symbols. The symbol-oriented activity may be distinguished from what Edelman calls "interest in tangible resources." The two varying types of group activity are summarized by Edelman in this manner:

> (1) Pattern A: a relatively high degree of organization—rational, cognitive procedures—precise information—an effective interest in specifically identified, tangible resources—a favorably perceived strategic position with respect to reference groups—relatively small numbers. (2) Pattern B: shared interest in the improvement of status through protest activity—an unfavorably perceived strategic position with respect to reference groups—distorted, stereotyped, inexact information and perception—response to symbols connoting suppression of threats—relative ineffectiveness in securing tangible resources through political activity—little organization for purposeful action—quiescence—relatively large numbers.[47]

Edelman's contribution to the theory of groups in politics, which consists essentially of a synthesis of Lasswell with more traditional interpretations, provides a useful guide to the study of certain types of political movements, especially the "extremist" type activity.

GROUP INTEREST AND PUBLIC INTEREST

In the popular vernacular, as well as in more academic discussions, the term *public interest* has come in for more than its share of interpretations. During the Eighty-first Congress, the House of Representatives created a Select Committee on Lobbying Activities (popularly referred to as the Buchanan Committee) to investigate the nature and extent of organized group pressures on the representative branch of government. George Galloway, a political scientist who testified before the Buchanan Committee, presented his view of the responsibility of Congress to the public interest: "The primary responsibility of Congress is to promote the general welfare. . . . No public policy could ever be the mere sum of the demands of organized special interests, . . . for there are vital common interests that cannot be organized by pressure groups."[48] The difficulty of assuming the existence of a public interest is very easily recognized. What are these vital common interests? The Buchanan Committee never undertook the task of specifying such overriding goals, nor has there ever been a clear formulation of the components of a hypothetical general interest. Indeed, even when we list values on which everyone would presumably agree, such as the survival of the nation or the education of the young, we find widely ranging conceptions of the true expression of the general will. In time of war there are pacifists, conscientious objectors, and others who apparently do not agree that the interest of the nation is best pursued by the waging of armed conflict. Can we say that proper education of our children is a common interest when the public authorities of Prince Edward County, Virginia, prefer no education to integrated facilities?

A realistic approach to the public interest

The subscribers to the group theory of politics do not agree that it is possible to isolate a national interest beyond that of the interests of the many social aggregates encompassed within the boundaries of the nation. There are, says Bentley, "always some parts of the nation to be found arrayed against other parts." Even before the development of an explicit group theory we find evidence of skepticism about the existence of a common interest. Over a century ago John C. Calhoun said that the general will "instead of being the united opinion of the whole community is usually nothing more than the voice of the strongest interest or combination of interests; and not infrequently a small but energetic and active portion of the people."[49] Compare Calhoun's statement with Bentley's claim that ". . . we shall never find a group interest of society as a whole. . . . The society itself is nothing other than the complex of the groups that compose it" and with Truman's synthesis: "In developing a group interpretation of politics . . . we do not need to account for a totally inclusive interest because one does not exist," and the position of the group theorists may be understood. Stated in its briefest version, the group theorists' doctrine maintains that every public policy helps someone and hurts someone; laws operate to the advantage of some groups and to the disadvantage of others.

The criticism of this aspect of group theory falls into two classes: (1) normative objections based on the assumption that the denial of a common interest undermines the foundations of democratic society; and (2) methodological objections claiming that the attribution of primary causal force to groups neglects the integrative function of institutions and political culture. The first charge, that group theory is anti-democratic, is well illustrated by Robert MacIver's criticism of Bentley which, as Richard Taylor points out, is based on a misunderstanding of *The Process of Government*.[50] MacIver interprets Bentley as believing that "a legislative act is always the calculable resultant of a struggle between pressure groups, never a decision between opposing conceptions of the national welfare." MacIver concludes that "the fact that the interest in the common welfare cannot be organized after the fashion of specific interest should not conceal from us either its existence or the need to sustain it. Democracy itself is the final organization of the common interest."[51]

Postponing for the moment the necessity of dealing with concepts of democracy, we may easily see that MacIver has attributed to group theory a far more deterministic nature than it actually possesses. Surely it would be useless to maintain that all public policy is a result of the conflict of organized "pressure groups." The slightest inquiry into empirical evidence would convince the student that many laws are passed not only without the support of organized groups but frequently in opposition to the demands of such organizations. When a congressman issues a press release announcing his intention to support or oppose a particular bill in "the interest of the public" in spite of the pressure of "minority interests," we cannot assume that this is merely a rationalization. Surely the congressman believes he is acting in the public interest. This is the key to the problem. Each legislator (or administrator) is an actor in the decision-making process. As an individual he is a member of many groups, yet none of these groups commands his total loyalty. His perception of a particular situation will be the result of the complex pressures of this variety of affiliations. For example, a congressman from a rural Republican district (to list only two of many possible affiliations) might well believe that the continuation of the foreign aid program is not in the "national interest."

Pendleton Herring adequately expresses a group interpretation of the public interest: "Its value is psychological and does not extend beyond the significance that each responsible [public] servant must find in the phrase for himself. . . ."[52] The evaluation that each person in a position of responsibility gives to opposing presentations of the public interest may well be heavily influenced by the activities of organized lobbying associations, but these associations are not the sole determinants of the content of a decision. In short, instead of public policy "never" resulting from opposing conceptions of the national welfare, as MacIver maintained, it is the position of the group theorists that opposing conceptions of the national welfare constitute the very heart of the political process.

The importance of institutions

The second criticism of group theory, that it does not provide an accurate account of the role of institutions and environmental conditions, is more valid. Writing at his particular period in the development of political science, Bentley perhaps overstated his case by urging that we "get hold of political institutions, legislatures, courts, executive officers, and get them stated as groups, and in terms of groups." Is it not possible that these institutions not only react to group pressure, but also help to mold the structure of group action? Later writers, particularly Truman, have given more importance to governmental institutions as actors in the political process. It would be a false realism which described the agencies of government as passive pawns rather than active participants. In many cases, government administrators have identified with the interests of unorganized segments of the population in opposition to cohesive and well organized interests as, for example, in the pursuit of antitrust litigation.

However, when group theorists are criticized for failing to give proper attention to institutions, the word *institution* is usually employed in a more general sense. In this broader use of the word, institution denotes a stable pattern of behavior. Defined in this way, institutions consist of stylized or regularized patterns of behavior. They reflect conformity in behavior. Merle Fainsod diagnosed the failure of Bentley to come to grips with the broader "institutional matrix" within which groups operate. He maintained that there are "conditional factors" which combine to form the institutional framework within which group conflict is waged.[53]

The institutional context may consist partially of broad, inclusive, or widely shared attitudes which may very logically be called a common interest. Various terms have been given to these widely shared attitudes. Truman refers to them as "rules of the game"; Austin Ranney speaks of "consensus" while Seymour Lipset prefers "legitimacy."[54] Whatever the term employed, the essential meaning is the same. In any society there is a "way of doing things." The continued stability of a political system rests on the degree to which there is a substantial agreement among the members of the community that they should continue to operate as a community. Truman has greatly improved the reliability of group theory by his recognition of the existence of a broad social system:

> We cannot deny the obvious fact that we are examining a going political system that is supported or accepted by a large proportion of the society. We cannot account for such a system by adding up in some fashion the National Association of Manufacturers, the Congress of Industrial Organizations, the American Farm Bureau Federation, the American Legion and other groups that come to mind when "lobbies" and "pressure groups" are mentioned. . . . Were such the exclusive ingredients of the political process in the United States, the entire system would have torn itself apart long since.[55]

What Truman is implying is that patterns of group organization and activity may be derived from factors other than an isolated or totally inclusive struggle among the groups themselves.

To summarize what we have learned about groups and the social system we must recognize that whether a group is successful in its quest for the fulfillment of its goals depends on its role within the "total way of life of the population." This includes not only widely shared attitudes but also more readily observable factors such as "the degree of separation of formal authority, the degree of legitimacy accorded formal authority, and the lack of representation of interests in the representative structure of government."[56]

From a brief outline of the historical development of group theory, it is obvious that group theory has limitations and is often contradictory. Indeed, much of the criticism of the group theory of politics is that none of its exponents have been able to agree on the nature of groups. Nevertheless, the activities of groups have a bearing on the shape of public policy. It now becomes our task to inquire into the manner in which interest groups are able to have some effect on the kinds of decisions made by the political mechanisms of a society. To do so requires that we first understand the milieu in which interest groups operate.

NOTES

[1]This is admittedly a departure from traditional definitions of interest such as a "*conscious* desire to have public policy, or the authoritative allocation of values, move in a particular general or specific direction" [Joseph G. LaPalombara, *Interest Groups in Italian Politics* (Princeton University Press, 1964), p. 16]. Nevertheless, the broader definition we have used is, in our opinion, more consistent with the phenomena we are studying. This fact should emerge more clearly in Chapter 3.

[2]Peter M. Blau, "Organizations," *International Encyclopedia of the Social Sciences*, ed. David L. Sills, XI (1968), pp. 297–98 (New York: The Macmillan Company and The Free Press).

[3]David Truman, *The Government Process* (New York: Alfred A. Knopf, 1951), p. 23.

[4]Henry W. Ehrmann, "Interest Groups," *International Encyclopedia of the Social Sciences*, VII, p. 486.

[5]See Charles A. Beard, *An Economic Interpretation of the Constitution of the United States* (New York: The Macmillan Company, 1913).

[6]Alexis de Tocqueville, *Democracy in America*, edited and abridged by Andrew Hacker, revised translation by Francis Bower (New York: Washington Square Press, 1964), p. 71.

[7]Heinz Eulau, "Political Science," in Bert F. Hoselitz, ed., *A Reader's Guide to the Social Sciences* (New York: The Free Press, 1959) p. 89.

[8]E. Pendleton Herring, "On the Study of Government," *American Political Science Review*, XLVII (Dec. 1953), p. 961.

[9]Arthur Bentley, *The Process of Government* (San Antonio, Tex.: Principia Press of Trinity University, 1949).

[10]David Easton, *The Political System* (New York: Alfred A. Knopf, 1953), p. 71.

[11]Theodore Woolsey, *Political Science or the State* (New York: Charles Scribner's Sons, 1878).

[12]Frank J. Goodnow, "The Work of the American Political Science Association," *Proceedings of the American Political Science Association*, I (1904), p. 37.

[13]C. H. Titus, "A Nomenclature in Political Science," *American Political Science Review*, XXV (Feb. 1931), p. 45. Cited in Easton, *op. cit.*, p. 107.

[14]In Raymond G. Gettell, *Readings in Political Science* (Boston: Ginn and Co., 1911), p. 19.

[15]W. W. Willoughby, *The Nature of the State* (New York: The Macmillan Company, 1896), p. 3. See also John W. Garner, "The Relations of Political Science," *American Journal of Sociology*, XII (Nov. 1906), pp. 341–66.

[16]See Seymour Martin Lipset, *Political Man* (Garden City, N.Y.: Doubleday & Co., 1959) for an analysis of the social requisites of democracy.

[17]George E. G. Catlin, *A Study of the Principles of Politics* (London: George Allen and Unwin, 1930), pp. 66–71.

[18]Woodrow Wilson, *Congressional Government* (Boston: Houghton Mifflin Company, 1885).

[19]For a history of the development of realism in political research see Bernard Crick, *The American Science of Politics* (Berkeley: University of California Press, 1959), pp. 95–117.

[20]Emory S. Bogardus, *The Development of Social Thought* (New York: Longmans, Green and Co., 1940), pp. 364–66.

[21]Cited in Barnes and Becker, *op. cit.*, p. 718. See also Albion Small, "Ratzenhofer's Sociology," *American Journal of Sociology*, XIII (Jan. 1908), pp. 433–38.

[22]Franklin Giddings, "The Basis of Social Conflict," *American Journal of Sociology*, XIII (Mar. 1908), p. 645.

[23]Charles B. Hagan, "The Group in a Political Science," in Roland Young, ed., *Approaches to the Study of Politics* (Evanston, Ill.: Northwestern University Press, 1958), p. 45.

[24]Arthur Bentley, *The Process of Government*, p. 176.

[25]*Ibid.*, p. 202.

[26]*Ibid.*, p. 211.

[27]Easton, *op. cit.*, p. 177.

[28]Bentley, *op. cit.*, p. 210.

[29]Peter H. Odegard, *Pressure Politics: The Story of the Anti-Saloon League* (New York: Columbia University Press, 1928).

[30]E. Pendleton Herring, *Group Representation Before Congress* (Baltimore: Johns Hopkins University Press, 1929).

[31]*Ibid.*, pp. 5–6.

[32]E. E. Schattschneider, *Politics, Pressures and the Tariff* (Englewood Cliffs, N.J.: Prentice-Hall, 1935).

[33]Bentley, *op. cit.*, p. 177.

[34]Vernon Van Dyke, *Political Science: A Philosophical Analysis* (Stanford, Calif.: Stanford University Press, 1960), p. 148.

[35]David Truman, *The Government Process*, p. 29.

[36]*Ibid.*

[37]This example is taken from *ibid*, p. 163. For other examples of overlapping affiliations see Paul Lazarsfeld, Bernard Berelson, and Hazel Gaudet, *The People's Choice* (New York: Columbia University, 1948), and Robert E. Lane, *Political Life* (New York: The Free Press, 1959), pp. 197–203.

[38]George Herbert Mead, *Mind, Self and Society* (Chicago: University of Chicago Press, 1934), pp. 6–7.

[39]Alfred de Grazia, "Interest Group Theory in Political Research," *Annals of the American Academy of Political and Social Science* (Sept. 1958), p. 116.

[40]Catlin, *Principles of Politics*, p. 69.

[41]*Ibid.*, p. 137.

[42]*Ibid.*, pp. 371–75. Much of Catlin's early writing has been reiterated in *Systematic Politics* (Toronto: University of Toronto Press, 1962).

[43]The first edition of *Psychopathology and Politics* was published by the University of Chicago Press in 1930. The paper referred to above was printed as an appendix to Harold Lasswell, *Psychopathology and Politics*, rev. ed. (New York: The Viking Press, 1960), pp. 269–319.

[44]Harold Lasswell, *World Politics and Personal Insecurity* (New York: The Free Press, 1950), p. 3.

[45]Harold Lasswell and Abraham Kaplan, *Power and Society* (New Haven, Conn.: Yale University Press, 1950), p. 240.

[46]Lasswell, *Psychopathology and Politics*, pp. 188–93.

[47]Murray Edelman, "Symbols and Political Quiescence," *American Political Science Review*, LIV (Sept. 1960), p. 701. The patterns of activity described by Edelman offer the possibility of comparison with the theory of William Kornhauser. In his *The Politics of Mass Society* (New York: The Free Press, 1959) Kornhauser distinguishes between mass or pluralistic movements and elites and suggests that the social strata with the fewest social ties are more responsive to mass movements. Some examples which Kornhauser gives of mass versus elites are new business versus old business, small business versus big business, unskilled workers versus skilled workers, and poorer farmers and farm laborers versus wealthier farmers. See p. 223.

[48]House Select Committee on Lobbying Activities, *Hearings, The Role of Lobbying in Representative Self Government*, 81st Cong., 2nd Sess. (Washington, D.C.: Government Printing Office, 1950), p. 99.

[49]John C. Calhoun, *A Disquisition on Government*, in Benjamin F. Wright, ed., *Source Book of American Political Theory* (New York: The Macmillan Company, 1929), p. 537.

[50]Richard W. Taylor, "Arthur F. Bentley's Political Science," *Western Political Quarterly*, V (June 1952), p. 219.

[51]Robert MacIver, *The Web of Government* (New York: The Macmillan Company, 1948), p. 220.

[52]Herring, *Public Administration and the Public Interest* (New York and London: McGraw-Hill Book Company, Inc., 1936), p. 24. For a stimulating analysis of perceptions of group interests by legislators see John C. Wahlke, William Buchanan, Heinz Eulau, and Leroy Ferguson, "American State Legislators' Role Orientations Toward Pressure Groups," *Journal of Politics*, XXII (May 1960), 203–27.

[53]Merle Fainsod, "Some Reflections on the Nature of the Regulatory Process," in Carl Friedrich and Edward S. Mason, eds., *Public Policy* (Cambridge, Mass.: Harvard University Press, 1940).

[54]Truman, *op. cit.*, p. 159, Lipset, *op. cit.*, pp. 77–83. Austin Ranney and Willmoore Kendall, *Democracy and the American Party System* (New York: Harcourt, Brace & World, 1956), p. 54.

[55]Truman, *op. cit.*, p. 51.

[56]De Grazia, *op. cit.*, p. 115. For criticism of group theory for failure to account for institutional factors see Samuel J. Eldersveld, "American Interest Groups: A Survey of Research and Some Implications for Theory and Method," in Henry W. Ehrmann, ed., *Interest Groups on Four Continents* (Pittsburgh: University of Pittsburgh Press, 1958), p. 187; and Roy C. Macridis, "Interest Groups in Comparative Analysis," *Journal of Politics*, XXIII (Feb. 1961), pp. 34-38.

two

The American Democratic Environment

Interest groups in the United States function in a many-faceted environment. It would be presumptive as well as foolhardy to attempt to specify all the environmental factors that affect interest group activities, for such factors are too numerous and transitory to be catalogued. Moreover, any systematic categorization of them is foredoomed to be somewhat arbitrary. Therefore, we do not claim that the following discussion of the American political environment is exhaustive, or that alternative conceptual schemes are wrong. We do maintain, however, that the discussion isolates the major categories of agents which affect the general functions of interest groups and lets us view those agents within the socio-political matrix in which they exist. We shall examine four areas of environmental factors—social evolution, the political culture, the social culture, and political institutions.

Social Evolution

In Chapter 1, we defined an interest group as an *organized* social aggregate which seeks political goods that it is incapable of providing for itself. Organization presupposes common goals and a minimal degree of formalization of the patterns of interaction among group members. Yet not all interests which are widely shared become bases for concerted group action. An outstanding example of such a "non-group" is household consumers. The consuming public share an interest in keeping the prices of consumer products low, packaging and advertising fair, and quality high. Individually, consumers often feel that they are being taken advantage of, yet little effort has gone into organizing them into a potent group. The few attempts at such organization have been either ineffective or extremely short-lived.[1] Consumers, although they share a common interest, remain only a potential, or latent, group. Why do some interests become centers for formalized, instrumental interaction patterns while others remain only latent? The best way to approach some understanding of the nature of formal pressure groups is to undertake a comparative description of cultures, both primitive and complex, in order to perceive common occurrences in the formation of political associations.

The most plausible body of theory suggests that increase in task specialization or division of labor provides the most frequent stimulation for the beginning and maintenance of new interaction patterns. The study of primitive societies suggests that, in most cases, associations of a subcommunity type do not exist. Such societies, described by William Graham Sumner as "small groups scattered over a territory," are characterized by a strong feeling of loyalty to the total group.[2] Because of acute physical isolation from other peoples, the primitive community usually develops a strong "we-feeling" directed against all out-groups. "Thus a differentiation arises between ourselves, the we-group or in-group, and everybody else, or the others-groups, out-groups."[3] Despite little communication with outsiders, the primitive community reinforces ethnocentrism by means of intimate internal patterns of communication. The people are very much alike; there is great homogeneity and not much division of labor. "What one man knows and believes is the same as what all men know and believe."[4] This strong feeling of solidarity, minimizing the development to subloyalties, can be seen in Radcliffe-Brown's description of the economics of the Andaman Islanders:

> Within the local group there is no such thing as a division of labor save as between the sexes. Every man is expected to hunt pig, to harpoon turtle, and to catch fish, and also to cut a canal, to make a bow and arrows, and all the other objects that are made by men.[5]

Such a society would afford little opportunity for the development of conflicting interests. In addition to the feeling of total solidarity, social relations within the community are highly ordered by custom and tradition, which also reduces the chances of conflict. If studying the precedents embodied in tribal lore can solve every new issue, legislation has no place in the development of social order. Succession to positions of authority in the social and political hierarchy is regulated in a similar manner and is subject to only minimal discussion. The final solution to most social or political problems that are liable to arouse conflicts of interests is found in the "cake of custom."[6]

This brief résumé of primitive political organization is an "ideal type" to which there are exceptions. Some primitive societies have developed more specialization than others. However, in such societies, associations are usually the product of relations that develop unintentionally or are the result of complementary usefulness to members of the group. They are not deliberately entered into to achieve ends implied in shared attitudes. Familial institutions, which are the most durable primitive subgroup, are of this type. In some cases these institutions, extended beyond the immediate family into clan-like groups, are able to restore equilibrium in the face of sudden change. Still, these organizations stem from involuntary characteristics rather than conscious efforts.

Societies which acknowledge subgroup loyalties only in terms of primary groups generally exhibit a paucity of formal associations. In some advanced situations, tenacity of primary-group identification reduces the possibility of the development of more broadly based groups. In Ceylon, for example, although rice and rubber form the base of the economy, there is sufficient diversity to allow for the development of conflicting attitudes. Nevertheless, interest groups on the formal level are almost nonexistent and certainly suffer a high mortality rate. The central government has attempted to develop trade associations and occupational groups among the villages, but most of these have become inoperative shortly after their inception. The growth of special interest groups has been difficult and tedious because the people are not "easy joiners" and have little inclination to organize beyond the primary group. Most interest groups in Ceylonese villages are actually informal leadership cliques serving the entire village. They function less as special interest groups within the community than as village leadership units directing activity for the entire population.[7]

Other attempts at organization under similar conditions produce comparable results. The transformation of a Navaho society from a pastoral to a wage-earning economy by the construction of a natural gas line over a reservation would seem to create a situation of sufficient challenge to the psychological equilibrium of individuals to require the formation of associations to restore balance. Undergoing their first experience as wage earners, Navaho males were subject to entirely new paths of interaction. However, an attempt to organize them for a strike was a total failure. The Navaho, who had never been accustomed to groups beyond kinship organizations, exhibited no tendency to identify with his fellow workers, felt no solidarity or "class consciousness," and remained unaffected by the appeals of organized labor.[8]

The same conditions proved true for a village in southern Italy and among the small farmers of rural Ireland where the nuclear family dominates.[9] In Ireland, the farm is the center of kinship relations. It is not an economic interest to be exploited, but rather an institution to contribute to the stability of the family system. Small farmers showed no feeling of solidarity with a rural community and felt no desire to interact with members of their occupational group. In spite of economic regressions, the small farmer has clung to traditional patterns of interaction, seeking equilibrium within the kinship system. The family is isolated and fiercely loyal in much the same way as the primitive tribe. "There has never been a vital community larger than the family to act as a focus of cooperation, motivation, or change."[10] On the other hand, larger farm owners, with more contacts outside the family, more specialization in products, and a continuous exchange of goods and services with other members of the rural community, are successfully organized into commodity groups and into a general association known as the People of the Soil.

These illustrations suggest that, while associational activity is the result of change in the life-styles of individuals, under some circumstances it is likely that an individual whose life-style has been disturbed will interact with people with whom he has already established tangent relations. "Individuals who need to interact with someone to compensate for the disturbances in the institutions in which they have habitually interacted, do so along channels already in existence."[11] The failure of the individual to interact beyond the traditional primary group in response to chance circumstances seems to depend on the intensity with which perceptions of crisis were geared to the family as an equilibrating mechanism. This intensity of perception may vary from society to society. Generally, however, there is a relation between rapid population shifts and the sufficient differentiation of society to permit the development of formal organizations. While this would lead us to expect that rapid growth of associations is to be expected as a characteristic of urban society, it is incorrect to assume that urbanization per se is a fundamental cause of interest groups. Farm organizations are generally conceded to be influential in some aspects of American politics. Nevertheless, the complexities and impersonalization of urban life do lay the groundwork for a rapid growth and greater diversity of organizations. To depart momentarily from primitive culture, the medieval synthesis of church and state made it improbable that the individual could be a member of any other organization. In the late middle ages, guilds developed as a response to the crumbling of traditional loyalties and increasing economic differentiation. Writing on the nature of voluntary organizations, Rose notes that "one of the most characteristic features of the shift from medieval to modern times is the rise of groups with specialized interests *within* the community."[12] One might add that formal interest groups are most likely to develop in the more democratic countries. In modern totalitarian societies there are, at least officially, no groups beyond the party or social mechanism that control the apparatus of the state.

Although emotional instability due to rapid urban migration is an incomplete explanation, it is nevertheless worthy of consideration. Studies of political organization in transitional societies are consistent in maintaining that the uprooted and transient feeling of portions of the population reduces the influence of traditional institutions, whether family, tribe, church, or community, and necessitates a substitution of formal associations (secondary groups) to restore stability. In many ways the nineteenth century Industrial Revolution created social and psychological needs that are again evident in the development of new African nations from tribes. Reduced influence of traditional group patterns and rapid growth of special interest groups are characteristic of both periods. Wirth has described the influence of urbanism on organized groups in these words:

> The distinctive features of the urban mode of life have often been described sociologically as consisting of the substitution of secondary for primary contacts, the weakening of the bonds of kinship, and the declining social significance of the family, the disappearance of the neighborhood, and the undermining of the traditional basis of social solidarity. . . . Being reduced

to a stage of virtual impotence as an individual, the urbanite is bound to exert himself by joining with others of similar interests into organized groups to obtain his ends.[13]

In West Africa, World War II served as the stimulus toward many different ways of earning a living and many more modes of life than existed in prewar days. As in the era of the Industrial Revolution, much of traditional life disintegrated, and new forms of organization, primarily occupational and professional, arose. Some of the immigrants to the Gold Coast have achieved sufficient solidarity to monopolize certain aspects of economic life. This development can be partially traced to the impersonality of relationships and to the psychological effect of isolation, which encourages the individual to exert himself with others of like interests through the medium of the formal organization.[14]

Perhaps the reason that secondary organizations serve well as reactors to change is that they are initially flexible and easily adjustable to changing circumstances. This explanation is offered by Robert T. Anderson and Gallatin Anderson as a result of their study of the role of voluntary associations in a Danish village facing the problem of relocation of economic enterprise. Technological advances reduced the traditional marine economy of the village to impotence in competition with large commercial fleets. The old form of economic organization, the family-owned fishing boat, could no longer provide a profit. In addition, the village was gradually becoming absorbed as a suburb of Copenhagen. The research indicates that the family unit, losing economic utility, declined in importance, while the special interest organizations assumed the responsibility of adjustment. These organizations met the emergence of changing channels of distribution and marketing by uniting people for concerted action on the basis of shared interests.[15]

The generalization to be abstracted from these examples is that organized groups begin in response to changes in the relationships between individuals when existing institutions are inadequate to provide a means for the reestablishment of stability. Key states, "Most pressure groups . . . originate in an effort to cope with some immediate problem and then persist as an organization to deal with new matters of concern to the membership."[16]

Urbanization is only one example of such change. Group activity occurs in rural areas, and there is considerable variation in the participation of urban peoples in voluntary associations. To suggest other variables, studies of large cities have shown that primary groups are not replaced by interest groups in all cases.

In the broad scheme of social evolution, then, organized secondary group activity develops as social functions become specialized. Specialization breeds social change, and secondary groups serve as an adaptive mechanism whereby individuals can cope more effectively with altered environmental relationships. Urbanization, industrialization, and democratic sociopolitical forms are all indicators of change. Each is at once a result of socially dynamic processes and a producer of further dynamic processes. Recognizing that in the United States each of these indicators of change abounds, it is not surprising that organized groups also proliferate here.

THE POLITICAL CULTURE

Almond and Verba have defined political culture as "the particular distribution of patterns of orientation toward political objects among the members of the nation."[17] Hence, "when we speak of the political culture of a society, we refer to the political system as internalized in the cognitions, feelings, and evaluations of its population."[18] Such perceptual and attitudinal patterns form one dimension of the American political environment within which interest groups must function.

Likewise, values—the states of affairs men think are desirable—are essential ingredients of the political culture. Those values agreed on by individuals throughout a society are powerful forces which affect the nation's political life. Moreover, they tend to be self-perpetuating. When consensus is approached or reached on a particular value orientation, that orientation becomes part of the political culture of that nation. As such it not only affects the political life of the present, but it is also passed on to succeeding generations through what scholars have referred to as the socialization process.

The political culture, in short, constitutes what might be called the psychocognitive dimension of the political environment. For our purposes, then, it is necessary to examine the American political culture as it shapes interest group activity. The intellectual history of the United States and, for that matter, of all Western democratic nations is characterized by an antipathy toward any political activity associated with special interests. This, in turn, has retarded the development of organized interests and restricted the scope of their activities. Although groups are now recognized as being firmly rooted in our political system, this has not always been the case. In fact, the interest group system as we know it has been granted what degree of legitimacy it now enjoys only in relatively recent years. Even now terms such as *lobbyist* and *special interest* tend to carry pejorative connotations when used popularly.

From the beginnings of the American republic, the assumption has been made that pressure groups, irrespective of their goals, are evil because they conflict with the fundamental attributes of democracy. James Madison's famous tenth essay in *The Federalist*, while acknowledging the inevitability of "factions," argued that one of the best features of the proposed constitution was its "tendency to break and control the violence of faction." Madison described the existence of factions as a "dangerous vice" and one of the most serious threats to popular government.[19] Since Madison's day there has been a prolific stream of anti–pressure group writings, in which some social scientists and public officials have stated the basic thesis that "minority interests" and "democracy" cannot coexist. Our literature is full of warnings that the influence of organized groups is becoming dangerous: "Group organization is one of the perils of our times"; the unfortunate fate of American government is that "there is nothing it can do to protect itself from pressures." From social scientists we have the warning that since the goals of pressure groups are at best the desires of a minority, any effort to implement them would tend to be undemocratic. The only logical conclusion from such a premise is that "... every pressure group tends inevitably to embrace the potentiality for evil."[20]

Official sanction was given to the hostility toward pressure groups by the United States Supreme Court when it refused, in the case of *Trist* v. *Child*, to uphold a claim for payment by a lobbyist against an individual who had hired him.[21] The basis for the decision was that lobbying was a practice "contrary to sound policy and public morals." Hugo Black, the late Supreme Court Justice, while chairing a Senate investigation committee in 1935, voiced the fear of organized groups in a cogent, if extreme, fashion:

> Contrary to tradition, against the public morals, and hostile to good government, the lobby has reached such a position of power that it threatens government itself. Its size, its power, its capacity for evil; its greed, trickery, deception and fraud condemn it to the death it deserves.[22]

This type of criticism is not based merely on the disapproval of some of the more harsh tactics sometimes employed by organizations, but specifies a rejection of the legitimacy of the very existence of such groups in our society.

Public hostility toward organized group political activity can be traced to two aspects of traditional democratic theory which are part of the civics curriculum in every American elementary school. The first is the concept of the public interest, the second that of rational individualism. Through the socialization process every generation learns these myths of popular democratic theory, so that they have become significant features of the political culture.[23]

The popular version of the public interest concept entails the following beliefs: (1) that the many individuals who are American citizens form a collective entity called the public; (2) that the public is homogeneous enough that there exists one state of affairs that is objectively "the best" for it; and (3) that for any given set of policy alternatives there is one which contributes more toward the realization of that "best" state of affairs than any of the others. Therefore, to act in the public interest is to serve the welfare of all. Public officials, according to the myth, are charged to act precisely in that manner to the best of their abilities. Clearly, anyone who believes in the public interest not only as a description of reality but also as a prescription for political decision-making must react negatively against the idea and existence of interest groups which promote the special interests of their members as opposed to the general welfare of the public.

Rational individualism, the second aspect of the political culture, inhibits the philosophical acceptance of interest group legitimacy in America. Autonomous, rational man is a central concept in traditional democratic theory. Government is not only conceived to promote his well-being, but it is also seen as an agent acting under his direction. Each individual, employing his natural faculties for rational thought, is supposedly able to determine what his own true interest is and to act accordingly. Each citizen, acting on his own behalf, expresses his political desires via the appropriate democratic channels. The collective will of the majority is taken to be the proper course of action because it reflects not only the desires of more people but also the *rational* choice of more. Thus, the principle of majoritarianism enjoys the double sanction of benefiting more persons in their capacity as recipients of governmental policies and of ensuring approval by the greatest number of individuals acting in their capacity as rational decision-makers. On both counts, the underlying belief is that men think and act freely and rationally.

Faith in individual responsibility, when amalgamated with the dogmas of traditional democratic theory, is another mechanism to prejudice the average citizen against collective action, and specifically against the pressures of organized groups. The view prevails that each person's effort toward the solution of his problems is more worthy than group effort through appeal to government agencies. Pressure groups, so the argument goes, are dominated by single "blind" impulses which tend to "undermine the honest and rational thinking on which democracy depends" and "sabotage the struggle toward objective reason."[24]

Individualism, as in the case of the public interest myth, has become both descriptive and prescriptive in America. As a prescriptive norm it has been reinforced by the doctrine of individual conscience and free will, which historically has been emphasized from the pulpits of American churches. Likewise, Americans have long revered almost religiously the economic tenets of free-enterprise capitalism, a primary concept of which is autonomous, rational, economic man.

The social history of the United States offers evidence supporting individualism as an objective description of man. Whether or not one accepts Frederick Jackson Turner's thesis that the American frontier experience uniquely determined our national character, it is difficult to deny that it did foster individualism.[25]

> The imagined frontier—the frontier of story, saga, and song—cast its spell over the American mind. Thus, a "frontier mentality" became a further characteristic of the American. And with this mentality went a frontier faith, a faith in common humanity that was rooted and expressed in the *spontaneous and autonomous strivings of the individual*. Recognizing man as a creative agent, this mentality sensed the *ultimate value of man as an individual member of society*; and in fact this insight into individualism often compensated for the cultural sterility that sometimes accompanied pioneering life.[26] (italics added)

It is interesting to note that, paradoxically the twin myths of the public interest and of rational individualism, which are so very much a part of our political culture, are themselves seemingly contradictory. To accept the former is to adopt a corporate image of society; to accept the latter makes one an advocate of social atomism. Scholars and theorists of democracy have long recognized this apparent inconsistency, but none has been able to resolve it satisfactorily. An articulate expression of this logical impasse, although one not optimistic about its resolution, was made by Ervin Laszlo, who wrote,

> A political theory based on the full and correct knowledge of the individual would just as surely satisfy the social animal as the theory based on the full knowledge of social requirements would fulfill the individual. Inasmuch

as full, verifiable knowledge of either man's being or existence is not possible, the difference between the individual and collective ideas lies mainly in the area of compromise.[27]

Logical inconsistency notwithstanding, a belief in the public interest and a concurrent faith in rational individualism conspire in the popular American political culture to create in many people an abstract distrust of interest groups. As a result, groups are often forced to defend their activities on the basis of their actually being "in the public interest."

A few years ago a state university, under the auspices of the Citizenship Clearing House, invited several people registered as lobbyists at the state capital to explain their work. Without exception, each began his remarks by explaining that his organization was not a pressure group since its goals were in the public interest. At the local level, civic groups often adopt the public interest guise. Consider, for example, this report:

> For years a hotbed of torrid politics, Santa Fe has suddenly seen the light. Last year a group of civic minded citizens, including the League of Women Voters and the Junior Chamber of Commerce, organized the Citizens Union of Santa Fe and enrolled some 400 members pledged to fight for good government and to vote only for able candidates regardless of party.[28]

Such a group would be appalled at the suggestion that it was organized to achieve a special interest; the goals of the group are those of the city. Another example of this peculiarity in our thinking is a statement of the Citizens' Council of La Grange, Illinois. The Citizens' Council was founded for the purpose of making nominations for local office. All who accepted membership were obliged to support the candidates of the Council. Yet in its articles of association the Council stated, "All members of the Council . . . act as representatives of the village as a whole and do not in any narrow sense represent any organization, business, or social group, or special interest. Each member acts solely in his or her individual capacity."[29]

Such examples point out not only that groups are constrained (at least in their public utterances) by the political culture, but also that such constraint applies primarily to group *behavior*, not to group *existence*. Americans, as Alexis de Tocqueville remarked, are joiners.[30] Few today argue to the contrary;[31] however, no one has been able to measure satisfactorily the exact extent to which this is true. Estimates of the percentage of persons belonging to voluntary associations vary from 36% to 64%.[32] Likewise, there is no absolutely definitive assessment of the actual number of such associations that exist.

> It is generally assumed that there are thousands of voluntary associations in the United States today, but we can only speculate as to the exact number. Not even an approximately complete complication of local and state associations exists; their number must greatly exceed 200,000, the majority purely local groups, few linked together by formal ties, and most short-lived. For national associations there is no complete compilation, but a combination of several sources provides an approximate list of those with any appreciable number of members. We have counted 8,000 national associations but estimate the total to be about 12,000.[33]

Whatever the correct figures may be, there is sufficient evidence of the prevalence of organized group activity. Of course, not all of the extant groups are politically active, yet all indications are that the majority are so engaged, if not as a primary activity at least as a secondary one. A very rough indicator of political activity at the federal level is that of lobbyist registration. Even since the Federal Regulation of Lobbying Act of 1946, all paid Washington lobbyists have been required to register themselves and the organizations they represent. Through 1968, 5,798 lobbyists representing 8,641 organizations had so registered.[34] No records have been kept which could tell us the number of those who have ceased lobbying activities or how many are reregistrations; however, when one considers that there are in all likelihood a large number of unregistered lobbyists as well, one cannot avoid concluding that group political activities are widespread in the United States. Furthermore, there is undoubtedly a substantial number of groups which engage in political activities of a nonlobby variety and many more which are active in only state or local political arenas.

THE SOCIAL STRUCTURE

We have discussed the paradox of concurrent beliefs in the abstractions of the public interest and of rational individualism. The critical reader might well have noticed the implication of a second paradox— that interest groups flourish within a nation that distrusts them. A curious aspect of our society is the tendency of many of us to use the word *lobbyist* to refer to something evil while engaging in the very tactics which we condemn. This means that we approve action by groups having goals with which we agree, while condemning as pressure similar activities by hostile groups. We see nothing ambiguous in demanding more freedom for business organizations while insisting that labor unions should be abolished. In almost all organizations it is good form to bemoan the evil of "pressure groups" while resolving to organize more effectively to combat this evil.

Before we too hastily judge ourselves a nation of hypocrites it might be advisable to seek an alternative explanation of this inconsistency. Research indicates that the answer is more likely an intellectual than a moral one. Many people simply fail to translate abstract principles into concrete action where they are themselves concerned.[35]

The inability to deduce behavioral cues from abstract belief is largely a function of one's degree of education. Likewise, the unquestioning acceptance of and the firm attachment to the secondary school civics text version of democratic myths is more likely to occur among those who have had little or no college than among the better educated. We know that education is highly correlated with socioeconomic status (SES); therefore, it is reasonable to assume that the greatest frequency of attitudinal–behavioral inconsistency occurs among those of lower SES.

On closer inspection, however, the inconsistency may not prove to be as great as a cursory glance may indicate—even with respect to those lower on the SES scale. Although membership in voluntary associations may be a widespread phenomenon in the United States, studies have indicated that it is more characteristic of those with high SES than of those with low SES. In analyzing data collected by the National Opinion Research Center (NORC) during the mid-1950s, Wright and Hyman found that

> . . . fully 76 per cent of the respondents whose family income falls below 2,000 dollars do not belong to any organizations in contrast to only 48 per cent of those whose income is 7,500 dollars or more. Furthermore, there is an increase in the percentage of persons who belong to *several* organizations as social status increases. For example, only 7 per cent of the lowest income group belong to two or more associations in contrast to 30 per cent of the highest income group. Similar findings are obtained from inspection of the data on education, level of living, occupation, and home ownership. . . .[36]

Moreover, Rose, citing a number of recent research reports, observed that while only a small proportion of the population is very *active* in associations, a very large proportion—at least in the towns and cities—are *members* of the associations. Several studies show, however, that Americans of middle and higher incomes are more likely to join associations than are people of lower income.[37]

We are forced to conclude, along with Schattschneider, that "the pressure group system has an upper-class bias."[38] Since it is among the lower classes that the abstract distrust of interest groups in general is more likely to occur, it appears that their behavior is somewhat more consistent with their attitudes than we initially suspected.[39] Thus, the socioeconomic structure of society affects the composition of interest groups in general and that of the active minority of group members in particular.

There are those who would decry the lack of lower-class participation in associational activity as being at once symptomatic of sociopolitical alienation and unhealthy for democracy. By and large such critics adhere to what contemporary political science refers to as the pluralist position.[40] At the core of pluralist theory is the belief that individuals can best convey their needs and desires to government through concerted group activity. In a large, complex society one person stands little chance of being heard—much less of being able to affect the governmental decision-making process. However, so the argument runs, when a number of individuals who share a particular concern band together, their collective voice speaks with more force than the sum of their individual voices. Thus, pluralists view interest groups as channels through which men realize the democratic goal of legitimate and meaningful interaction with government.

Individuals are presumed to have a variety of interests, so that it is thought unlikely that any single group will circumscribe all of the salient interests of its many members. Moreover, a sizable number of persons who agree on one issue will more than likely not agree on a host of other issues in the political system. Therefore, groups not only proliferate, but they also tend to restrict the scope of issues with which they are concerned in order to focus on one relatively concentrated issue area in which all members share a common interest.

It is further argued by the pluralists that groups help to integrate their members with society at large by reducing their feelings of isolation and insignificance and by giving them the opportunity to participate in public policy formation through the group.

Pluralists do not contend that all that is needed to affect a desired policy decision is to organize a few kindred beings and collectively petition the government. The pluralist world is one of conflict. It is inhabited by as many groups as there are interests to represent. It is assumed that if an organization crystallizes around an interest, an opposing group will also form in reaction to it (provided, of course, that there are persons who perceive their own interest to be at variance with that of the organized group). Since only the most general and most abstract interests are common throughout a polity, pluralist democracy is characterized by many groups, each in competition with another, and each seeking to maximize its own interests. However, the pluralist view of politics cannot be likened to a chaotic free-for-all. We hasten to point out that the interests represented by voluntary associations tend to be of limited scope; therefore, the vast majority of interest groups will be ambivalent toward any given issue which enters the political arena. Only a small number of groups enter the conflict in the course of most policy debates.

The above description of pluralism differs little from the traditional theory of democracy, nor is there any reason for us to expect that it should. Pluralism is basically nothing more than a restatement of classical democratic thought modified somewhat in an attempt to make it square with the observable conditions of modern industrial mass society. One major change in the theory was the intercession of the voluntary association on behalf of the individual. Since the pluralistic theory is based on the traditional theory of democracy, it contains the same basic strengths and weaknesses as the democratic theory. It attempts to be at once normative and descriptive, it is still individualistic in that groups are created by and act on behalf of the many individuals whose interests they represent, and it remains unalterably committed to the goals and norms of participatory democracy.

Confronted with the evidence of a relatively small but active political elite and widespread political apathy among the masses, pluralists further modify both the normative and the descriptive aspects of the traditional theory.

According to the pluralists, the most significant function of the interest groups is that they afford political elites and the masses the opportunity to influence and control each other in concrete, constructive ways, rather than in abstract and destructive ways. The mostly apathetic masses can exercise their indirect control over the nomination and election of the elites within their own organizations, and within the state as a whole. (Direct, "active" interference by the masses in politics is held to be undesirable.) The masses can learn the art of "responsible self-government" with leadership by participating in these voluntary, intermediate groups. They can better perceive social reality and relate themselves to the social and political structure concretely and constructively through these organizations. Since no group exercises an inclusive, total control over its members, the masses can maintain their personal autonomy, and check the conduct and policies of the elites. The political elites for their part benefit as well, because they are free from direct intervention from the mass in taking initiatives, in formulating programmes, and in executing policies. In other words, they can contain "fantasy" or "mass" politics.[41]

Regardless of their commitment to democratic norms, pluralists have been found to recognize, and to account for, the existence of an elite–mass dichotomy. Perhaps they have done so by "stretching" the concepts of democratic theory, but they have not destroyed them. Man remains rational and autonomous, although not all men exercise their autonomy to the fullest. Participation in politics remains both fact and ideal, although most people participate only indirectly. The faith remains that out of the clash of opposing interests the public interest is best served by the principle of majoritarianism, although the majority is no longer that of individual wills but of group resources of power. Thus, even pluralists, the intellectual torchbearers of the democratic creed, recognize the distinction between elites and masses—a distinction which reflects the effect of the social structure of the nation on its political life, and one which cannot be obliterated even by focusing attention on group activity.

POLITICAL INSTITUTIONS

Formal democracy is not dependent on any given set of governmental institutions. Although we are accustomed to equate our unique political forms with the basic necessities of a stable democracy, there are many ostensibly democratic countries with governmental institutions different from our own. Nevertheless, there are formal patterns of authority which coexist with American democracy. Pressure groups not only must cope with the political culture and the social structure of a nation, but they must also operate within the framework of its political institutions. Let us consider the relation of pressure groups to the following American institutions: (1) federalism, (2) separation of powers, and (3) the party system.

Federalism and the separation of powers

Federalism and the separation of powers are closely related. Federalism may be defined legally as a system of government in which power is divided between a central government and regional govern-ments, each of which is supreme in its own area of jurisdiction. This system is to be contrasted with the unitary system, in which the central government is supreme and all powers held by regional gov-ernment are delegated. Of course, such delegated powers may be withdrawn. In the American federal system the states are formally recognized as existing independently of the national government.

The Constitution, as every schoolboy knows, does not contain a formal definition of federalism. However, the Constitution does specify the powers held by the national government and provides, in the Tenth Amendment, that "the powers not delegated to the United States by the Constitution, nor published by it to the States, are reserved to the States respectively, or to the people." The Con-stitution also includes a system of separation of powers or "checks and balances" among the three branches of the national government. The theoretical argument for these provisions is centered on the assumption that political power is potentially dangerous. Therefore, the best way to reduce the danger is to provide for a balancing of authority between the nation and the states and between the legis-lative, executive, and judicial branches of the national government. Although one should avoid being so presumptuous as to speak with authority about the *motives* of the framers of the Constitution, it is possible to ascertain from their writings that the system of diffusion of power was designed to provide a barrier to the dominance of "factions" (whether interest group or party). Presumably it would be possible for a faction to gain control of one branch of government only to be thwarted by another; or to control a state government but not *all* the states. As Professor Arthur W. Macmahon states: ". . . federalism lessens the risk of a monopoly of political power by providing a number of independent points where the party that is nationally in the minority at the time can maintain itself while it formulates and partly demonstrates its policies and capabilities and develops new leadership."[42]

To what extent has the diffusion of legal authority succeeded in developing a dispersal of actual or social power? We must be cautious in answering this question, to avoid becoming overly legalistic. First, there is little doubt that actual power is diversified in American society. Still, there is no way in which we can assert that federalism and the separation of powers cause this diversification.[43] The best that can be done is to provide illustrations of the problems en-countered by pressure groups in a system of legal dispersion of authority.

In our system of government we observe groups which, although unsuccessful in achieving their goals on a national level, have established positions of power among state governments. One reason for this occurrence is the variation between the responsibilities of state legislatures as opposed to the national Congress. The state legislature has a narrower set of interests within its area of jurisdiction, whereas the national legislature is responsible to the vast array of interests spread among the entire United States.

One of the best examples of an interest group operating from a position of strength at the state level is the perennial conflict between chain stores and independent retailers.[44] In the years following World War I, chain stores had increased their activities to such a point that the economic lives of thousands of independent merchants were threatened. The coming of the depression of the 1930s added to the menace of the chains and increased the fear on the part of the independent businessman that he would be driven from business. The problem was most intense among grocers because chain operations had been most successful in this field. However, other types of retailers and some wholesalers were also affected. Whatever the type of the business, the mass buying techniques of the chains and the subsequent lower prices charged to consumers were weapons against which there was no economic defense.

To meet this threat the retail and wholesale merchants tried unsuccessfully to prevent chain store growth by boycotting manufacturers who sold directly to chains. Next, independent merchants tried to "educate" the public via mass media to the "evils" of chain stores. However, chain sales continued to rise. Finally the problem was attacked by seeking governmental aid. However, even though chain operations directly injured millions of retailers, no national organization arose to ward off the "chain store menace." Instead, the problem was approached on a state-by-state basis with no connection between the activities of retailers from one state to the next. In most of the states the legislature was urged to enact tax legislation sharply restrictive on the activities of chains. As early as 1927 four states had adopted special taxes on chain stores and thirteen other bills had been introduced but failed to pass. In 1931 the Supreme Court upheld the constitutionality of the chain store tax, and the floodgate was opened. By 1935, 225 chain tax bills had been introduced and 13 had passed; by 1939, 27 states had enacted such taxes. One commentator ruefully remarked that "wherever a little band of lawmakers are banded together . . . you may be sure that they are . . . thinking up things they can do to the chain stores."[45]

For our purposes, the significance of this episode is the fact that every success in retaliatory legislation occurred at the state level.

Joseph C. Palamountain notes that "taxes vary so extremely from state to state as to show that no national group was able to coordinate the activities of its state and local units. . . ."[46] In fact, there is considerable evidence to suggest that, had the proponents of restrictive chain store taxation not worked through the states, the anti-chain campaign would have been much less successful. By the middle 1930s the chains had developed a counterattack program through the use of effective public relations. By skillful propaganda they converted potential supporters to active participants. Housewives, farm organizations, and food processors combined to ebb the tide of tax legislation. In 1936 California voters, in a popular referendum, voted down a chain tax. Thereafter few states considered chain-tax legislation.

The conclusion of the anti-chain drive occurred when an effort was made to have the national Congress adopt a nationwide restrictive tax in 1938. This would have seriously hampered the operations of chains doing business in several states. However, in the arena of Congress, the chains were at less of a disadvantage than they had been before the state legislatures. At the state level, home-town sentiment against "foreign big business" went a long way toward balancing out the lack of money or organization on the part of the independent merchants. Nationally, the independents did not have the resources to compete with the vast potential of the chain stores. Only the National Association of Retail Druggists worked consistently for the legislation, although a few other retailers' groups testified at committee hearings. The chains, however, marshaled a formidable coalition to oppose the bill. The chains gained the support of the American Farm Bureau Federation, the National Association of Real Estate Boards, and many large food manufacturers. In addition, the support of labor unions figured prominently in the chain store coalition. Chain stores also had the backing of the Departments of Agriculture and Commerce.

The independent merchants were outmanned once they sought to expand their sphere of influence to the nation as a whole. The chain-tax bill, introduced by Representative Wright Patman of Texas, was lost in a maze of parliamentary delays. No hearings were held until 1940 and the bill never cleared the committee hearing stage. Thus, the federal system of government played a part in the solution to a problem of public policy. Although the anti-chain interests were able to secure federal legislation in the form of the Miller–Tydings amendment to the Sherman Act in 1937, the existence of two levels of decision-making bodies enabled one interest to maintain a position of strength that might not have been possible under a unitary system.

The chain store episode is an example of a conflict within the business community in which each had access to a different decision-making area. In this particular case the larger business group, the chain stores, found a more satisfactory environment in the national legislature. Often, however, corporate interests find it more compatible with their goals to advocate the expansion of state jurisdiction at the expense of the national government. Some large corporations have financial resources greater than many state governments. With respect to the regulation of business, many states lack the necessary administrative machinery to provide thorough supervision. Under these circumstances, the cry of "states' rights" has become an important part of the struggle among pressure groups. As Donald C. Blaisdell has noted, "Federalism is particularly pleasing . . . to the managers of industrial enterprise. While their charters to do business are obtained not from the federal but from state government, under federalism they get the benefits of a trade area of continental proportions, at the same time escaping effective federal regulation."[47]

The use of states' rights as a symbol or propaganda device is important not only because it serves to clarify the relation of interest groups to the structure of government but also because it plays on the myths of American society. Indeed the "specter of a centralized federal bureaucracy invading the reserved rights of the states" is invoked on the assumption that our values are biased toward a commitment to "grass roots" democracy.[48]

The use of the states' rights argument by interests seeking to avoid the intervention of the national government into certain economic and social matters began with the surge of industrial expansion after the Civil War, although some businesses still feared the erraticism of the state legislatures and preferred federal regulation. This was the period in which popular reform movements, such as the National Grange, advocated strict regulation of business activity to ameliorate the dangers of monopoly. In defense of their status, business interests argued that regulation by the federal government infringed on the reserved rights of the states while simultaneously maintaining that state regulation was a violation of the right of Congress to regulate under the powers of the commerce clause. A large part of this activity serves to illustrate the use of the doctrine of separation of powers. The normal pattern was for business to challenge regulatory legislation through the courts. Such memorable decisions as *Hammer* v. *Dagenhart,* in which the Supreme Court invalidated the Child Labor Act as an invasion of the reserved rights of states, reflect this tech-

nique.[49] While legislative arenas mirrored the values of those supporting regulation, the courts became the citadel of business.

The technique of "divide and rule," in which federalism was used
as a vehicle to produce inaction, made it possible for corporations
to turn themselves into clusters of private power, sometimes to the
extent of dominating the state governments. Many examples from
contemporary economic life illustrate this technique. Oil companies
interested in controlling the vast reservoirs of tidelands oil have
relied extensively on the doctrine of states' rights. Robert J. Harris
has written with perception that "the solicitude of the oil companies
for states' rights is hardly based on convictions derived from political
theory but rather on fears that federal ownership may result in the
cancellation or modification of state leases favorable to their interests, their knowledge that they can successfully cope with state
oil regulatory agencies, and uncertainty concerning their ability to
control a Federal agency."[50]

The position of large dairy chains is comparable to that of the oil
companies. Because the marketing of milk is usually perilous due to
the highly perishable quality of the product, many states have created
agencies to regulate the distribution of milk. These agencies have
usually been ineffective in dealing with the huge intrastate chains,
such as Sealtest, Borden's, and Foremost, which dominate the market.
On occasion, overtures have been made to the Federal Trade Commission by states to assist them in the task of regulation, only to face
the determined opposition of the dairies.

These examples should illustrate that federalism does not involve
a struggle between the nation and the states, but rather a struggle
among interests which have favorable access to one of the two levels
of government. The recent controversy over integration fits this
assumption. After the Supreme Court had ruled against the continuation of the practice of segregation in public schools, the states' rights
argument was well suited for groups of people in the South who
sought to defend their regional customs against the dominant attitudes of the rest of the nation. Local and statewide organizations,
known variously as White Citizens Councils and States' Rights
Councils, demanded, in the name of the right of each sovereign state
to exercise the authority of self-determination, that attempts to end
segregation cease. Their efforts are given the official sanction of the
state governments. State officials regularly attend meetings and
pledge the support of the administration. Letters urging support of
these movements are mailed from governors' offices. In Mississippi
the state legislature established the State Sovereignty Commission
in 1956 to combat integration efforts. The governor, Ross Barnett,

became chairman of this commission and also served as chairman of the Citizens Council, a private organization with the same aims as the official State Sovereignty Commission. The relations between the two bodies became so intimate that the private nature of the Citizens Council was blurred. The legislature actually allocated state funds for the propaganda efforts of the Citizens Council, thus making it a quasi-official body.

In contrast to the warm reception given segregationist groups by the southern state governments, the National Association for the Advancement of Colored People and related organizations have been subjected to constant harassment. Attempts to gain legal access to NAACP records, challenge of tax-exempt status, and other similar tactics continually frustrate the efforts of pro-integration groups. Under these circumstances it is only natural for these organizations to concentrate their efforts at the national government level. The argument between the opposing groups is not, whatever the verbalization, one of the rights of states against an ever-encroaching federal government. Rather the argument concerns more basic values. The states' rights argument is an example of the manipulation of symbols for the purpose of creating a satisfactory attitudinal framework for the achievement of political goals. When one realizes that the southern states regularly pay into the federal treasury less than they get back in the form of grants-in-aid, the issue may be seen in a more complete perspective.

Turning to separation of powers, we are confronted with the same patterns of activity expected under any system of divided authority. Access by a particular group to one branch of government does not necessarily mean access to another. Examples of congressional overturning of decisions by the Supreme Court come most readily to mind. The problem of differential access was brought into focus by two recent instances of judicial decisions which damaged the economic security of trade associations that were influential in Congress.

In 1948 the Supreme Court, in the case of *Federal Trade Commission* v. *Cement Institute*, held that the basing-point system of pricing was illegal. Under this system, prices were determined by formulas which eliminated the right of the consumer to choose between competitive producers. The basing-point system provided that the price of a commodity delivered anywhere in the United States included shipping charges estimated from a geographical basing point, irrespective of the actual point of departure of the merchandise. The Cement Institute, a trade association organized in 1929, had administered such a system rigorously. The assumption which guided the tenacity with which the Institute held to its pricing system was that "ours is an industry above all others that cannot stand free competition, that must systematically restrain competition or be ruined."[51]

The reaction to the Court's decision was swift and decisive. The steel industry, which also used the basing-point system, soon began to work for legislation that would legalize the system. Representatives from the state of Pennsylvania, national center of steel production, introduced resolutions calling for a moratorium suspending further action under the decision. United States Steel abandoned the basing-point system and raised the price of steel seven dollars per ton, although there is evidence suggesting that the change in pricing systems actually reduced the cost to the steel companies by one dollar per ton. The strategy was to raise a demand for legislation among the customers of the steel companies. The clamor finally resulted in the passage of S.1008. This bill provided that the Federal Trade Commission Act be amended so as not to regard the absorption of freight charges by sellers as an unfair trade practice. Thus, the Congress had minimized the effects of the Supreme Court's decision.

However, the political process does not stop with the passage of a law. There was still another branch of government which had a role to play. President Truman's sympathies were not usually in accord with the desires of big business, which had guided the legislation through Congress. In addition, his political strength was believed to rest among the lower-income groups. Consequently, the opponents of the basing-point legislation, unable to bring their desires into reality in Congress, were in a more favorable position when they appealed to the President. The congressional delegation which urged Truman to veto was composed entirely of Democrats long conspicuous in their championing of vigorous enforcement of antitrust legislation, such as Senators Kefauver of Tennessee and Douglas of Illinois. In addition, organizations such as the United Automobile Workers of America, the National Association of Retail Druggists, and the United States Wholesale Grocers Association met with the chairman of the Democratic National Committee. The net result of this activity was a Presidential veto in 1950.

The case of the basing-point legislation gives us a situation in which group interests fought for their goals through the entire national government. Those interests which failed in one area succeeded in another. A similar development can be seen in the Supreme Court decision in *Federal Maritime Board* v. *Isbrandtsen*, handed down in 1958.[52] In this case the Supreme Court struck down the legality of the "dual rate" or "exclusive patronage" contract employed by steamship conferences. Oceangoing carriers have for years been organized into voluntary conferences. These conferences consist only of those vessels furnishing regular service and not the independent lines and "tramps." The principal purpose of these conferences is to establish cargo rates and conditions of carriage. Under normal circumstances such agreements might violate the antitrust legislation. However, the Shipping Act of 1916 exempted agreements between oceangoing carriers from antitrust penalties, provided these agreements are approved by the Federal Maritime Board. By 1959 110 conferences had negotiated agreements which had subsequently been approved.

One such type of contract was the "dual rate" agreement. This is an agreement binding shippers to transport all cargo loaded or discharged at ports served by the conference in vessels belonging to conference members. The rate charged to shippers who refuse to sign is higher, even for identical items. The "spread" between contract and noncontract rates sometimes was as high as 20%.

However, there was always the question of whether such obviously discriminatory measures did not violate section fourteen of the Shipping Act, which forbids unfair or discriminatory agreements. Although the dual rate agreement had been before the Supreme Court on numerous occasions beginning in 1932, the Isbrandtsen case was the first time that the Court had faced the question of its legality. This decision literally was felt around the world since over sixty conferences were affected.

Since the decision of the Court threatened serious economic disruption to the shipping industry, an almost frantic appeal was made to Congress through the American Merchant Marine. On the same day that the decision was issued, a bill was introduced in the House legalizing all dual rate agreements. During a hurriedly arranged series of hearings, the only opposition came from a few scattered small traders who were hurt by dual rate agreements. As far as the reaction of congressmen can be ascertained, the shipping industry was believed to present a united front. In approximately one month Congress established a two-year period of immunity for all contracts operative at the date of the Isbrandtsen decision. The Shipping Act was amended, with only one opposing vote in either house, to read that "nothing in this section or elsewhere in this Act shall be construed or applied to forbid or make unlawful any dual rate contract arrangement in use by the members of a conference on May 19, 1958. . . ." The stated purpose of the law was to "defer the impact of the Court decision."[53]

These examples of interest groups and separation of powers are not intended to provide an exhaustive account. Indeed, instances such as those cited above could be described almost *ad nauseam*. However, one further point should be made. In the interplay between groups and formal institutions the executive office of the president may be checked by strong concentrations of power in the other branches. The famous struggle between President Franklin D. Roosevelt and the Army Corps of Engineers, perhaps the most widely discussed case of successful pressure group opposition to executive goals, will conclude our analysis.[54] The Army Corps of Engineers is legally responsible to the president as commander-in-chief. However, the Corps of Engineers has built a close relationship with Congress primarily through the mechanism of the National Rivers and Harbors Congress, an organization to which many members of Congress belong. The Corps has performed river development tasks since the beginning of the nation's history, when it was the only agency with engineers trained for such work. However, since the increasing expansion of government services, the Corps has been almost incessantly involved in struggle with other agencies doing the same thing. The Hoover Commission drew attention to these jurisdictional disputes and concluded that, irrespective of the legal position of the president, the executive branch could not marshal sufficient power to coordinate a water program against the wishes of the influential "rivers and harbors bloc."

The independence of the Corps of Engineers is strikingly borne out in the struggle over the Kings River Project in California. Both the Corps and the Bureau of Reclamation wanted to develop a program to provide more adequate water supply for the arid area surrounding the river. President Roosevelt decided that the project was primarily one of irrigation and consequently should be handled by the Bureau of Reclamation. However, at Congressional hearings on the project the Corps continued to urge that it be given authority. It was supported by its loyal following in Congress, and the final solution had both the Bureau and the Corps authorized to undertake the development of the river. Even though the president's 1945 budget contained an appropriation for the Bureau and none for the Corps, the appropriation acts passed by Congress reversed these positions. President Roosevelt, usually classified as a "strong" president, could not cope with the entrenched strength of the Corps of Engineers built upon Congressional loyalties and close relationships with the National Rivers and Harbors Congress.

The political party system

If the formation of pressure groups is the core of the democratic political process, then the existence of political parties is significant.

Pressure groups and political parties are both representative of efforts by a substantial number of people to play a role in the formation of public policy. Although the surface similarities between the two types of organization are apparent, there are differences both in technique and in types of goals. The main difference is that political parties seek to have their membership elected to positions within the formal framework of government while pressure groups do not. In addition, the parties' key to success is their ability to convince a majority of the electorate that their particular position is worthy of support. The pressure group takes its demands to legislators, administrators, or judges who are already in office. Admittedly the distinction is frequently blurred. Some pressure groups participate in both types of activity. Some organizations whose interests are far too narrow to attract a majority still persist in running candidates for public office in addition to maintaining the regular type of pressure operation. Also, many influential organizations attempt to have their members appointed to positions on key administrative agencies, usually in advisory capacities.

However, the essential validity of the distinction may be seen in the kinds of programs adopted by political parties. A party which is a serious contender for political influence must present a more general program than the pressure group, and must have a far broader basis of support. Purely on practical grounds, it is impossible for the party to enter into a commitment with the electorate on the thousands of decisions that will be undertaken during its term of office. All the party can do is pledge itself to general approaches to the major issues it expects to face. In this case the voter who supports, for example, a conservative candidate for president can assume that the specific decisions made by the administration will conform to the general precepts represented in the attitudes held by the candidate and his supporters.

In addition to the impracticality of detailed party programs, there are more fundamental reasons. Since the political party is not the sole organizational representative of popular attitudes and goals, but must share its functions with pressure groups, the party must try to direct or control the activities of these groups. Operating in a highly specialized and pluralistic social framework, the party is forced to adopt a program broad enough to satisfy the many narrow demands of diverse and sometimes conflicting interests. For this reason it is very unlikely that a party which is rigidly committed to a set of doctrines or dogmas will succeed. This is true of democratic societies in general, but is particularly true of the United States. Both major parties tend to blur sharply divisive issues and reach a compromise from among the claims of competitive groups.

The thesis that parties serve as "smoke screens" for potentially explosive issues should not be carried so far as to allow one to conclude that there is no difference between the basic programs of the major parties. In Congress there are certain issues on which there is substantial disagreement between Democrats and Republicans. However, since the firmness of party lines varies from issue to issue, it is impossible to generalize. In determining how he will vote on a certain bill, the congressman's perception of his party affiliation will certainly be one of many pressures operative. Further, despite the notion that parties gravitate toward the blurring of issues, their active party workers appear to be separated by significant differences in their perceptions of programs. These differences agree with the "popular image in which the Democratic party is seen as the more 'progressive' or 'radical,' the Republican as the more 'moderate' or 'conservative' of the two."[55] In a survey of the attitudes of governors, senators, national committeemen, precinct workers, and local officials of both parties, Herbert McClosky and his associates found that these leaders were far apart on many issues. The Republicans strongly opposed government ownership of natural resources while the Democrats were equally vociferous in favoring it. Republicans favor a reduction of farm price supports; Democrats do not. On the questions of federal aid to education, slum clearance, social security, and minimum wages the leaders have widely divergent attitudes.[56]

It must be remembered, however, that such differences are between party leaders—the active political elite. Among the mass public to whom parties must appeal there is, if not less ideological conflict, at least a poorer crystallization of issue positions. The vast majority of American voters constitute an amorphous, consensual mass. Their allegiance to either party appears to be unrelated to policy positions of the respective party leaders or, for that matter, to specific issues at all. In their monumental study of the American voting public, Campbell et al. found that "if we focus upon the total range of individuals represented in the national electorate, we find almost no correlation between a general disposition that we would expect to be of prime political relevance and variation in issue attitudes or partisanship."[57] Similarly, McClosky et al. found after shifting their attention from party elites to their mass followers that

[w]hereas the leaders of the two parties diverge strongly, their followers differ only moderately in their attitudes toward issues. The hypothesis that party beliefs unite adherents and bring them into the party ranks may hold for the more active members of a mass party but not for its rank and file supporters.[58]

To succeed, parties must appeal to diverse sectors of the population and at the same time remain well within the vague limits of the mass consensus; hence, they are rarely able to put forth candidates or platforms that truly reflect the desires and values of the party leaders. The most recent attempt to do so on a nationwide scale—the Goldwater candidacy in 1964—ended in a disastrous defeat for the Republican Party.

Occasionally a third party which attracts sizable numbers of voters and departs significantly from the dominant consensus in its candidates and policies may appear on the scene. The Dixiecrat revolt in 1948 was one such example, as was George Wallace's American Independent Party in 1968. Such phenomena might more correctly be labeled "movements" than "parties." The emotional nature of their appeals is geared more toward the release of frustration than toward positive programs. They have arisen at times when sizable portions of the populace are confronted with demands for change which they are either unprepared or unwilling to accept. Widespread anxiety, fear, and alienation place strains on the dominant consensus. At such times evocative rhetoric substitutes for reasoned debate in winning the allegiance of many. The threat that such "third parties" present is not that of winning a few seats in state or federal legislatures—the American Independent Party did not even offer candidates for such offices in 1968—but rather that of polarizing society into two mutually antagonistic, intolerant camps. Under such conditions little if any social or political progress can be achieved, for every policy debate or political act is accompanied by sanguinary conflict. No society can long tolerate such conditions and remain free in any meaningful sense of the word.

Fortunately, the American political system has proved itself sufficiently flexible (with only one notable exception—the Civil War) to attenuate the intensity of conflict during crisis periods. In so doing the two major parties have either "ridden out" the crisis until the conditions which led to its occurrence have passed, or they have shifted their ideological position toward that of the dissident faction, thereby reducing the intensity of social conflict. Just such a shift occurred during the Roosevelt administration when the Democratic Party adopted a social welfare character. The Republican Party, too, was forced to abandon its laissez-faire ideology to attract a mass following. Now, although Republican leaders are generally somewhat more conservative than their Democratic counterparts, their conservatism is largely directed at the administration of social welfare programs and policies rather than at the philosophy behind social welfarism. Parties not only reflect America's underlying value consensus, but they also help to maintain it by accommodating themselves to challenges from without.

In addition to contributing to the maintenance of consensus, the political parties perform the necessary function of supplying leadership. It can be suggested that although the parties are not the sole or even the best instruments for the development and formulation of policy, they are ideally suited for the supplying of governmental majorities. It is generally assumed that the United States has a two-party system, but this is an oversimplification. It might be more realistic to say that in any contest for public office there are seldom more than two serious contenders. In fact, in approximately half of the congressional districts, the minority party is too insignificant to finish better than a poor second. In these districts a single party has a monopoly on election victories and the true opportunity for choosing among contenders for public office occurs in the party primary rather than in the general election.

The decentralization of American parties is most apparent in connection with the nominating function. Although it is obvious that a federal system of government would tend to buttress the diffusion of power in the party system, such structural considerations are not in themselves adequate causal factors. A consideration of the complex array of socioeconomic variables which contribute to the form of party organization might lead one to inquire if the American party system would have developed its present characteristics even if the framers of the Constitution had adopted a unitary government. Looking briefly over the sweep of American history reveals several possible reasons for decentralization. The heterogeneous qualities of the social structure are to a considerable extent regionalized, and domestic conflicts have maximized these regional diversities. In the absence of issues of great significance which may intersect sectional differences, domestic politics takes full cognizance of attitudes and interests which vary along sectional lines.[59]

In a very real sense, states and some cities are cultural entities. North Dakota, economically dominated by wheat farming, is a strong center of agrarian radicalism. In Utah about 60% of the people are Mormons and the influence of the Church of Jesus Christ of Latter-Day Saints is a telling force in the politics of the state. In Michigan, a highly industrial state, organized labor is prominent within the Democratic Party. In most southern states urbanization and industrialization have lagged behind and labor is generally regarded as less important than, for example, the state Farm Bureau Federations.[60] An element of localism has also been built into the pattern of American politics by the flow of immigration. With the exception of the Negro question, ethnic issues have not had much of an impact on national politics. However, the tendency of ethnic groups to follow similar paths of migration and concentrate in particular areas has "constituted a means to power and influence for locally oriented political organizations outside and inside their own ranks."[61]

Since the electoral system in the United States is designed to ensure the supremacy of local units, it often happens that regional conflicts are dealt with on a relatively low level. Each party organization will be more responsive to the dominant interests in the community. For example, the Americans for Democratic Action, an organization dedicated to "liberal" principles, became so aggressive in striving for municipal reform in Philadelphia that it actually assumed control of the machinery of the Democratic Party. The political activists who operated under the Democratic label in this election of 1950 were surely not similar in attitude to the Democratic politicians of the South. Similarly, the Los Angeles Democratic party faction which supports Mayor Sam Yorty is unique even within the context of California's factionalized Democratic Party. However, such differences are usually submerged at the national level, where pragmatic necessity dictates that resources be pooled in order to elect a president. The political maverick who fails to endorse his party's candidate for the presidency is such a rare animal that a good deal of newsprint is expended whenever one does make an appearance.

Since the Constitution requires that a president receive a majority of the electoral votes, it is necessary for the loose coalition of local and state organizations to forge themselves into a temporary alliance for the purpose of placing their candidate in the White House. This alliance is not based on shared values. Rather, the seeking of office acts as a catalyst. Even in the selection of candidates, localism plays a vital role. The presidential nominee will be a person who can appeal to the undecided voters while avoiding the alienation of social groupings. Consequently a national platform may be logically inconsistent but satisfying to group demands. Also, those aspiring to presidential nomination are aware that their best path to success lies in cultivating the support of the state organizations.

An outstanding example of the importance of state party organization can be found in Eugene McCarthy's attempt to win the 1968 Democratic presidential nomination. Delegates to national party nominating conventions are, with few exceptions, selected by their state party organizations. Thus, their actions at the conventions can be construed to be representative of state party leaders. In spite of his respectable showing in preconvention primaries and public opinion polls,[62] support for McCarthy at the Chicago convention was low.[63] Despite concerted efforts either to capture the machinery of state party organizations or to win their backing, the McCarthy forces failed in their crucial endeavor.

Once a presidential election is over, the national organizations continue to function in preparation for the frequent elections which occur beneath the national level. The isolation of state party organizations makes it possible, and indeed likely, that the interests which coalesce every four years to nominate a president will not continue to function in harmony. This is especially true when the national party organization, personified by the president, attempts coercion of deviant factions within the party. The most remarkable example of the ability of local power structures to resist national pressures toward conformity is the Roosevelt "purge" of 1938.[64] President Roosevelt, in an effort to reduce intraparty opposition to his legislative program, entered selected candidates in state Democratic primaries and lent the full weight of his personal prestige to their campaigns. In addition, he worked behind the scenes to develop local organizations in support of these candidates. The purge attempt resulted in a victory for the state organizations, who resented bitterly what they regarded as an intrusion into the right of each state to select its own candidates. In Georgia, where Roosevelt campaigned vigorously against Senator Walter F. George, the president suffered his worst defeat. Senator George, with the full support of the state party organization and the financial backing of industrial interests such as the influential Georgia Power Company, won over the New Deal candidate by a two-to-one margin. That the voters, while soundly trouncing Roosevelt's choice in the senatorial contest, elected a governor running on a New Deal–type platform indicates that the resentment of interference was a crucial factor.

The essential conclusion of this section is that the political parties, operating on the necessity of a broad base of support, achieve more cohesion in the selection of candidates than in the formulation of public policy. On the other hand, the ideological fuzziness of American parties should not blind us to the fact that each party tends to be more responsive to particular sets of interests within the community. Both in terms of leadership recruitment and hard-core support the Democratic party has relied on industrial, urban, low-income groups while the Republicans have traditionally been more representative of financial and manufacturing interests. Translating bases of support into demands for governmental action would lead us to conclude that people of a conservative inclination gravitate toward the Republican Party while the "radicals" find a more congenial atmosphere within the Democratic Party.

If for no other reason than to avoid stereotyping party followers, it should be stressed that each party attracts a membership with a broad range of political orientations. Such diversity among party members would lead us to expect little or no internal agreement over any issue or candidate if it were not for two facts. First, parties are basically state and local organizations, and greater homogeneity is to be found *within* such sublevels than *between* them. Therefore, what appears to be great diversity at the national level is often diminished when the lower levels of party organization are examined. Second, only a small number of individuals are actually active in party work at any level, and recruitment patterns are such that these few leaders find less difficulty in reaching agreement than would the mass membership which they ostensibly represent. As Sorauf observed,

> [d]espite recent trends the American parties remain largely skeletal, "cadre" organizations, manned generally by small numbers of activists and involving the general masses of their supporters scarcely at all. . . . American party organization continues to be characterized by its unusual fluidity and evanescence, by its failure to generate activity at non-election times, and by the ease with which a handful of activists and public office-holders dominate it.[65]

Given the vague, amorphous policy positions which parties are forced to adopt to launch a general appeal to the public, and given that parties, by their nature, are more concerned with electing office-holders than with enacting issues, it is small wonder that interest groups are formed to serve the function of "representing" specific policy concerns within the American political arena. Pragmatic considerations dictate that parties must default in adopting such roles. Just as nature abhors a vacuum, so it might be said that democratic politics abhors interest inarticulation. Voluntary associations, functionally independent from political parties, have filled this breach.

NOTES

[1]At the time of this writing there appears to be increased activity in the area of consumer protection, yet no mass-based association reflecting the full scope of the consuming public has emerged, and it remains to be seen whether such an association will develop.

[2]William Graham Sumner, *Folkways* (New York: Mentor Books, 1960), p. 27.

[3]*Ibid.*

[4]Robert Redfield, "The Folk Society," *American Journal of Sociology*, LII (Jan. 1947), p. 297.

[5]H. R. Radcliffe-Brown, *The Andaman Islanders* (London: Cambridge University Press, 1933), p. 43.

[6]Raymond Firth, "Succession to Chieftanship in Tikopia," *Oceania*, XXX (Mar. 1960), pp. 161–80; Redfield, *The Folk Culture of Yukatan* (Chicago: University of Chicago Press, 1941).

[7]Bruce Ryan, *Sinhalese Village* (Coral Gables, Fla.: The University of Miami Press, 1958), pp. 148–52.

[8]Gordon F. Streib, "An Attempt to Unionize a Semi-Literate Navaho Group," *Human Organization*, XI (Spring 1952), pp. 23–31.

[9]Edward C. Banfield, *The Moral Basis of a Backward Society* (New York: The Free Press, 1958), p. 89.

[10]Ralph Lane, "Change and Organization in Rural Ireland," *Human Organization*, XIV (Summer 1955), p. 6.

[11]Eliot D. Chapple and Carleton S. Coon, *Principles of Anthropology* (New York: Holt, Rinehart & Winston, 1942), p. 418.

[12]Arnold Rose, *Theory and Method in the Social Sciences* (Minneapolis: University of Minnesota Press, 1952), pp. 54–55.

[13]Louis Wirth, "Urbanism as a Way of Life," *American Journal of Sociology*, XLIV (July 1938), p. 20. Cf. S. N. Eisenstadt, "Primitive Political Systems: A Preliminary Comparative Analysis," *American Anthropologist*, LXI (1959), pp. 200–220.

[14]Kenneth Little, "The Role of Voluntary Associations in West African Urbanization," *American Anthropologist*, LVII (1957), pp. 579–95.

[15]Robert T. Anderson and Gallatin Anderson, "Voluntary Associations and Urbanization: A Diachronic Analysis," *American Journal of Sociology*, LXV (Nov. 1958), pp. 265–73.

[16]V. O. Key, Jr., *Politics, Parties, and Pressure Groups* (New York: Thomas Y. Crowell Company, 1958), p. 49.

[17]Gabriel A. Almond and Sidney Verba, *The Civic Culture: Political Attitudes and Democracy in Five Nations* (Boston: Little, Brown & Co., 1965), p. 13.

[18]*Ibid.*

[19]James Madison, *The Federalist*, No. X.

[20]Edward M. Freeman, "The Pattern of Pressure," *Sociology and Social Research*, XXXVII (Jan. 1953), p. 187. For an excellent summary of literature on pressure groups and democracy see Lewis A. Bayles, "Are Pressure Groups Threatening American Democracy?" *The Midwest Quarterly*, 11 (Oct. 1960), pp. 49–66.

[21]*Trist* v. *Child*, 21 Wallace 441 (1875).

[22]Cited in Thomas B. Mechling, "Washington Lobbies Threaten Democracy," *Virginia Quarterly Review*, XXII (Summer 1946), p. 341.

[23]The use of the term *myth* does not necessarily connote disapproval; it is used here to mean a belief about the "real" world—the way things actually are—regardless of the empirical validity of that belief. If they are woven into the basic values of individuals, myths may continue to survive irrespective of their objectivity in describing reality.

[24]Freeman, *op. cit.*, p. 185.

[25]See Frederick Jackson Turner, *The United States, 1830–1850: The Nation and Its Sections* (New York: Holt, 1935).

[26]Gerald N. Grob and Robert N. Beck, eds., *American Ideas*, Vol. I: *Foundations (1629–1865)* (New York: The Free Press, 1963), p. 247.

[27]Ervin Laszlo, *Individualism, Collectivism, and Political Power* (The Hague: Martinus Nijhoff, 1963), p. 47.

[28]"Civic Group Scares Parties Into Nominating Good Candidates," *National Municipal Review*, XLI (June 1952), p. 317.

[29]The Citizens' Council of La Grange, Illinois, "Articles of Association and By-Laws," revised May 15, 1957 (mimeograph).

[30]Alexis de Tocqueville, *Democracy in America*, Vol. I (New York: Vintage Books, 1954), p. 199.

[31]Among those who do not accept Tocqueville's assertion as applicable today are Charles R. Wright and Herbert H. Hyman. See their "Voluntary Association Memberships of American Adults," *American Sociological Review*, XXIII (1958), reprinted in Betty H. Zisk, ed., *American Political Interest Groups: Readings in Theory and Research* (Belmont, Calif.: Wadsworth Publishing Company, 1969), pp. 300–315.

[32]Arnold M. Rose, *The Power Structure* (New York: Oxford University Press, 1967), p. 220.

[33]Frank C. Nall II, "National Association," *The Emergent American Society*, Vol. I: *Large-Scale Organizations*, ed. W. Lloyd Warner (New Haven, Conn.: Yale University Press, 1967), p. 280. Nall's estimate of 12,000 national associations appears to be conservative, but reasonably accurate. In 1964 there were over 12,500 such organizations existing in America, according to *Encyclopedia of Associations* (4th ed., Detroit: Gale Research Co., 1964).

[34]*Congressional Quarterly Almanac*, Vol. XXIV (Washington, D.C.: Congressional Quarterly Service, 1968), p. 891.

[35]Many studies substantiate this assertion. A summary of some of them and a fuller discussion of the phenomenon in question is contained in Chapter 4 of Thomas R. Dye and L. Harmon Zeigler, *The Irony of Democracy: An Uncommon Introduction to American Politics* (Belmont, Calif.: Wadsworth Publishing Company, 1970).

[36]Wright and Hyman, "Voluntary Association Membership . . . ," p. 306.

[37]Rose, *The Power Structure*, p. 222.

[38]E. E. Schattschneider, *The Semi-Sovereign People: A Realist's View of Democracy in America* (New York: Holt, Rinehart & Winston, 1960), p. 32.

[39]It should be observed, however, that this consistency probably results more from apathy on their part than from a conscious desire to make their actions congruent with their attitudes.

[40]The discussion of pluralism which follows is admittedly abbreviated. For a more explicit and detailed treatment of the subject, refer to some of the more eloquent statements of modern pluralism, such as Edward C. Banfield, *Political Influence* (New York: The Free Press, 1961); Robert A. Dahl, *Pluralist Democracy in the United States: Conflict and Consent* (Chicago: Rand McNally, 1967), and *Who Governs? Democracy and Power in an American City* (New Haven, Conn.: Yale University Press, 1960); Suzanne Keller, *Beyond the Ruling Class* (New York: Random House, 1963); William Kornhauser, *The Politics of Mass Society* (New York: The Free Press, 1959); and David Truman, *The Governmental Process* (New York: Alfred A. Knopf, 1951).

Additional insights can be gleaned from some recent critiques of pluralism. See Peter Bachrach, *The Theory of Democratic Elitism: A Critique* (Boston: Little, Brown & Co., 1967); Thomas R. Dye and L. Harmon Zeigler, *The Irony of Democracy* (Belmont, Calif.: Wadsworth Publishing Company, 1970); Henry Kariel, *The Decline of American Pluralism* (Stanford, Calif.: Stanford University Press, 1961); Grant McConnell, *Private Property and American Democracy* (New York: Alfred A. Knopf, 1966); and various selections contained in William E. Connolly, ed., *The Bias of Pluralism* (New York: Atherton Press, 1969).

[41]Shin'ya Ono, "The Limits of Bourgeois Pluralism," *Apolitical Politics: A Critique of Behavioralism*, eds. Charles A. McCoy and John Playford (New York: Thomas Y. Crowell Company, 1967), pp. 103–4.

[42]Arthur W. Macmahon, "Problems of Federalism: A Survey," in Arthur W. Macmahon, ed., *Federalism Mature and Emergent* (Garden City, N.Y.: Doubleday & Company, Inc., 1955), p. 11.

[43]See Franz Neuman, *The Democratic and the Authoritarian State* (New York: The Free Press, 1957), pp. 216–32 for a discussion of the limitations of the concept of federalism as an independent casual factor.

[44]This description is drawn from Joseph C. Palamountain, *The Politics of Distribution* (Cambridge, Mass.: Harvard University Press, 1955), pp. 155–87.

[45]Quoted in Merle Fainsod, Lincoln Gordon, and Joseph C. Palamountain, Jr., *Government and the American Economy* (New York: W. W. Norton & Co., Inc., 1959), p. 545.

[46]Palamountain, *op. cit.*, p. 163.

[47]Donald C. Blaisdell, *American Democracy Under Pressure* (New York: The Ronald Press Company, 1957), p. 50.

[48]Robert J. Harris, "States' Rights and Vested Interests," *Journal of Politics*, XV (Nov. 1953), p. 466.

[49]*Hammer* v. *Dagenhart*, 247 U.S. 251 (1918).

[50]Harris, *op. cit.*, p. 467.

[51]Quoted in Latham, *op. cit.*, p. 56.

[52]*Federal Maritime Board* v. *Isbrandtsen*, 356 U.S. 481 (1958). This account is taken from Jerrold L. Walden, "The Dual-Rate Moratorium—End of the Isbrandtsen Odyssey," *Journal of Public Law*, X (Spring 1961), pp. 78–99.

[53]House Report No. 2055, 85th Cong., 2nd Sess., 1946, p. 2. Quoted in Walden, *op. cit.*, p. 78.

[54]See Robert de Roos and Arthur Maas, "The Lobby that Can't be Licked," *Harper's Magazine*, Aug. 1949, pp. 20–30 for a more complete description of this episode.

[55]Herbert McClosky, Paul J. Hoffman, and Rosemary O'Hara, "Issue Consensus among Party Leaders and Followers," *American Political Science Review*, LIV (June 1960), p. 410.

[56]*Ibid.*, pp. 411–13.

[57]Angus Campbell et al., *The American Voter* (abridged ed., New York: John Wiley & Sons, Inc., 1964), p. 121.

[58]McClosky et al., *op. cit.*, p. 426.

[59]David Truman, "Federalism and the Party System," in Macmahon, *op. cit.*, pp. 131–32.

[60]Charles Adrian, *State and Local Governments* (New York: The Macmillan Company, 1960), p. 4. See also John Gunther, *Inside U.S.A.* (New York: Harper & Row, Publishers, 1947).

[61]Truman, *op. cit.*, p. 132.

[62]A Gallup poll conducted immediately prior to the convention showed Democrats to favor Humphrey over McCarthy 46%–42% with 12% undecided. However, the same poll indicated that in a showdown among McCarthy, Nixon, and Wallace, 62% of the Democrats favored McCarthy; whereas only 56% favored Humphrey in a similar showdown. *Gallup Opinion Index* (Sept. 1968), pp. 10, 11, 18.

[63]Humphrey was nominated on the first ballot. The delegate votes received by each candidate were Humphrey—1,761¾, McCarthy—601, McGovern—146½, Rev. Channing E. Phillips—67½. *Newsweek* (September 9, 1968), p. 36.

[64]See L. Harmon Zeigler, "Senator Walter George's 1938 Campaign," *Georgia Historical Quarterly*, XLIII (Dec. 1959), pp. 333–52 for a more detailed account.

[65]Frank J. Sorauf, *Party Politics in America* (Boston: Little, Brown & Co., 1968), pp. 79–80.

three

Interest Group Structure

We have examined the intellectual history of the group as a concept in social science, the liberal democratic theoretical tradition underlying much of the study of interest groups to date, and the sociopolitical milieu in which interest groups exist in America. Let us now begin to analyze the internal dynamics of interest groups. In subsequent chapters we will isolate specific groups and types of groups for more intensive scrutiny; for the present, however, our concern is with interest groups in general—why they are formed, how they are formed, and how they survive.

GOALS AND BENEFITS

Before proceeding with our discussion we need to introduce and define some of the concepts that will be used. *Goals* are the stated or unstated values for which groups or individuals strive. *Benefits* are the rewards, or values, which groups or individuals actually receive. Both concepts can be subsumed under the general heading, *goods*. Many types of goods exist in the sociopolitical market. Since a thing becomes a good merely by virtue of people placing a value on it, a variety of disparate entities (abstract as well as existential) can be goals and/or benefits. The subjective nature of the evaluation procedure combined with the heterogeneity of the goods themselves renders them virtually incomparable for purposes of rigorous scientific analysis. We can, however, deal with them in a somewhat more precise manner by categorizing them according to some consistent method of classification. To develop a consistent classificatory scheme it is necessary that we select some general characteristic common to all political goods, which may vary in the precise manner in which it is manifested. A concrete example with which we are all familiar is the parlor game "Twenty Questions." To begin a round of Twenty Questions the person who is "It" gives the other players a hint concerning the object he has in mind; he tells them whether it is animal, vegetable, or mineral. In doing so he has performed the act of classification. The general characteristic in this case is the organic structure of all potential objects that could be guessed; every object may be placed in one of the three categories. Two important aspects of classification are highlighted in this illustration. First, the characteristic according to which classification is to be made is sufficiently general that *all* objects are encompassed by it. And second, there are two or more mutually exclusive categories of that characteristic into which objects may be divided.

In Twenty Questions the characteristic according to which objects are classified is defined by the rules of the game. But since the study of interest groups is not a formal game, there are no official rules for us to follow in identifying the characteristic for classifying group sociopolitical goods. Although this lack of restriction gives us discretionary latitude in selecting a classification characteristic of our own choosing, it also means that any we do select is wholly arbitrary. The only guide we can follow in such a situation is that of theoretical richness. In other words, we must select a characteristic which has meaning in terms of the analytic framework with which we are working. It would be pointless to employ organic structure as used in Twenty Questions to classify interest group goals, for instance. We are left with the problem of selecting an appropriate classification scheme for our purposes.

Fortunately, others have confronted this problem before us, so that we have a legacy of literature from which to draw. The several extant categorization schemes employ different criteria for classification and therefore focus attention on different attributes of socio-political goods. We shall not restrict ourselves to the use of any one to the exclusion of all others; instead, we shall use that which has the most theoretical utility within the context in which it is employed.

In the abstract, each typology is composed of mutually exclusive categories; however, in application the boundaries of categories may become somewhat blurred. Let us return to the Twenty Questions illustration to clarify this statement. Assume that a piece of woolen material is the object to be guessed. Wool is clearly animal in its organic structure. Assume also that the particular piece of fabric in question is dyed with a vegetable dye. The wool is animal to the exclusion of being vegetable or mineral; likewise, the dye is vegetable to the exclusion of being either mineral or animal. Abstractly, the two substances are distinct; however, in applying the single classification scheme to the concrete object—the particular piece of fabric—the distinction becomes blurred, and the players are given the hint that the object is both animal and vegetable.

Although categories are analytically distinct *within* each of the typologies to be employed, there may be a degree of overlap between any two categories from *different* typologies. This is so because different typologies are based on different characteristics which may themselves overlap. If, for example, we were to group substances according to whether they were solids, liquids, or gases in their natural states, we would classify coal as a solid and petroleum as a liquid. Were we to use an entirely different schema in classifying the same substances, however, coal and petroleum might fall into the same category; for example, if the animal, vegetable, or mineral classifications were used.

Let us now proceed with a brief discussion of each of the categorization schemes that will be used in analyzing goals and benefits related to interest group activity. Bear in mind that conceptually each is composed of mutually exclusive categories, but in reality a given category in one is not necessarily wholly distinct from the categories in another.

Collective goods versus selective goods

Economists have long employed the distinction between collective goods and selective goods. The former are goods which are not amenable to discriminatory distribution within a given categoric group; the latter are those which do lend themselves to contingent distribution. For example, a city that purifies its water is providing a collective good, for all who use the city water supply benefit equally. There can be no discrimination among water users concerning the relative purity of the commodity. On the other hand, if the city distributed home purification devices to some but not all water users, those devices would be selective goods. In the latter instance, not all members of the water-using public would benefit equally from the good in question. It will presently become apparent that a categorization of goals according to those involving collective goods and those involving selective goods will help to understand the rationale behind someone's decision whether to join an organization. For the present, however, we need only be concerned with grasping the distinction between goods categorized according to this characteristic.

Whenever we differentiate collective from selective goods, it is wise to identify explicitly the group to which we are referring, for the universality of benefit is relative to the particular set of individuals in question.[1] By way of illustration, let us define a categoric group as being composed of all college students in the United States. Suppose Congress were to enact a law which provided for a $300 per month cost of living allowance to all college students. Such a stipend would be a collective good with respect to college students as a categoric group. However, if one were to define the categoric group as being all persons of college age in the United States, then the stipend would be a selective benefit. Additionally, one must realize that even when a collective good is made available in equal amounts to all persons, it is not necessarily valued equally by all recipients. Thus, the $300 stipend may be of less value to students from wealthy families than to those who are less well off.

Source of value

Another scheme for classifying individual benefits from group association has been proposed by Blau.[2] It groups such rewards according to their source. His twofold scheme divides rewards into those which are *intrinsic* and those which are *extrinsic* to the group in question. Persons receive intrinsic rewards solely by virtue of association itself; extrinsic rewards result from enjoying the goods attained through group activity. In the former instance the group is perceived as being an end in itself, whereas in the latter case the group is a means to an end. Frequently benefits received from group association are a mix of intrinsic and extrinsic rewards. As Blau observed, "Workers participate in unions not only to improve their employment conditions but also because they intrinsically enjoy the fellowship in the union and derive satisfaction from helping to realize its objectives."[3]

Clark and Wilson have proposed a threefold typology of socio-political goods according to their substance.[4] Goods are divided into *material*, *solidary*, and *purposive* categories. Material goods have monetary value or can be readily converted into goods of equivalent monetary value. Solidary benefits, on the other hand, are intrinsic to associated individuals.

> They derive in the main from the act of associating and include such rewards as socializing, congeniality, the sense of group membership and identification, the status resulting from membership, fun and conviviality, the maintenance of social distinctions, and so on. Their common characteristic is that they tend to be independent of the precise ends of the association.[5]

Purposive benefits, like material ones, tend to be extrinsic, but like solidary ones, they tend to defy monetary evaluation. They are derived from the goals and objectives of the group and are altruistic or "suprapersonal" in nature. Salisbury writes,

> Although, of course, the benefits of such [suprapersonal] achievement may accrue to particular individuals they are not ordinarily divisible into units of value allocated to specific persons or charged against unit costs. Nor can purposive benefits always be confined to the parties seeking them. Thus "good government" or "peace" or "states rights" or "civil liberties" are all desired by individuals and benefit individuals, but the benefits cannot readily be cost analyzed and they accrue to all sorts of people who took no part in the efforts to secure them.[6]

Thus, purposive benefits appear to overlap collective goods.

A related distinction is that between *symbolic* and *tangible* goods.[7] Tangible rewards are material (in the above scheme) and are valued for their utilitarian potential. Symbolic rewards may also stem from material objects; however, their value cannot be expressed in material or monetary terms. They are abstract values resulting from psychological responses evoked by some stimulus which may or may not be a manifest object. Although symbolic and tangible rewards are analytically distinct, they may result simultaneously from a single object. For instance, an American flag is a corporeal object possessing monetary value; the acquisition of a flag provides a tangible reward. Additionally, its acquisition may stimulate strong positive emotional responses in those to whom the flag is the abstract symbol of patriotism. Nonmaterial stimuli such as words are capable of evoking similar responses.

Expressive versus instrumental actions

We now concern ourselves with the value that individuals and groups receive from their goal-seeking activity rather than from the actual acquisition of a good. Blau first called attention to the difference between *expressive* and *instrumental* action.[8] Robert Salisbury, too, has employed the distinction. Salisbury observed,

> Expressive actions are those where the action involved gives expression to the interests or values of a person or group rather than instrumentally pursuing interests or values. Presumably one cannot *express* material values; one must pursue them and achieve them.... But one can often derive benefits from expressing certain kinds of values.... Whether the expression is instrumentally relevant to the achievement of the values in question is, for the moment, not at issue. The point here is that important benefits are derived from the expression itself.[9]

Most of the scholarly work that has been done on interest groups has focused on their instrumental activities in pursuit of material goods. Little attention has been devoted to the expressive aspects of interest groups.

INTEREST GROUPS AND THE STATUS QUO

Organized activity may frequently be directed *against* something as well as toward a goal. Organizations may seek either to bring about a change in a situation (Students for a Democratic Society, for example) or to prevent a change (Daughters of the American Revolution). Often, the establishment of an organization to institute change will provide the necessary spark to set a status quo–oriented group on its feet.

Having distinguished between these two types of groups, it is plausible to suggest that the organization which seeks to prevent a change, to keep things as they are, has a better chance of keeping its original purpose in the forefront because of the essentially negative orientation of its operations. It is easier to be in opposition without assuming the responsibility of offering alternative courses of action. Many such organizations concentrate their attention on a perceived threat which may be high in emotional content and unfluctuating even though the conditions which produced the threat have ceased to exist. Negative groups frequently develop precise symbolization of threats that "resist the discipline of external events."[10] Thus, a group may identify "internal communist subversion" or "Wall Street" as a basic threat, not only to the group itself, but to the total society. That there may be little evidence to substantiate these fears does not alter the continued perception of the danger as immediate.

While the intention to act, whether for or against something, results from some event or series of events impinging on a value, the direction which an organization takes over time may follow one of three courses: (1) it may decline in activity and eventually disappear as the threat becomes less serious; (2) it may continue to perceive the threat as real, irrespective of its actual seriousness; or (3) it may develop new issues and "causes" to keep itself alive.[11] A good example of a negative organization which maintains stable goals in the face of changing circumstances is the Ku Klux Klan. The revival of the Klan took place in an atmosphere of steadily rising tension and hostility following the *Brown* v. *Board of Education* decision of 1954 which declared unconstitutional continued segregation of Negro and white students in public schools. In 1956 the crisis temporarily abated and the integration forces instituted a corresponding reduction in their efforts. Accordingly, the White Citizens Councils, relatively new organizations, entered a temporary period of relative inactivity. The Ku Klux Klan, on the other hand, continued to operate with its original zeal. While the rapid growth and equally rapid decline of the White Citizens Councils seemed to be hinged to the perception on the part of members of the imminent probability of integration, the Klan apparently functioned independently of the reduction of the external threat. There was no observable correlation between Klan activities and Negro counteractivities.

SOCIAL CLASS AND GROUP PARTICIPATION

The explanation of the Klan's deviation from the common-sense assumption that organization breeds counterorganization is to be found in the social background of Klan members. Klan membership is largely marginal, both socially and economically. Most members are from working-class backgrounds, usually in the lower brackets of the labor market, and they have been uprooted from traditional life-styles by the rapid industrialization of the South. While the White Citizens Councils membership is predominantly rural, the strength of the Klan is in large cities such as Birmingham, Atlanta,

Jacksonville, and Tampa. Klan members are experiencing a transition from one mode of life, that of the rigidly ordered rural community, to another, more ambiguous one, that of the city. Vander Zanden concludes that a failure of the individual to define his role, to "learn his place," causes him to overconform to what he believes are the values of traditional middle-class America. Ambiguity about one's social role is relieved by the solidary group identification provided by the elaborate secret rituals and symbols of the organization. Klan programs are anti-Negro, but they are also much broader in that they represent a conscious effort to convince the members that they do not occupy an inferior status. The exaggerated emphasis of status symbols (mostly those of "pure" Americanism) in Klan literature helps to placate more extensive anxieties than those produced by the integration question. Hence, the Klan goals remain unchanged year after year, since there is no specific action that could be undertaken to satisfy the needs of the members.[12]

The benefits that individuals receive from organizations of the Ku Klux Klan variety are largely symbolic, consisting primarily of psychological value received from camaraderie and from the emotional release of pent-up frustrations and anxieties engendered by the members' ambiguous social roles. Edelman explains this type of attachment as follows:

> For those whose identification with work, political party, and community is slight and unsatisfying, the yearning to escape from isolation and responsibility becomes very strong. The alienated man, who feels little sense of belonging to any group and cherishes no organization as an extension of his own personality, will . . . predictably become authoritarian. He will seek strong leadership, personalize, stereotype his environment, and will react to distortions and abstractions rather than to concrete people and things.[13]

Such persons tend to be from the lower socioeconomic strata.[14] It is not sufficient, however, merely to assert that such a relationship exists without attempting to explain it, for it is illogical to assume that a low-status, low-paying job or poor education leads directly to the alienation syndrome. One hypothesis that has been offered, which also accounts for the upper-class bias in interest group activity, is that the working conditions and life-styles of those in the lower socioeconomic strata foster feelings of alienation. Workers are divorced from the products on which they work, they enjoy little autonomy, and they depend on others to produce the things they consume. Whereas their work may be instrumental in that it contributes to the creation of some product, it involves only one marginal (and repetitive) step in the creative process. Such conditions do not contribute to the worker's identification with the final product. As a result he does not take pride in his work, nor, for that matter, does he experience the feeling of actually producing a material good. In short, he does not develop an image of himself as an instrumental actor.

People in higher socioeconomic strata, by virtue of the roles they play in society, have a greater opportunity to develop their assertiveness.

> A great many people, particularly specialists, professionals, and managers in industry, develop a tie to their work that is relatively rational and efficient. Their effectiveness derives from their special ability to devise methods of accomplishing desired ends, and they experience deep satisfaction as they exercise such ability. . . . [S]uch rational and effective manipulation of resources is in part a function of the opportunity to work with the concrete environment and to see the results of one's work. . . . It may be that only people who have learned through some such gratifying association how to deal effectively with men and objects are likely to respond to political leadership and movements in a way that serves their objective interests and brings them tangible results.[15]

Admittedly, one cannot explain all differences between types of group membership in terms of occupational roles alone. To attempt such a total explanation is to be guilty of gross oversimplification. Nevertheless, the evidence is sufficient to warrant the conclusion that one's vocational experiences do affect one's general feeling of efficacy and are at least a partial determinant of political attitudes and the style in which they are expressed.

We have noted that the ideal type of instrumental interest group organized around a specific tangible goal rarely exists. Many groups do not confine themselves to a single issue but take an active interest in several, thereby diluting the consensus they can command from their members on any one issue. Such groups are also found to avoid specifics and to adopt more general positions on issues to appeal to broad membership bases. The result of such dilution and generalization is that the tangible goals are more difficult to agree on and the tactics suitable for the attainment of such goals are difficult to execute. The further a group departs from the pragmatic interest group ideal, the greater the likelihood that it will seek and attain only symbolic rewards. Such rewards are more satisfying for those in the lower socioeconomic strata than for those in the upper classes, who tend to be oriented more toward tangible rewards. It follows, then, that groups which reap mostly symbolic benefits should appeal more to a mass following than to an upper-class (elite) membership. Conversely, it is to be expected that groups organized around a tangible interest embraced by those in the upper classes will have limited memberships and highly articulated goals of limited scope. Furthermore, the nature of their goals conspires with the pragmatic character and instrumental capabilities of their members (along with the members' relatively high resource level) to place such small elite interest groups in a favored position. It is not too surprising, therefore, to find that groups which are the most successful in attaining tangible policy outputs from the political system are relatively small and composed of members from the elite socioeconomic strata of the nation.

SOCIAL MOVEMENTS AND EXPRESSIVE GROUPS

One type of social aggregation which is frequently (but in our view erroneously) thought to be within the interest group universe is the social movement. Social movements involve a much broader area of concern than do interest groups, which, you recall, are not primarily involved with capturing public office or changing the fundamental nature of the political regime.[16] Their principal function vis-à-vis the political system is to extract desired goods, not to restructure it. Most groups, therefore, are essentially conservative institutions which operate within the political system.[17] Social movements, on the other hand, have ideological bases which transcend specific issue concerns. They tend to seek purposive goals through expressive action. This is not to say that material policy decisions are not included within the goal structure of social movements. However, such goals are valued only in the short run as things which contribute to the movement's fundamental aim of providing channels for its members' expressive action.

Furthermore, social movements can be differentiated from interest groups on the basis of their respective organizational structures. Little or no central coordination or leadership can be perceived in the case of social movements. Isolated, fragmented, and possibly conflicting centers of control may be identifiable, but the very nature of a movement renders stable, consolidated control virtually impossible. The membership of a movement is vague and rather amorphous. One rarely joins a movement by formally signing up and paying dues. In fact, it might be more accurate to speak of "supporters" or "followers" of social movements than of "members."

Conceivably, a number of interest groups could be encompassed within any given social movement. For example, the civil rights movement is properly classified as a social movement, yet the NAACP, CORE, SCLC, the Urban League, and many other formal interest groups are part of that movement. Thus, one might want to argue that formal membership in a social movement is possible by virtue of membership in an included interest group. We shall leave such arguments to metaphysicians and semanticists; the fact remains that movements and interest groups are analytically distinct entities. Support for the former is therefore different from membership in the latter.

Support for a movement may fluctuate rapidly, for emotional commitment is the major investment that one makes in becoming involved in a movement. Little of material value is lost if a shift in one's attitudes or in the political climate precipitates a lessening of emotional commitment. Moreover, the purposive nature of a movement's goals does not offer a potential material payoff to supporters sufficient to maintain the interest of many. But the same factors that make it easy for supporters to drop from the fold also facilitate ease of entry for others. Thus, social movements are characterized by relatively loose bonds among supporters and rather high turnover rates.

Many of the distinguishing characteristics of social movements are applicable to a greater or lesser extent to interest groups in general. In fact, all of our criteria for defining an interest group are met by social movements, with the exception of organization. It is our contention, however, that more factors differentiate them than this one characteristic. The ideological content of social movements causes them to act consistently in an expressive manner, to provide benefits almost exclusively of the purposive variety, and to seek primarily symbolic goals. These qualities, when considered collectively and in conjunction with the lack of central coordination and the amorphousness of their supportive public, are sufficient to justify the exclusion of social movements from the interest group universe.

We do not mean to give the impression that interest groups never engage in expressive action, symbolic goal-seeking, or the provision of purposive benefits. Most interest groups, although they may be engaged *primarily* in instrumental activity and concerned *primarily* with material goals, do in fact incorporate some degree of purposive or ideological content within their issue interests and do in fact engage in expressive behavior on occasion. For instance, the American Legion falls within our definition of an interest group. It does not seek to capture political office or to change the social or political order; it does take positions on bills pending in Congress and in state legislatures, and it does seek to affect political decision-makers when issues it deems important are raised. Yet the American Legion is not devoid of ideology. It is a strongly patriotic group with an interest in maintaining the "American way of life" and the symbols thereof in addition to its more specific material interests in veterans' welfare. Perhaps the most realistic way of viewing the situation is to place groups on a continuum. On one end are transitory ad hoc groups which have no apparent ideological position and which are concerned with a single tangible policy goal. Once their goal is attained or once it becomes obviously unattainable, they no longer have a raison d'être and cease to exist. At the other extreme are groups which have at most a peripheral interest in the tangible effects of specific policy decision but an overriding concern with changing or defending the institutions of society. The American Legion, representing as it does a mixture of tangible and ideological interests, would fall somewhere near the midpoint of such a continuum.

A further distinguishing feature concerns the nature of the rewards received by members of the two extreme types of groups. The existing political system is designed to process instrumental demands for the allocation of tangible goods; therefore, those groups which operate within the system and which express instrumental demands tend to measure their rewards in material terms. Ideological groups and social movements, on the other hand, tend to be more concerned with expressive behavior in pursuit of purposive values, and they frequently operate outside the political system, sometimes seeking to change it. But whether they are committed to the existing political system or demand changes in it, social movements are less concerned with tangible resource allocations through institutional channels than they are with signs of ideological rectitude. The vast majority of groups in the United States which have any degree of "politicalness" tend to fall somewhere between these two extremes.

GROUP SIZE

Although the distinction between large, mass-membership organizations which perform primarily symbolic political functions and small, elite groups which rationally pursue tangible political goods is an oversimplification of the interest group universe, it is not as great a distortion of reality as one might at first suspect, and it is heuristically defensible. One might object to the lumping together of such apparently dissimilar attributes as the quantitative factor of group size and the qualitative factor of rationality in the establishment and pursuit of goals. Such an objection would find strong support in much of the traditional literature dealing with interest groups, for, as Mancur Olson has observed,

> [I]n so far as the traditional theory draws any distinction at all between small and large groups, it is apparently with respect to the scale of the functions they perform, not the extent they succeed in performing [them]. . . . It assumes that small and large groups differ in degree, but not in kind.[18]

Traditional theory notwithstanding, recent writers, many of whom have drawn heavily from economic exchange theory, have implied that the size of an organization is integrally related to the type of program it develops.

The size of a group has much to do with determining the type and amount of resources available to the group. Resources, in turn, affect the tactical options open to groups in their pursuit of particular policy goals. For instance, large groups, such as labor unions, have many members. To the extent that they can control the votes of their members, their sheer size constitutes a resource in that a vast number of votes can be delivered or withheld from selected candidates at election time.[19] Similarly, large groups provide manpower for launching time-consuming public opinion campaigns, letter-writing drives to political representatives, and myriad other tactical maneuvers including public demonstrations.

Large memberships usually mean sizable monetary resources, although this is not always the case. Large organizations may be relatively impoverished, while many small elite groups may command substantial financial resources. The type of interest represented by a group can also be expected to affect its level of financial support. Groups such as labor unions and the National Association of Manufacturers, which are organized around the material economic interests of their members, are generally able to command a greater share of their members' economic resources than are groups of comparable size which are organized around purposive or expressive interests. Dues or contributions to the former type of organization are, in a sense, like investments which may result in increased economic benefits, whereas dues or contributions to the latter type of organization may result in benefits whose values cannot be fiscally counted. Because most individuals are concerned about their personal financial situations, it is not surprising that they tend to place more restrictive limits on contributions which "buy" noneconomic benefits than on contributions toward benefits which will have a positive effect on their bank accounts.

Furthermore, as Salisbury has noted, individuals will not only devote more of their personal resources to groups which seek material benefits, but they will be more consistent in that support over time.

For most people the act of joining an expressive group—contributing dues to ACLU or signing a Vietnam protest petition—is a marginal act. The benefits derived from value expression are seldom of great intrinsic worth. Consequently, even if civil liberties remain equally endangered, a slight change in the member's resources or social pressures may lead to his failure to renew his membership.[20]

We can summarize by saying that, when all other variables are held constant, large groups tend to be richer than small ones. However, factors other than sheer size also determine the availability of such resources: (1) greater per capita contributions can be expected in the case of economically oriented interest groups than in the case of others, and (2) interest groups whose members tend to be economically well off can be expected to receive greater per capita contributions than those whose members are relatively poorer. Thus, size is one, but by no means the sole, determinant of financial support for a group.

Earlier we made the point that for a group to appeal to a large number of supporters it is highly probable that it will either have to offer a wider range of benefits than if it were to limit its appeal to a smaller public, or it will have to adopt a more ambiguous, more general rhetorical appeal. This is so because heterogeneity tends to increase as numerical size increases even if the persons in question are nominally alike with respect to a particular attribute or interest. Obscuring the clarity of focus on a single central issue may result in an expanded membership; however, the costs are not incurred without risk, for they may alienate the original members without appreciably attracting others. A case in point is provided by the various Vietnam Moratorium organizations that sprang up around the country in the fall of 1969. They were loosely confederated at the national level but remained primarily local organizations. Since central coordination was minimal, we cannot generalize to all local organizations; although we suspect that similar experiences occurred nationally, our point of reference is the one Moratorium organization that we observed personally.

Originally only one goal was enunciated—that of terminating America's involvement in the war. In October a protest march was held in which over 5,000 persons participated. The march was composed largely of persons associated with the university community, but significant numbers of participants from diverse walks of life were in evidence as well. A desire to see a speedy end to the American presence in Vietnam was the sole interest that these people had in common. There were many reasons why the supporters of the Moratorium had come to this point of view. Some were philosophic pacifists; some objected pragmatically to the war as an unwise instrument of American foreign policy; others objected on the grounds that it was a waste of precious human and economic resources. The only requirement for participation in, and support for, the Moratorium was this one interest; other politically relevant attitudes and interests were immaterial as far as the October demonstration was concerned. An explicit effort was made by the leaders of the Moratorium to disassociate it from other organizations which objected to the war, but which also had adopted positions with respect to other issues. Participation by members of such groups was welcomed and indeed encouraged, but they were offered no opportunity to "contaminate" the Moratorium observances by injecting additional ideological or issue concerns into it.

Following the October Moratorium, which was considered a success by most observers, the leadership of the organization adopted a different policy. For some reason—perhaps as a conscious attempt to expand their base of support or because opposing pressures caused them to lose sight of their original goal—the leaders expanded the scope of the Moratorium's interest. Prior to the second march, which was scheduled for mid-November, the Moratorium committee publicly expressed support for workers who were striking a local manufacturing concern. At the second march, in which there were fewer participants than there had been on the previous occasion, speakers attacked not only America's involvement in the war but "police harassment" of minority-group members, and intolerance on the part of the management of a local industrial plant (not the firm which was being struck) as well.

As a result of the expansion in the scope of the organization's interests, many persons who were originally sympathetic and supportive became disaffected. Whereas a large heterogeneous group could be in consensus on the single issue of the war in Vietnam, when other issues were introduced which resulted in cleavages along different socioeconomic axes, consensus could be attained among only a relatively small portion of that original group. By January support for the Moratorium was reduced to a mere handful of sympathetic individuals, and thereafter the group ceased to exist.

The object of this historical anecdote is not to present a chronicle of the Moratorium efforts, but rather to illustrate that an expansion of issues embraced by a group does not automatically ensure a wider membership base but may in fact have the reverse effect. When multiple issues are compatible—that is, when they create parallel cleavages within a group—it is likely that they will attract more members than if only a subset of such issues were embraced. However, the determination of how potential group members will react to any given issue is at best a difficult task to perform, for individual value orderings and perceptions of salient aspects of issues are rarely amenable to quick and easy assessment. Perhaps we can best illustrate the importance of crosscutting and parallel cleavages through the use of abstract diagrams.[21]

Let the area inside the square in Figure 1 represent a policy. The area inside the circle labeled "Issue A" represents that subset of persons who have an interest in Issue A. The diagonal line cutting through Issue A demarcates those who favor Issue A (the subset labeled "A+") from those who oppose it (the subset labeled "A−"). Assume that an interest group has been organized which has as its sole objective the adoption of Issue A. Such a group has a potential membership of all those persons who fall into the A+ sector of the circle. This sector is marked by horizontal lines shading the area.

Since the A+ sector is larger than the A− sector one might conclude that Issue A will probably be enacted. This conclusion would be correct (1) if policies were made only by those who are directly interested in the issues at stake, and (2) if only numerical superiority were required for decision-making. However, neither of these conditions holds uniformly in the American democratic political system.[22]

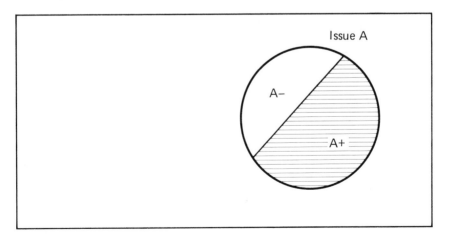

Figure 1.

Citizens rarely have the opportunity to determine public policy directly. Moreover, their representatives, who do formulate such policies, are frequently forced to consider many more factors than the raw numbers of constituents who are actively interested in an issue. Furthermore, one must not overlook the vast numbers of citizens who fall outside the circle of interested parties. Although they may not be initially concerned with an issue, they may become so as a result of factors such as propaganda, increased information, "logrolling," and so on.

Now let us imagine an interest group composed of all of those persons who fall into the A+ sector. Suppose that the group decides to expand its scope of involvement and to take a position on a second issue, Issue B. Such a decision might be based on a desire to expand its membership, on moral or ideological grounds, or on other tactical or material considerations. The results of issue expansion in terms of membership support will depend on several factors. Four distinct types of situations may result.

The first is illustrated in Figure 2. Issue B is salient to a totally different set of individuals than is Issue A. Our hypothetical interest group has taken a position favorable to Issue B (vertical shading) in addition to its pro-A position. Thus, although the A+ people have little in common with the B+'s, they can unite for purposes of mutual benefit. Such a group could be called a confederated interest group. The A+'s lend their support to the B+'s, in whose issue they have no

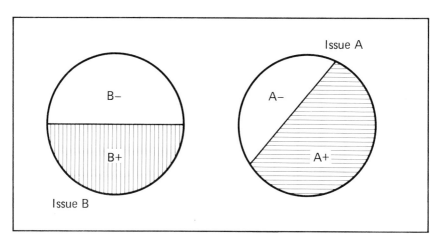

Figure 2.

intrinsic interest; in return, they benefit from like support on Issue A, in which the B+'s have no intrinsic interest. This is a classic example of logrolling.

Figure 3 shows a different type of situation that may result from the group's expansion of issues. Issue A and Issue B are salient to exactly the same subset of individuals. However, in this example, the lines of cleavage are crosscutting, that is, they bisect the group along different axes. Therefore, the result is four sectors or subsets rather than two. In the northern sector fall those who are opposed to both issues; in the south are those who favor both; and in the east and west are those who favor one but oppose the other. Clearly, only the southern crosshatched sector, which is composed of A+, B+'s, contains persons whose interests are congruent with the avowed position of the interest group. Some individuals who are either A+, B−'s, or A−, B+'s may be attracted to the group if they place a greater weight on the issue on which they are in agreement with the group position than on the one on which they disagree. Such persons, however, even if they retain membership in the group, must be considered marginal members, for their commitment to the goals of the group is less than absolute, and they might easily withdraw their support from it without greatly violating their own self-interest. This is an obvious example of how groups can decrease their support by expanding their scope of interests. It is an example of what we will call the "crosscutting case" as opposed to the logrolling case discussed above.

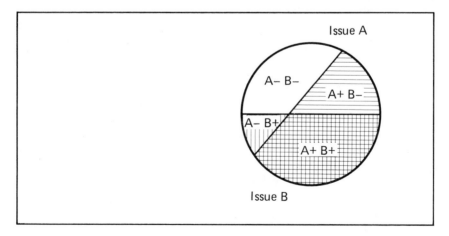

Figure 3.

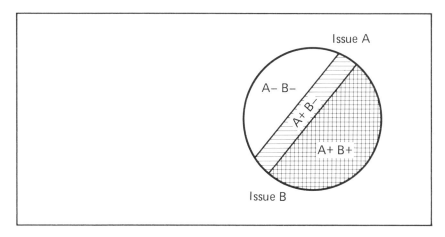

Figure 4.

Figure 4 represents a special type of the crosscutting situation. The sole difference between Figures 3 and 4 is that the axis along which the Issue B cleavage exists has been rotated so that it is parallel to that of Issue A. Both issues are salient to a coincident set of individuals, but instead of four distinct subsets, parallel cleavage results in only three. Once again, those in the crosshatched A+, B+ subset find the positions of the group consistent with their own interests, while those in the A−, B− subset find the group positions wholly at odds with their own. The A+, B−'s will be divided into nonsupporters and marginal supporters.

The situations represented in Figures 2, 3, and 4 are rather pure abstractions of what may take place in the existential world. More frequently than not, however, political phenomena are not as simple as our abstract models would indicate. Figure 5 is probably more representative of the majority of instances in which multiple issues are embraced by groups. Unfortunately (at least for purposes of analysis), it is also more complex. We will call it the "mixed case."

In the situation represented in Figure 5, Issues A and B are salient for distinct but overlapping sets of individuals. Those persons who are favorably disposed toward one issue and who have no interest in the others (the A+'s and the B+'s) should react to the group as did their counterparts in Figure 2, that is, for them the group functions as an umbrella under which interests are confederated for mutual advantage. Group membership for such persons takes on the quality of logrolling for tactical advantage.

Within the intersection of the two subsets, however, the situation is reminiscent of Figure 3, for four distinct orderings of issue orientations occur within the area of overlap. The A+, B+ subset is obviously in agreement with the group goals just as the A−, B− subset is in disagreement. Support can be expected from the former and opposition from the latter. As was the case in Figure 3, those who are either A+, B− or A−, B+ can be expected to be only marginal members at best.

The reader is encouraged to experiment with various combinations of overlapping sets and lines of cleavage, for an infinite number of possibilities exist. Although we have presented only examples involving two issues, those involving three or more can be constructed, resulting in appreciably more complex situations. In all instances, however, the effect of multiple issues on group membership can be analyzed (at least in the abstract) in terms of five factors:

1. The number of issues on which the group adopts a position.
2. The population (size of the set) for which each issue is salient.
3. The size of the respective pro and con subsets within each issue set.
4. The extent of overlap when two or more issue sets intersect.
5. The relative angles between lines of cleavage in intersecting issue sets.
   a. The closer the cleavage lines are to congruence, the more compatible the issues are.
   b. When cleavage lines are not congruent, the closer they come to being

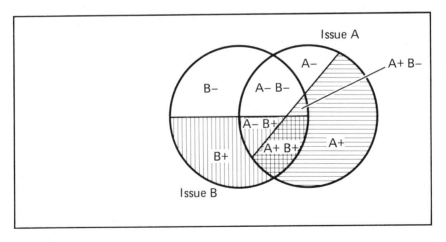

Figure 5.

parallel, the more compatible the issues are. In other words, the more nearly the angles between lines of cleavage approach 90°, the more pronounced will be the conflicting cross-pressures felt by potential group members.

While the above approach to interest group analysis may aid in explaining the *aggregate* level of support for a particular organization, it tells us nothing about the process by which *individuals* decide whether to become members. If we are to understand fully the structure of American interest groups it is imperative that we view the determinants of group membership from as many perspectives as possible, for no vantage point commands an unobstructed view, and relationships that are masked from one may become apparent from another.

Olson has developed a theory which offers insight into the factors involved in individual decisions to join or not to join a given interest group.[23] He posits the existence of a relatively large number of individuals who share a common interest in a collective good, but who are as yet unorganized—a latent group. He assumes that these individuals act rationally; that is, they carefully weigh the costs of an action against its expected benefits and behave on the basis of that evaluation. His thesis is that the mere existence of a joint interest in a collective good is not a sufficient condition for rational individuals to unite in organized group activity unless they constitute a relatively small latent group. The argument in support of this thesis rests squarely on the rationality assumption, for a rational man will perceive that if others organize, the value added to the group by his membership will be insignificant. Moreover, since the good in question is a collective good, he will benefit from an organized group's acquisition of the good regardless of whether he participated in that acquisition. Inasmuch as group membership is never without cost to the individual, Olson deduces that no rational person will incur the costs of organizational participation unless (1) the anticipated payoff resulting from such participation is appreciably higher than the probable payoff resulting from his nonparticipation, *and* (2) that payoff exceeds the costs of group membership.

When an organized or latent group is large, the rational man will see his contribution to be costly to himself but without measurable effect on the probability of the group's success. Only when selective goods are derived from membership in such groups, when membership is compulsory, or when the group is so small that the weight of one member might make a difference will Olson's rational individual join in collective activity.

The closed shop and union shop are examples of compulsory membership in labor groups. Olson discusses at some length the development of organized labor groups and contrasts the early unions, which "sprang up, not in the factories being spawned by the industrial revolution, but mainly in the building trades, in printing, in shoemaking, and in other industries characterized by small-scale production"[24] with later, large-scale national unions, which were made possible only by compulsory membership.

Examples of groups stimulating membership by providing selective benefits on a "members only" basis are legion. Farm groups are among the many which do so. Cooperative businesses and mutual insurance companies limit dividends, if not patronage rights, to members of parent organizations. The Grange in particular offers social and recreational benefits to its members. Many other types of interest groups provide selective benefits in the form of particular services, financial opportunities, and social rewards. Even in the case of unions in which membership is compulsory, active participation is not. Selective benefits can stimulate participation above the minimum level required by membership. As Blau has observed,

> Workers participate in unions not only to improve their employment conditions but also because they intrinsically enjoy the fellowship in the union and derive satisfaction from helping to realize its objectives. Indeed, these are the primary inducements for active participation, since the material rewards the union provides are not contingent, for any one individual, on active participation.[25]

Selective benefits, as the quotation indicates, need not be confined to the realm of material rewards alone. Solidary and purposive rewards may function as selective goods to stimulate participation in an organization which seeks material collective goods.

It would appear, then, that size affects not only the external programs of an organization but its internal programs as well. If Olson's model is a reasonably accurate description of reality, then large organizations are forced to direct a portion of their resources internally for the provision of selective benefits for members. When one considers the additional fact that organizational costs increase as size increases, it is obvious that the proportion of resources available for expenditure in pursuit of external goals to the total amount of group resources diminishes as size increases. In terms of external goal-directed activity, large groups are clearly less efficient in their resource allocations than are small groups, given comparable levels of leadership acumen. This fact, coupled with our earlier observation that small elite groups tend to be more instrumental in their orientation and more effective in their goal-seeking activities than do large mass-membership organizations, leads to the conclusion that size is, if not a determinant, at least an indicator of the quality of interest group activity.

LEADERS AND FOLLOWERS

It is one thing to discuss the *effects* of group goals and of the rewards groups offer (as we have done with respect to membership recruitment and stability); it is yet another, however, to discuss the *origins* of goals and rewards. In the former context—in which goals and benefits are accepted as "givens" for analytical purposes—group leadership could remain undifferentiated from the group itself, for both are, in a sense, prior to the articulation of goals and the provision of goods. Now, however let us focus our attention on the process by which such articulation and provision are conducted. We must discriminate between the general notion of group behavior and the more precise concept of organizational leadership. Groups do not articulate goals and control rewards (other than perhaps solitary rewards); it is the *leaders* of groups who perform such functions.

It is convenient to employ the economic exchange analogy to our examination of the interaction between group leaders and followers. Instead of conceiving of the transactions as occurring between members and the group as a whole, we shall view members as exchanging support for leadership in return for leadership-provided goods. This support can take many forms ranging from cash dues to acquiescence in the actions of leaders. Leaders, on the other hand, invest the resources at their disposal to procure benefits for group members, which are subsequently exchanged for continued support.

Salisbury has gone well beyond the simple exchange model proposed above in his theoretical work dealing with interest groups.[26] He differentiates the types of benefits primarily offered by leaders to members—whether they are material, solidary, or purposive—and traces the implications of each. Although he recognizes that few leaders deal exclusively in only one type of benefit, Salisbury treats exchanges as if they were conducted in only a single currency, for purposes of simplicity and analytic clarity. We see no need to depart from this practice. Solidary benefit organizations are discounted, for groups based on strictly social values have little politically relevant content. Groups in which solidary benefits are exchanged, and which are political in nature, are so only by virtue of some other material or purposive benefits offered in addition to the solidary ones. Thus, we are left with a comparison of material benefit groups and those that are purposive.

Expressive benefits are relatively cheap to acquire. Causes can be promoted, ideology can be articulated, and rhetoric can be disseminated without much capital outlay. Leaders who offer such benefits to the members of their groups frequently do so with little material cost to themselves.[27] Depending, of course, on the conditions of exchange, it is easy to see how leaders of purposive groups could realize a sizable "profit" from their enterprise. Such profits may take the form of a salary for the leader as the group's chief executive officer if the exchange extracts membership dues in excess of that which is required to provide the purposive benefits. But profit may also take the form of permissiveness, which allows the leader to use group-supported media for his own expressive gratification.

As Salisbury correctly points out, the low cost of organization and the profit potential in purposive groups contributes to their instability. Just as in the business world, when profits are high, competition can be expected. In the case of successful purposive organizations, splinter groups frequently compete for the allegiance of members. On the other hand, material benefit groups are more difficult and more expensive to establish, but once established they are relatively stable, for the costliness of entering the market discourages opportunistic speculation.

Whether a leader realizes a profit as an organization entrepreneur depends on a number of considerations, foremost among which are (1) market competition, (2) the demand curves of potential members, and (3) the cost of providing group benefits.

Market competition

A competitive market exists whenever two or more leaders or would-be leaders attempt to attract a single potential group to their respective organizations. Since potential members will attempt to receive maximum benefit at minimal cost, each leader is forced to minimize his profit to provide a more favorable exchange rate than his competitor, thereby attracting more members. It is to be expected that any purposive group market will be characterized by a fairly high degree of competition, since the political goods involved can be obtained relatively easily by leaders.

Demand curves

Demand curves determine the amount of benefit an individual requires before he is willing to incur a given cost. Figure 6 is a graphic representation of an individual demand curve. Along the Y-axis is measured the support currency price per unit to the "buyer" of the good in question.[28] The quantity of units desired is measured along the X-axis. Curve A represents the amount of the good that hypothetical individual A will demand at each price level. It is readily apparent from Figure 6 that if the good were offered at a support currency price of three, individual A will want ten units but no more. Alternatively, if the price were one, individual A would want twenty units.

All individuals can be thought of as having a unique demand curve, similar to that in Figure 6 for any conceivable good. Some may not desire a given good at any price (in which case their curves would be vertical lines congruent with the Y-axis); others may strongly value a good and have sufficient resources at their disposal so that their demand curves are offset to the right of that of individual A, curve less sharply downward, or both. Such a curve is illustrated by B in Figure 7. Curves such as A's, which are relatively vertical, are said to be *inelastic*; relatively horizontal curves, such as B's, are said to be *elastic*. Inelastic demands are relatively stable and are less sensitive to price differences than are elastic demands, which may fluctuate widely as prices are altered.

Figure 6.

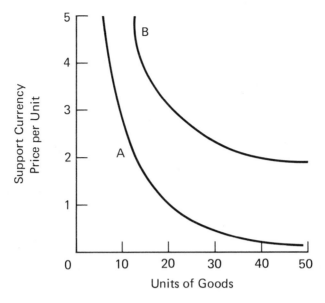

Figure 7.

Obviously, the shapes of the demand curves of group members substantially affect the character of transactions between group leaders and followers and potential members. Leaders must be exceedingly careful in establishing an acceptable balance among support price, quantity of goods offered, and the demand characteristics of followers.

Unlike apples in a supermarket, which consumers can buy in discrete quantities depending on their price, group benefits are offered as prepackaged bundles. For instance, an organizational entrepreneur may offer to members twenty units of political goods at a set support price. If a potential member accepts the price, he receives the full twenty units of goods. He cannot pay half the support price and receive ten units of goods. If the twenty-unit bundle were offered at a support price of three per unit (point X in Figure 8) the total cost of the sixty units would exceed individual C's threshold of acceptability, and C would therefore refuse the exchange. To make the terms of exchange acceptable to C, the entrepreneur would have to reduce the price per unit of the goods he offers, reduce the quantity of goods in the package, or both.

To make the exchange attractive to C and yet retain the unit price of three, the quantity offered would have to be reduced to five (point

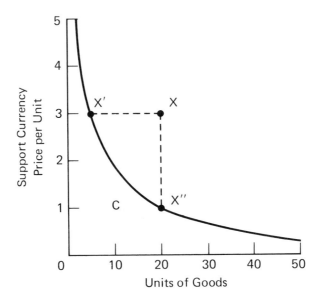

Figure 8.

X' in Figure 8). Alternatively, if the entrepreneur wished to maintain the quantity of goods he offered at twenty units, he could reduce the unit price to one. In the former case, five units of goods are offered at a total exchange price of fifteen; in the latter, twenty units of goods cost a total of twenty support currency units.

Cost of goods

Of course, no entrepreneur is so free from constraint as to have unlimited flexibility in choosing quantities of goods provided, for they may be in limited supply, thereby imposing an upper limit on the quantity to be offered. Moreover, few such goods are available to the entrepreneur at no cost. Therefore, since he must at least break even to avoid political bankruptcy, no interest group leader can long exchange goods at a net loss to himself to maintain a following. Thus, the cost of providing goods combines with market competition and the demand characteristics of members in determining the profitability of organizational leadership. Profitability, in turn, determines whether the organization itself will continue to exist. For just as a bankrupt businessman is a financial entrepreneur without a business, so is a bankrupt organizational entrepreneur a leader without an organization.

NOTES

[1]Mancur Olson, Jr., *The Logic of Collective Action: Public Goods and the Theory of Groups* (Cambridge, Mass.: Harvard University Press, 1965), pp. 14–15.

[2]Peter M. Blau, *Exchange and Power in Social Life* (New York: John Wiley & Sons, Inc., 1964), pp. 34–38.

[3]*Ibid.*, p. 37.

[4]Peter B. Clark and James Q. Wilson, "Incentive Systems: A Theory of Organizations," *Administrative Science Quarterly*, VI (Sept. 1961), pp. 129–66.

[5]*Ibid.*, pp. 134–35.

[6]Reprinted from "An Exchange Theory of Interest Groups," *Midwest Journal of Political Science*, XIII (February 1969), p. 16, by Robert H. Salisbury by permission of the Wayne State University Press.

[7]See Murray Edelman, *The Symbolic Uses of Politics* (Urbana, Ill.: University of Illinois Press, 1964).

[8]Blau, *Exchange and Power in Social Life*, pp. 5–6.

[9]Reprinted from "An Exchange Theory of Interest Groups," *Midwest Journal of Political Science*, XIII (Feb. 1969), p. 16, by Robert H. Salisbury by permission of the Wayne State University Press.

[10]Harold Lasswell, *Psychopathology and Politics* (New York: The Viking Press, Inc., 1960), p. 314.

[11]For a more complete discussion of ideological conflict and of changes in that conflict resulting from altered social conditions, see Lewis A. Coser, *The Functions of Social Conflict* (New York: The Free Press), pp. 95–119.

[12]This analysis is drawn from James W. Vander Zanden, "The Klan Revival," *American Journal of Sociology*, LXV (Mar. 1960), pp. 456–62.

[13]Edelman, *op. cit.*, p. 181.

[14]For substantiation of this point and for a fuller discussion of "working class authoritarianism," see T. W. Adorno et al., *The Authoritarian Personality* (New York: Harper & Row, Publishers, 1950); Seymour Martin Lipset, *Political Man* (Garden City, N.Y.: Doubleday & Co., 1959), pp. 87–126; and Herbert McClosky, "Consensus and Ideology in American Politics," *American Political Science Review*, LVIII (June 1964), pp. 361–82.

[15]Edelman, *op. cit.*, pp. 179–80.

[16]We use *regime* in the sense of the established fundamental rules and relationships of the political system. See David Easton, "An Approach to the Analysis of Political Systems," *World Politics*, IX (April 1957), p. 392. Further elaboration on the concept of the political regime is contained in the next chapter.

[17]This is no doubt largely a result of the preponderance of small, elitist interest groups that embrace the norms of the elites. No such group is likely to present a fundamental challenge to the system under which the elites attained their elevated status. Not only is elitehood defined within a context provided, in part, by the extant political system, but, pragmatically, those who comprise an elite stratum do so by virtue of their relative effectiveness in making the system operate to their advantage. Thus, the elites and those who adopt elite norms have a commitment to the existing regime.

For the time being we shall confine ourselves to considerations of elitist-oriented interest groups, recognizing as we do so that marginal organizations exist led by counterelites which do not balk at the notion of systemic change. This and related points will be pursued in greater depth in the following chapter, when we take up the topic of the external interactions of interest groups.

[18]Olson, *The Logic of Collective Action*, p. 20. For additional elaboration on this point see Schattschneider, *The Semi-Sovereign People*, pp. 35–36.

[19]This point will be expanded in subsequent chapters. Let us merely say here that the discipline necessary to deliver large blocs of votes is conspicuously absent in most interest groups.

[20]Reprinted from "An Exchange Theory of Interest Groups," *Midwest Journal of Political Science*, XIII (Feb. 1969), p. 19, by Robert H. Salisbury by permission of the Wayne State University Press.

[21]In constructing the models which follow we have tacitly assumed that individual values are constant over time. We concede that this is a distortion of reality and that, in some cases, a change in organization policy may result in changes in the values of some members. However, models of the sort we are proposing are primarily heuristic devices and are not to be taken as strict representations of real-world phenomena. Our objective is that of explicating abstract relationships. In view of this goal, parsimony dictates that certain simplifying assumptions be made.

[22]For some outstanding theoretical discussions pertinent to these two points, see James M. Buchanan and Gordon Tullock, *The Calculus of Consent* (Ann Arbor, Mich.: University of Michigan Press, 1962); Charles E. Lindblom, *The Intelligence of Democracy* (New York: The Free Press, 1965); and William H. Riker, *The Theory of Political Coalitions* (New Haven, Conn.: Yale University Press, 1962).

[23]Except where otherwise noted, the following discussion is based on Olson, *The Logic of Collective Action*, pp. 5–52.

[24]*Ibid.*, p. 66.

[25]Blau, *Exchange and Power in Social Life*, p. 37.

[26]Salisbury, "An Exchange Theory of Interest Groups," pp. 1–32.

[27]Leaders of many purposive groups are able to provide cost-free expressive benefits to followers merely by staying in the news. Mimeographed newsletters, group meetings at which rhetorical speeches are delivered, public demonstrations, and civil court actions are all examples of relatively inexpensive means of providing expressive benefits. Furthermore, once a capital outlay has been expended in establishing a vehicle for disseminating such goods, an increase in the intensity of evocative content of the goods can result in an increase in the value of benefits at no increase in dissemination costs.

[28]We are using the term *support currency* in our discussion rather than the more traditional *dollars* or *utiles* to make the presentation more intuitively understandable within the present context. Since support can take a variety of forms, we hope that our terminology is less confusing than one which would indicate a single specific exchange currency.

four

Interactions
with the
Political System

Eugene Meehan has written that "without a conceptual framework, description is impossible. The meaning and significance of facts derive from the conceptual structure employed by the observer."[1] We have suggested an interpretive framework for the purpose of analyzing and understanding the internal dynamics of interest groups. We will now propose a similar conceptual scheme for viewing them in their interactions with agents of the political system. The accent is on theoretical abstractions and the relationships that can be deduced from them, and the reader is warned against confusing concept with fact. We believe that these theoretical considerations are useful in the interpretation of many empirical observations relevant to the study of interest groups, but we make no claim that they have the power to explain all phenomena. Nor should they be taken as necessarily accurate portrayals of reality.

> Perhaps the most common error found in handling descriptions is a failure to differentiate adequately between fact and concept. Indeed, the confusion of fact and concept may well be a more serious hazard in political science than the widely heralded confusion of fact and value. Strictly speaking, a fact is the sum of an observed set of properties, whereas a concept is a rule for dealing with such observations.[2]

LEVELS OF THE POLITICAL SYSTEM

Our point of departure in the present phase of this undertaking will be the concept of the political system, which is so abstract that it can be and has been used to represent a wide variety of actors and institutions which perform political and quasi-political functions. The concept was introduced in 1953 by David Easton.[3] Briefly, the political system is taken to be the entire set of formal and informal institutions in a society which take part in the authoritative decision-making processes of that society. Outputs from the systems are public policies; inputs to it are of two types—demands and support. Demands are the requests by members of society for particular policy outputs. Support inputs are the acceptances on the part of society of the legitimacy of the political system. In one sense, political systems theory can be viewed as being a type of exchange theory, in which the system exchanges policies which satisfy social demands for continued social support.

An alternate conceptual scheme which has received much attention by political scientists would substitute power or influence for exchange as the primary source of energy for the system. This school emphasizes a unidirectional process in which one actor influences the behavior of another by exerting power to induce a desired response by the other. Nothing in this view is incompatible with exchange theory, for the exertion of political power is equivalent to exercising discretion concerning the expenditure of political resources over which one has control. Resource expenditure (or power application, if you wish) is an integral part of the exchange process. Therefore, to say that actor A *influenced* actor B is tantamount to saying that A mobilized sufficient resources to consummate a desired transaction with B.

Easton has identified three levels on which the political system exists.[4] In increasing order of conceptual abstraction, these are the government, the regime, and the community. Demands at the government level pertain to the establishment and administration of public policy through existing political institutions. Support at this level involves accepting the existing occupants of roles in the system as legitimate decision-makers.

As we noted earlier, the regime concept refers to the established fundamental rules and relationships of the political system. The regime comprises the set of institutions through which demand inputs are processed and the rules by which policies are made; in short, it is the functional constitution of the political system. Regime-level demands are requests for the political system to reconstitute itself. In the national political arena the form of such changes may range from explicit constitutional amendments to subtle alterations in the decision-making process. The latter, for example, occur when a president establishes a new cabinet post, restricts his communication with key legislators, or comes to rely heavily on one or more particular advisors to the exclusion of all others. Support for a regime consists of acceptance of the rules by which the political system determines public policy, although it need not imply support for the government currently making such policy.

The concept of community is roughly equivalent to what we have called society. It is the body politic—that is, the aggregate of people within a geographically defined area served by a single political system. Members of a political community share a political culture that includes, at minimum, a common desire for a single policy-making agent. Community-level demands are desires for the contraction or expansion of the scope of citizenship along some dimension. The admission of a new state is an example of expansion of the political community of the United States along the geographical dimension. The enfranchisement of women might be considered an expansion along the social dimension.

A breakdown in support for the political community results from severe cleavages within the body politic. In such instances disaffected social elements no longer recognize the legitimacy of the social bonds that unite them with other segments of the policy. Therefore, they are no longer willing to confer legitimacy on the political regime that serves the whole polity. The Civil War resulted from just such a situation. It should already be obvious that support at the regime level necessarily implies support at the community level, although the converse need not be true. Likewise, support at the governmental level implies both regime- and community-level support.

Exchanges between interest group leaders and the political system can occur at any of the three levels. Typically they occur at the governmental level, from which emanate policies directly pertinent to the distribution of tangible goods. In recent years, however, increasing demands have been placed on the system at the regime and even the community level. Anti–Vietnam War groups have functioned at the governmental level in demanding policy changes from Washington, and they have at times challenged the regime by questioning the president's authority to make and execute war policies. Civil rights groups have operated on all three levels. Specific demands such as school integration, equal employment opportunities, and fair housing codes are governmental demands. Other demands, such as for the decentralization of urban school authority and for minority group representation in government councils, are directed toward the regime. Furthermore, in many areas Negroes and other minorities have been denied voting rights and equal protection of the laws—two determinants of functional citizenship. Demands to rectify these situations and to grant such persons equal de facto citizenship must be considered a call for expansion of the political community.

THE COOPTATION OF COUNTER-ELITES

The level at which interest groups articulate demands can be viewed as the result of a strategic decision on the part of group leaders. Assuming that the objective of a given group is the enjoyment of some predefined tangible good, its acquisition may be deemed impossible under the existing political regime (implying, of course, that regime-level support is weak). Therefore, strategic considerations may dictate that to achieve its ultimate goal, the group initially has to engage in regime-level activity directed toward altering the governmental decision-making process so that the desired policy would be likely to follow. University students who wish to change one or more aspects of their school's policy are engaging in this type of strategic regime-level activity when they seek representation on faculty and administrative decision-making bodies.

It would be appropriate at this point to observe that whereas elitist-oriented organizations tend not to tamper with the political system at the regime or community levels, these are precisely the levels at which marginal groups led by counter-elites direct their demands. Counter-elites such as civil rights leaders, political radicals, or spokesmen for the urban poor have by definition little or no legitimate power within the existing political system. Therefore, if they are to seek and receive *continuous* benefits from the system, they must first attempt to change its character. While it is true that such groups are from time to time the beneficiaries of governmental policy decisions, it is also true that such decisions tend to be more on the order of stop-gap gestures than they are indicative of coherent programs which provide tangible benefits. In other words, elites occasionally grant benefits to marginal groups, but they do so seemingly out of a sense of *noblesse oblige* or a desire to pacify these groups and "keep them in their place." Benefits thus granted therefore tend to be more symbolic than real.

Examples of this type of phenomenon abound. Recall that the freeing of the slaves and the conferral of full de jure citizenship on blacks was done not at the instigation of the blacks themselves, but was due largely to northern whites. Although many whites were probably moral abolitionists, it is doubtful that moral conviction alone would have been a sufficient cause to have precipitated the Civil War, had not the northern industrial and commercial elites realized that the perpetuation of slavery and the plantation agricultural economy was detrimental to their economic and political interests. In any event, the Emancipation Proclamation and the Thirteenth through Fifteenth Amendments to the Constitution were made the law of the land by those elites, and de jure equality was thereby conferred on black Americans—a marginal categoric group. Yet today, over a century later, de facto equality has not been fully realized. The aforementioned legal enactments, regardless of their respective wordings, were *not* incremental parts of a coherent policy to materially affect the station of American Negroes. They were in part salve for the conscience of the nation and in part tactics which effectively undermined the previous power of the Southern agricultural elite. But since the blacks were unable to organize an effective counter-elite of their own and since no established elite adopted their cause, the symbolic benefits they received were never realized in tangible follow-up policies. Not until the 1960s, when civil rights counter-elites began actively pursuing their cause, did any appreciable material changes begin to take place. Even so, material change has been very slow. Many of the "victories" of the sixties were symbolic. Yet, by focusing their demands at the regime level (by demanding to be represented in decision-making councils) and at the community level (by demonstrating their desire and ability to take an active and responsible role in American participatory democracy), blacks have begun to win some of the material benefits they desire. As long as the leadership elements of marginal groups see themselves in the role of counter-elites, they will typically act to withhold their support from the political system at the governmental, regime, and possibly the community levels while concomitantly articulating demands. Once a counter-elite begins to identify with the system—that is, once marginal group leaders perceive the political system as responsive to their demands and believe that its policies will result in their receiving tangible benefits—it is no longer a counter-elite, but part of the established elite. In the jargon of social science such a transformation is called cooptation.

Cooptation commonly has a pejorative connotation roughly equivalent to "selling out." However, before we too readily condemn a coopted counter-elite we should scrutinize the means of their cooptation carefully, for there are two dissimilar conditions under which leaders of marginal groups may come to identify with the political system. A counter-elite which is consistently and fundamentally concerned with maintaining its group of followers is bound by that concern to enter into transactions which will secure from the political system the type of goods that can subsequently be exchanged for support from its followers. Therefore, such goods must be consistent with the goals and values of the group as a whole. It follows that if a counter-elite is true to the values of the marginal group it leads, then for it to be coopted means that its demands (or at least a significant portion of them) must have been met by the political system. This, in turn, implies that the system has been made responsive to the marginal group, thereby coopting both leaders and followers. Cooptation of this sort should not be evaluated negatively, for it is precisely the group's initial goal. Once within the system, such groups will exchange support for benefits at the governmental level and their once radical counter-elites will become relatively more conservative segments of the political elite.

Cooptation of a sizable sector of the population is never a facile or a placid undertaking as history will attest, yet it does occur. As economic and social conditions change, so do the lines of cleavage within society. New social categories which have new values and norms emerge. Old categories vanish. Such changes tend to be gradual rather than cataclysmic, so that they frequently go undetected for some time. The nascent values are not even recognized —much less articulated—and political demands based on them fail to achieve coherent integration. When the magnitude of change reaches a level at which it becomes salient, all too frequently the dynamic social conditions have changed far more than has the relatively static political system. Thus, the process of social evolution continually creates marginal groups, which eventually develop their respective counter-elites. If these marginal groups are not just temporary aberrations, their counter-elites will eventually force a change in the political system, the marginal group will become an element in a new social synthesis, and the counter-elite will become a segment of the conservative, system-oriented elite stratum of the polity.

The history of organized labor in the United States exemplifies this process. At the beginning of the twentieth century, America was in the throes of the Industrial Revolution. The working classes, which had been relatively small and concentrated in the northeast prior to the Civil War, were becoming not only numerous but widespread as well. Industrial technology defined the new social category of the laborer. Population growth accompanied by territorial growth and increased transportation facilities created ready markets for the products of industry, thereby swelling the demand for labor. By the 1920s labor constituted a sizable and a vocal marginal group in America. The industrial, commercial, and agricultural elites had all won their places within the political system, and they were reluctant to expand the system to process the demands expressed by the labor counter-elite. Pro-labor legislation was occasionally enacted, but its value was largely symbolic, for even the minimal material benefits it provided were either left unadministered or overturned in the courts. Labor leaders during these years were clearly a counter-elite.

Gradually, however, the system became more responsive to labor's demands as expressed by the leaders of strong unions. By the end of the New Deal era, labor had been fully coopted into the system. Today, labor is one of the most supportive segments of the populace with respect to the community and regime levels of the political system. Policy demands, of course, continue to be directed toward the governmental level, but they are expressed through established channels, and they are satisfied enough to ensure the continued support of the labor elite as well as their mass followings. Labor, having thus won its fight for a role within the political system, has adopted a conservative, status quo–oriented attitude with respect to more newly emergent marginal groups which have yet to penetrate the system.

The dialectic nature of society is such that as new social categories gain recognition and become absorbed within the system, newer categories are emerging. Marginal groups are constantly being created and systemic change is constantly being called for. Only when the lag between marginal group–creation and systemic response becomes too great does social conflict threaten to result in social disruption. In short, cooptation of a counter-elite, if it is accompanied by the absorption into the political community of that counter-elite's following, is politically and socially healthy. We shall call this type of cooptation *functional*.

Unfortunately, not all cooptation is functional. Recall that one necessary condition for it to be so is that the counter-elite must adhere to the norms and values of the marginal group it leads in order to extract the requisite regime- and community-level benefits from the system. When members of a counter-elite are appeased by goods other than those which contribute to the material satisfaction of their followers, unhealthy, *dysfunctional* cooptation occurs.

Dysfunctional cooptation may result from selfishness on the part of counter-elites which allow themselves to be coopted for their private gain, or it may result from their lack of wisdom in failing to see that their cooptation is inconsistent with the original goals of their marginal group. In either situation, however, the results are the same—leadership of the marginal group becomes both beneficiary and supporter of the ongoing political system, and the mass followers remain excluded from the system and are denied many of the benefits distributed by it.

GROUPS, ISSUES, AND EXCHANGE MEDIA

In his outstanding book, *Power and Discontent*, William A. Gamson presents an enlightened theoretical analysis of political phenomena that is of value for students of interest groups.[5] In so doing he develops several concepts and typologies which we must now review to receive the full benefit of his thought. What follows is only a highlighted version of Gamson's work; the reader who wants to pursue it further is encouraged to turn to the original.

Instead of the threefold hierarchical conception of the political system which Easton proposed, Gamson perceives a four-level system. The governmental level (which he calls that of "incumbent authorities") and the level of the political community are the equivalent of Easton's. The regime level, however, is separated into political institutions and public philosophy, the former being manifestations of the latter.[6]

Support ("trust" in Gamson's terminology) is necessary at each level if the system is to function effectively. There are two underlying dimensions of support: (1) the system's efficiency in achieving collective goals, and (2) the system's bias in defining goals and in processing demands.[7] In other words, support reflects the expectation that demands will be converted into the desired policies. Although groups can be placed anywhere along a support continuum running from low to high, Gamson abstracts three general types of groups according to their support orientation. These are *confident* groups, which perceive a high probability of favorable outcomes; *neutral* groups, which expect no systematic bias for or against their policy demands; and *alienated* groups, which see the system as unresponsive to their demands.

Although Gamson does not pursue this line of thought, it seems unreasonable to assume a priori that a given group will hold a consistent support orientation toward all elements or subsystems within the political system with respect to all issues. Obviously, an issue which is unrelated to the interests of a group will find that group neutral and apathetic toward the manner in which the issue is resolved, regardless of the group's support level for issues with which it is *concerned*. Furthermore, different classes of issues are processed by different political subsystems. Therefore, it is conceivable if not probable that a particular group might be confident about one issue being processed by its associated subsystem while at the same time it was neutral toward or alienated from a different issue being processed by a second subsystem.

The NAACP, for example, may be confident with respect to a pending voting rights bill in Congress and simultaneously alienated with respect to school desegregation policies in Georgia. Different support orientations may as likely exist between different branches of government at the same level as between different levels. Thus, at the same time it is confident of congressional action on the voting rights bill, the NAACP may be alienated or neutral with regard to the Justice Department's enforcement of a Supreme Court desegregation order. Moreover, since different categories of bills pass through different legislative committees within Congress, thereby resulting in the processing of demands by different political subsystems, it is conceivable that the NAACP's confidence on the voting rights measure may coexist with alienation on a pending appropriations bill affecting a low-cost housing program.

Although it is possible to talk about the general level of support a group manifests toward the political system as a whole, it appears more useful for the political analyst to specify the particular subsystem involved when he attempts to explain interest group behavior. Federalism, the separation of powers principle, and the procedural rules within decision-making bodies all ensure many such subsystems.

The support orientation of a group is seen as an independent variable which affects the means by which groups attempt to influence political decision-makers. The means, in turn, can be construed as the currency with which groups attempt to enter into exchange transactions with agents of the political system. The three general types of currency available to groups are *persuasion, inducements,* and *constraints.*[8]

Persuasion is the use of resources in an attempt to make a decision-maker evaluate the merits of an issue in the same manner as the persuader does. Control over resources is not exchanged, although it is conceivable that the value of the persuasive resources at the disposal of a group may be altered as a result of their having been employed. Thus, a group which uses the resources of expertise in persuading a political decision-maker that a pending policy will have a particular result may enhance its reputation for expertise if the predicted result occurs. Conversely, it may lose much of that value if its prediction turns out to be inaccurate. In neither instance, however, was control of the persuasive resource—expertise—exchanged. Rather than construing persuasion as a means of exchange proper, it is more appropriate to view persuasion as strategic interaction prior to exchange which is designed to affect the terms of subsequent exchange. The successful application of persuasion by a group will alter the value structure of decision-makers to make them seek the same immediate goal as the group. Subsequent policy decisions will therefore be "purchased" at a lower cost in political resources by that group.

That persuasion and expertise can be powerful resources is attested to by the comments of one state legislator interviewed by Zeigler and Baer. Referring to a lobbyist whom he described as helpful, he said,

> I relied on him because I think he knows what he is talking about. I think he has expertise in his field. This is what I want from a lobbyist—information.[9]

The persuader's integrity and knowledge are his keys to success with public officials. Milbrath quoted "one of the oldest and wisest men in Congress" in exemplifying this point:

> If a lobbyist misrepresents something, he is through. Then there are those who don't know very much, too. Those are soon dismissed, and we pay little attention to them. Maybe birds-of-a-feather flock together, but not one human in my life—and I have been holding public office since I was twenty-five and I am now seventy-five—has ever asked me to do an indecent thing. The fellow who does differently from this just doesn't have a chance.[10]

An inducement represents an exchange in which positive goods are transferred or promised to a decision-maker subject to his acting in a desired manner.

Inducements are the addition of new advantages to the situation or the promise to do so, regardless of the particular resources used. The authority acts as the partisan group desires in exchange for some resource which they have received or will receive. There is a specific good or service involved as a *quid pro quo* in such exchange.[11]

Such exchanges may be explicit or implicit. A legislator who votes for a measure with the understanding that his vote will pay off a political debt to a colleague or satisfy an interest group which contributed to a previous campaign fund has just as surely entered into this type of exchange as one who explicitly exchanges his vote for some present or future political good. The terms of most political transactions, in fact, are rarely made explicit, for to do so would be to make political authorities vulnerable to charges of graft, at worst, or improper behavior, at best.

Constraints are costs or disadvantages which a group threatens to impose on decision-makers unless the latter act according to the group's desires. They are usually employed with extreme discretion, for while their ability to influence a decision-maker in the desired direction is uncertain, their ability to incur his animosity is almost assured. The following statement by a legislative lobbyist illustrates how inducements and constraints are evaluated in practical political circumstances:

If it is an important bill, one that we just about have to get passed, usually I'll go to somebody and say, "Look, this is one I have to have and I want you to vote on this bill." I am calling in a debt. However, I don't use this very often because you can only use it once in a while. And you can only use it on a legislator once during a session. It is best to avoid an overt feeling of obligation, but every lobbyist does have certain legislators that he can go to if he really needs a vote. I'll probably do this two or three times during a normal session. You just don't put on the pressure every day. You save it until you need it.

I will also ask a legislator to get a vote that I can't get. This is the kind of pressure that you use, but you just don't go to a legislator and say "You do it or else." That is the poorest tactic you can use. Remember that we know most of these people very well, and in some cases have gotten them to run for office. We have worked with them in their campaigns. Even so, if I go to him and he says "I can't do it," then I'll say, "Okay, I'll get somebody else," and forget it. You don't do it by using threats or being cute. You do not campaign against them. If they are consistently against you, they know that we would like to see them defeated, and they know that we will try to get somebody to run against them, but that is as far as it goes. I would never say to a legislator that I will try to find a candidate to oppose him, but the feeling is there.[12]

It is equally important to considerations of both inducements and constraints that the group attempting to exert influence must actually control the resources or costs in question. If no such control exists, threats and promises are nothing more than predictions of consequences that will result from certain decisions. As such they properly fall into the category of persuasion attempts. For instance, imagine an interest group leader who "threatens" to divert the entire bloc of votes to be cast by his constituent group from candidate A to candidate B unless A commits himself to a particular policy position during the campaign. Such a group leader is not imposing constraints on candidate A unless he actually controls the way group members will vote and they would not otherwise have voted for B. The ability of organizational leaders to mobilize such resources effectively is indeed questionable. Schattschneider has assessed the extent to which group leaders actually control the votes of their members. Despite the fact that many politicians and newsmen constantly refer to the "labor vote," Schattschneider deduced that of approximately sixteen million members of the AFL–CIO, only about 960 thousand votes are delivered to the Democratic Party as a direct result of group membership even though the Democrats receive the official endorsement of the organization. He concludes that while his calculations offer less than conclusive proof, it is reasonable to assume that "pressure politics and party politics are two different things, and the impact of the one on the other is not what it seems to be in a superficial analysis."[13]

A final typology which we will borrow from Gamson's work concerns the nature of political decisions over which interests clash. Gamson isolates four major categories for purposes of analysis. These are (1) issues which deal with alterations in the scope of authority, (2) those pertaining to the bias of the system, (3) questions of personnel selection, and (4) content decisions.[14]

Decisions affecting the scope of authority alter the substantive area over which particular agents of the political system have competence. The transfer of a federal agency from one department to another, for example, would represent a decrease and an increase respectively in the scopes of authority of the departments involved.

Likewise, the creation of a new agency under an established department would increase its scope of authority. Such decisions have definite implications for interest groups in that not all decision-making systems are equally receptive to the demands and resources of a given group. As Schattschneider has observed,

> In politics as in everything else it makes a great difference whose game we play. The rules of the game determine the requirements for success. Resources sufficient for success in one game may be wholly inadequate in another.[15]

The locus of authority over a given issue area largely determines the rules of the game. But identifying the appropriate seat of authority is not always as easy as it may first appear to be. One of the factors which confounds this identification process is the delegation of authority. Suppose that a state government has delegated its authority regarding the selection of texts to the various local school boards within the state. A local citizens' group desiring to influence the selection of books to be used in its schools has the option of dealing with its local school board or going over the board's head in an attempt to wring a binding policy out of the state system.

Rarely is authority delegated to the extent that the body doing the delegating relinquishes all control over the issue area in question. Normally, limits are imposed on the discretionary latitude of the delegatee; frequently, his decisions are subject to review by the superior authority. Such review may be either procedural or substantive. In the former instance the reviewing authority merely ensures that the decisions of lower agents were made in conformity with the rules by which decisions should be made. For example, when the state delegates authority over textbook selection to the local boards it may also set forth a formal procedure by which such selection should be made. It may stipulate that public hearings be held prior to the adoption of any new text, it may require that school administrators sit on text selection committees, or it may impose any of a number of potential formal requirements. When review is strictly procedural, as long as the local boards conform to the formal rules, the reviewing authority merely rubber-stamps their decisions. In such cases an interest group concerned with a content decision has no recourse but to operate at the local level.[16] Substantive review, on the other hand, has different implications for interest groups, for discretion is exercised by both the superior and the inferior decision-making bodies. Thus, if a group loses over a content issue at the local level, it still has the option of attempting an exchange at the state level without incurring the additional costs of first effecting a decision as to scope.

Generally, the lower the level, the smaller and more homogeneous is the public which it serves. Therefore, one can expect that fewer opposing interests will develop at the lower levels and that communication costs between groups and decision-makers will be reduced. Thus, political goods purchased at the lower levels are acquired at less cost to interest groups than is the case at higher levels. The practical implication of this fact is that, all other things being equal, interest groups will tend to interact with the lowest-level political system that has de facto authority over issues salient to the group.

As a rule of thumb this deduction, although less than startling, is reasonably accurate. However, as with most rules of thumb, this one contains a qualification—"all other things being equal." In actuality, all other things are rarely equal. Among the inequalities with which interest groups must contend are the types of resources at their disposal. More on this topic in subsequent pages. For the time being, however, we should reiterate that resources vary in exchange value from market to market. A given level of resource X may "buy" more political goods within one political system than within another. The episode of anti–chain store interests related in Chapter 2 illustrates this fact. The resources available to opponents of chain operations were sufficient to bring about desired policies when they were exchanged within the various state political markets. But when the issue was injected into the national arena, their resources were substantially discounted while those of the chain store forces increased in value.

Decisions concerning the bias of the political system are those which alter the structural arrangements and the procedural rules by which the system allocates political goods.

> [It is not] surprising that some of the most historical power struggles in the House of Representatives have centered around the Speaker and the Rules Committee. The procedures by which a bill reaches the floor of Congress for a vote are fraught with implications for the influence of various partisan groups. Those which increase the authority of committee chairmen as gatekeepers on proposed legislation strengthen a bias toward potential partisans from one-party districts—in the South and in large, urban districts in the North, for example.[17]

Personnel decisions are those which directly determine the occupants of formal and informal roles in the political system. Since no two individuals act exactly the same under similar circumstances, personnel decisions affect the bias of the system. Although Gamson treats personnel decisions as a unique category, we see no reason why they should not be treated here as merely a special case of issues concerning bias. Therefore, unless otherwise noted, whenever we refer to issues of bias, personnel decisions are to be considered as lesser included phenomena. The appointment or the election of individuals to political office are obvious examples of such decisions.

Content decisions are directly concerned with the allocation of goods. The goods may be symbolic or tangible, but they represent the category of policy outcomes which give meaning to the other types of decisions. In the final analysis, all political conflict can be reduced to opposing desires over the allocation of goods through the political system. The importance of issues of scope, bias, and personnel devolves from their indirect influence on the content of subsequent distributive decisions.

By employing the above distinctions it is possible to deduce a number of hypotheses concerning the behavior of interest groups with respect to the political system.[18] Confident groups perceive the system to be biased in their favor and efficient in its allocative procedures. Therefore, they will see little need to expand resources to influence the quality of its decisions. Of course, if an opposing group (presumably one which is either neutral or alienated) undertakes to exert influence, a confident group is likely to attempt to counteract such influence. Since the group will see itself as enjoying a favorable relationship with authoritative decision-makers, persuasion will be the most probable means employed. Persuasion for such groups will involve relatively little resource expenditure and will have a relatively high anticipated chance of success. Moreover, resorting to another means of influence might jeopardize a confident group's favored position. The application of constraints would obviously result in resentment and opposition from decision-makers, and inducements would tend to destroy the group's privileged status and place it in the position of being a quid pro quo bargainer. Although either constraints or inducements might win an immediate victory for a confident group, they may also make future exchanges more costly.

A confident group can be expected to be most easily aroused on issues concerning system bias and scope of authority. Any attempt to change the status quo in either area will normally be perceived as a threat to the group's strategically favorable position, and it will be opposed. Occasionally, however, confident groups may take the initiative to expand the authority of a political subsystem. When environmental conditions change so as to create new sets of issues over which no political unit has competence, and the interests of a particular group are affected by the new issues, it can be expected to exert its influence to place the emergent issues under the cognizance of a subsystem in which it is confident. Likewise, if a group holds disparate support orientations toward different political subsystems, it may expend resources in attempting to reduce the scope of that in which it is least confident while increasing the scope of that in which it is most confident.

Alienated groups, on the other hand, have neither faith in the efficiency of the system nor trust in its fairness. They see authoritative decisions emanating from it as systematically biased against their interests. Therefore, they will favor modifications in bias and scope, but like confident groups, they will not be too likely to bring influence to bear where matters of content are concerned. Since the system as they perceive it is unresponsive to their demands and, in fact, ambivalent if not hostile toward gaining their support, resources expended in attempts to influence content decisions will be judged as having a low probability of payoff. Resources will be most effectively used in changing the political system itself.

Since alienated groups do not enjoy good relations with authorities, they will deem persuasion inappropriate and ineffective. Inducements may be employed; however, an element of mutual trust is necessary for any type of exchange and it becomes increasingly important in political exchange, for the terms of few bargains in that marketplace are explicitly stated and even fewer are backed by binding sanctions. Therefore, we may conclude that inducements will not be employed by alienated groups to the extent that constraints will be. Contrary to the situations for other types of groups, alienated groups do not run the risk of creating resentment and hostility in authorities by resorting to constraints, for they see authorities as already being, if not resentful and hostile, at least unresponsive.

A word of caution: remember that our discussion in this chapter is limited to considerations of exchanges between groups and the political systems from which they desire policy outputs. This, as we pointed out earlier, does not exhaust the types of activities in which interest groups engage. Many actions which at their face value may appear to be geared toward external exchange with political decision-makers are in reality designed to mobilize internal support from group members and are therefore properly seen as internal exchanges. For example, the leaders of an alienated group may visibly and actively expend resources in pressing for a particular policy which has little or no chance of being adopted. They may do so for a variety of reasons independent of the substance of the policy in question. Their actions may be designed to show their constituents how hard they are working in their interest, or they may hope to convert more potential group members into active members by demonstrating the need for concerted action against an unresponsive system. A leader of an alienated group will be most effective in mobilizing the support of his constituency and thereby enhancing the resources at his disposal if he is able to instill among potential group members a low sense of trust in the political system while at the same time giving them a moderately high sense of political efficacy. Many actions of such leaders can better be evaluated in terms of these dual goals than in terms of their immediate effects on policy outcomes.

> With a relatively unorganized constituency, the problem of mobilizing support is likely to dominate the concerns of the interest group and short-run influence may be willingly sacrificed to this goal. In such cases, defeats may actually be preferred to victories if they occur in ways that diminish trust in authorities and increase group solidarity and personal investment in interest groups.[19]

Neutral groups, as opposed to alienated and confident ones, perceive the political system as unbiased with respect to their interests. Therefore, questions of bias and scope tend not to be salient to them. Content issues which affect their interests, however, are matters over which they will become intensely concerned. Since the political system is not assumed to be predisposed one way or the other, neutral groups will not attempt to bargain with constraints for fear of increasing resistance on the part of decision-makers. Persuasion may be tried, but since there is no assurance that authorities are oriented toward pleasing or lending credence to the arguments of neutral groups, persuasion is not the major type of influence they will employ. Inducements are the primary tool of neutral groups in exchanges with political decision-makers, and they have the secondary function of favorably affecting future exchanges by creating a precedent for good relations with authorities. Over time, repeated exchanges in positive goods may result in mutual trust and faith in the integrity of both sets of participants. This, in turn, may transform a neutral group into a confident one.

In summary, we can predict that confident groups will be most active with respect to issues of scope and bias and that they will rely primarily on persuasion as a means of achieving their goals. We expect alienated groups also to be aroused most over issues of scope and bias, but predict that they will tend to employ constraints rather than persuasion in attempting to conduct exchanges with authorities. Finally, we anticipate that neutral groups will be most active in the area of content issues, where we expect them to use inducements as their primary exchange currency.

Summary of Chapters 3 and 4

We have outlined some of the major conceptual and relational considerations necessary for an understanding of interest group behavior in the political arena. If social scientists are to make sense of the welter of social and political phenomena they observe, they must employ an analytic framework which imposes order on their observations. It is just such a framework which we, relying largely on the work of others, have proposed for the study of interest groups.

The basic unifying concept is that of political exchange, in which a political act is seen as one element in a reciprocal relationship involving the transfer of X amount of political goods from party A to party B in return for Y amount of political goods from B. The exchange paradigm can be applied with equal utility to the internal dynamics of interest groups and to their external relations with agents of the political system. In the former instance, organization leaders are analogous to merchants in that they provide collective goods which satisfy the common interests of group members in return for support resources from the latter. External exchanges are those in which organization leaders, employing the support resources they acquire from their constituents, "buy" goods in the form of policy decisions from political decision-makers. There is no abstract qualitative difference between internal exchanges and those that are external to interest groups; there are only differences in the respective marketplaces and in the parties who participate. With respect to internal exchanges, organization members "buy" political goods from interest group leaders with support currency. Those leaders, in turn, "buy" political goods from agents of the political system with the support resources at their disposal. In the former case, group leaders exercise authority over the distribution of goods to members; in the latter case, agents of the political system exercise authority over the distribution of goods to group leaders.

Goods involved in political transactions may be placed on a number of dimensions. These dimensions are not mutually exclusive, nor are they equally meaningful for all analyses. Each can be profitably employed for particular types of questions. Questions dealing with the inherent substance of goods lend themselves to either the symbolic–tangible dichotomy or the material–solidary–purposive typology. Questions of generality imply categorization of goods as collective or selective. Goods may also reflect the nature of the want they satisfy, in which case they are placed along an expressive–instrumental continuum. Finally, goods may be either intrinsic or extrinsic, depending on the source from which they emanate.

Goods, or resources, are employed in one of three means of exchange with authorities. They may be used in persuasion attempts, as inducements, or as constraints to elicit a desired policy. The means of resource application depends largely on the level at which a group supports the political system. Confident groups are most likely to use persuasion, whereas neutral and alienated groups are most likely to resort to inducements and constraints, respectively. Support is specific to the particular subsystem with which exchange is undertaken and is appropriately conceived of as existing on three levels simultaneously—that directed toward the political community, that manifested toward the political regime, and support which has as its object the government, or political authorities.

Support not only affects the means by which groups exert influence; it also affects the type of issues with which groups will be most intensely interested. Confident and alienated groups are most active on regime-level matters. Confident groups will attempt to influence decisions in the direction of maintaining the status quo whenever matters affecting the bias or the scope of authority of a political subsystem are called into question. Alienated groups, on the other hand, will attempt to promote exchanges which alter the existing regime. Neutral groups are less concerned with regime-level issues but will be most active where content issues affecting their interests are concerned.

NOTES

[1]Eugene J. Meehan, *Contemporary Political Thought: A Critical Study* (Homewood, Ill.: The Dorsey Press, 1967), p. 13.

[2]*Ibid.*, p. 11.

[3]David Easton, *The Political System* (New York: Alfred A. Knopf, 1953).

[4]David Easton, "An Approach to the Analysis of Political Systems," *World Politics*, IX (April 1957), pp. 391–94.

[5]William A. Gamson, *Power and Discontent* (Homewood, Ill.: The Dorsey Press, 1968).

[6]*Ibid.*, p. 50.

[7]*Ibid.*, p. 53.

[8]*Ibid.*, pp. 75–81.

[9]L. Harmon Zeigler and Michael A. Baer, *Lobbying: Interaction and Influence in American State Legislatures* (Belmont, Calif.: Wadsworth Publishing Company, 1969), p. 110.

[10]Lester W. Milbrath, *The Washington Lobbyists* (Chicago: Rand McNally, 1963), p. 289.

[11]Gamson, *Power and Discontent*, p. 77.

[12]Zeigler and Baer, Lobbying, p. 116.

[13]E. E. Schattschneider, The Semi-Sovereign People: A Realist's View of Democracy in America (New York: Holt, Rinehart & Winston, 1960), pp. 51–52.

[14]Gamson, Power and Discontent, pp. 146–54.

[15]Schattschneider, The Semi-Sovereign People, p. 48.

[16]It could, of course, attempt to expand the power exercised by the reviewing authority to include considerations of substantive content; however, that would entail an initial exchange over the scope of authority and a subsequent exchange concerning the specific content issue. The process would be very costly, and only rarely will groups undertake such an ambitious project.

[17]Gamson, Power and Discontent, p. 152.

[18]The remainder of this section is based on Gamson, ibid., pp. 154-71.

[19]Ibid., p. 47.

five

Groups,
the Public,
and Elections

Within the interpretive scheme we have outlined, two general
types of organizational activity are dominant: first, interactions which are internally oriented and which can be
analyzed as organization-building transactions; and second,
externally-oriented activities which are viewed as exchanges
between groups and the political system. Among the latter
must be counted those interactions that occur between interest groups and the public at large as well as more direct
exchanges with public officials. Indeed, in their attempts to
win favorable policy decisions from authorities, interest
groups have increasingly come to recognize the resource
value of public opinion and have courted it accordingly.

Not all organizations, of course, resort to this type of
strategy to attain their goals. In some instances, the cause of

a particular group is furthered by the avoidance of publicity and the use of the advantage of surprise. The army, for example, in seeking to establish military control over the creation of atomic energy, worked in absolute secrecy in close cooperation with the War Department to draft legislation before the atomic scientists, who were anxious to impose civilian control, were even aware that legislation was being contemplated. Consequently, when a bill assuring military control was introduced in the House, those who opposed the legislation had to work at a feverish pace to try to recoup what had been lost because of lack of access to information about the opposition's activities.[1] Nevertheless, a general trend in the direction of increased attempts to influence public opinion can be discerned.

Organization size is one factor which some argue is related to the technique of mass propaganda. Key has suggested that smaller groups, such as business organizations, would be more attracted to extensive reliance on public relations since "they command directly the support of only a few people, and they can readily subscribe to the doctrine that they must carry their cause by the generous support of propaganda to shape the opinions of the general public."[2] However, Lester Milbrath's research based on interviews with lobbyists reveals that mass membership organizations, particularly farm and labor, rated public relations campaigns highest in comparison with other groups.[3] Mass organizations also ranked letter-writing campaigns higher than did other types of groups. The obvious assumption is that the mass membership organizations apparently view public relations as a device to mobilize *membership* behind the position of the organization, while the smaller organizations are aiming toward "general" public opinion. As Monypenny argues, the smaller group can expect more internal cohesion than the larger group, and hence would expend more of its energy outward.[4] Indeed, business groups such as the National Association of Manufacturers place primary reliance on public relations.[5]

If we consider the techniques of mass propaganda, we should not be victimized by the vast amount of attention given to the idea that private groups can control or even shape opinions. Although the effects of a public relations campaign are difficult to measure, a body of firm generalizations developed in the social sciences states that it is very likely that the consequences of propaganda efforts are negligible. It is one thing to sell a particular brand of soap through advertising; it is another matter to sell a candidate or a legislative proposal by the same techniques. In the case of soap, most Americans are sufficiently convinced that personal cleanliness is a desirable attribute; the particular brand they use is of no great importance. On the other hand, propaganda which deals with more complex situations comes into contact with more deeply rooted values.[6] In the case of ethnic prejudices, for example, propaganda would not reshape basic attitudes to any appreciable extent. Further, the attempts of organized labor to show that "union workers are nice people" would have little impact unless the recipients of the propaganda were already inclined to accept this premise.[7] It is the function of propaganda, whether recognized by practitioners of the art or not, to mobilize, reinforce, or channel pre-existing, but possibly latent, attitudes. It is interesting to note Milbrath's comments on the lobbyists' perception of the effect of propaganda in view of these conclusions. Some lobbyists, while they were not convinced that the message of their organization was penetrating very deeply, rationalized that governmental decision-makers might believe that a particular campaign was persuasive and might possibly alter their position to conform to an expected reaction from the "outside world."[8]

TECHNIQUES IN MOBILIZING PUBLIC OPINION

Generally, the propaganda campaigns of organized groups are of two types: defensive efforts to ward off some immediate threat, such as the campaign of the American Medical Association to defeat the King–Anderson bill; and generalized, long-range programs to create a favorable image of the organization without reference to any immediate objectives.[9] In both types of campaigns there are similarities, one of the most obvious being the use of symbols. If the group is trying to establish its legitimacy, or its conformity to generally held societal norms, it will use "good" symbols. Organized labor, to illustrate, seeks to create an association of the words *labor* and *America,* an identification of unions with "freedom" and "neighbors." The AFL–CIO Industrial Union Department's brochure entitled "The All Union Family" describes a family as living at "99 Shady Lane, Anytown, U.S.A." The members of the union family are "Mr. and Mrs. John Q. America and their two wonderful kids."[10] Labor, which we have described as essentially a protest movement, has to try to integrate itself more fully into the mainstream of American life. Its program is, of course, long-term. It begins with the assumption that labor has to carve out a niche for itself and, in so doing, faces an uphill struggle. Attention has already been given to the absence of unions as a discernible part of the mass, or popular, culture. By contrast, an association such as the American Bar Association, whose membership operates with less of a handicap, sees its job to be one of *restoring* confidence.

If the goals of an organization are to prevent the establishment of a program judged detrimental to its organizational interests, the technique is to identify the proponents of the program with "evil" symbols. No symbol is more exhausted by constant usage than the old reliable, "socialism." This symbol, made famous by its repeated use by the American Medical Association, has become almost standard in the operating procedure of nearly all organizations whose objectives can, without a thoroughly implausible stretching of the imagination, be associated with free enterprise. Real estate organizations, such as the National Association of Real Estate Boards and National Association of Home Builders, played heavily on the theme of socialism in their efforts to defeat public housing legislation. Electing to concentrate propaganda dissemination at the local level, where the impact of public housing would be apparent, the Realtors' Washington Committee (which served as coordinator) distributed "kits" to local realtors which spelled out in some detail the approach to be taken. The advice was to equate public housing with "statism," "socialism," or any other "scarism," and "wherever possible stir up religious and racial prejudice."[11]

These instructions did result in advertisements in local papers stressing the drastically simplified alternative: "Do you believe in socialism? No! Is public housing socialism? Yes!"[12] However, there were organizations equally concerned with supporting public housing. If there had been little counterpropaganda there would have been, theoretically, a greater possibility that the symbolism of the realtors could have effected at least a mobilization of opposition. Monopolization of media for the promulgation of specified objectives is a rarity, and, with the existence of opposing propaganda, the probable result of the entire effort was neutralization.[13]

Stimulating the efforts of opposing groups is not the only adverse consequence that can result from widespread public opinion campaigns. Communications from groups, regardless of the extent to which they are designed to put their interests in a favorable light, may have exactly the reverse effect on the cognitive apparatus of the recipient. People tend to hear what they want to hear, that is, an individual is a complex organism with a host of beliefs, attitudes, and values through which new sensory stimuli are processed. Communications received are interpreted in terms of such preformed cognitions, and when the two are not compatible, it is frequently the case that the new inputs are disregarded, distorted, or evaluated negatively to make them fit the established cognitive pattern. Doubtlessly, individuals vary in the extent to which their cognitive patterns are inflexible, but in any event, dissonant communications are not readily accepted. The implications of this are clear. Interest groups attempting to stimulate public opinion invariably run the risk of unintentionally violating a latent but widespread value or belief. Instead of making a particular issue salient to the public *and* creating a desired attitude toward it, they may succeed only in making it salient, thereby bringing the latent and undesired attitude to the fore.

A current research project in which the authors are participating has resulted in findings that illustrate this phenomenon. In studying the political aspects of educational policy-making, it was found that teacher organizations and the League of Women Voters are consistently among the groups most active on issues involving school finances. Both organizations are presumably pro-school and for the passage of financial referenda, yet the direction of influence their activities had on the outcome of such referenda was the opposite. The campaigns they waged apparently increased public awareness over the issue, but increased awareness resulted in stimulating relatively more individuals predisposed to vote against than for financial propositions.[14]

Likewise, Bauer, Pool, and Dexter found a similar situation in their study of federal tariff policy.

[W]e found that, among the general population, liberalism on foreign trade was highly correlated with education and social status. The lower in the social spectrum one looked, the more latent protectionists one found and also the more people unaware of the foreign-trade issue. Under such conditions, any propaganda campaign which increased popular attention to the issue would probably thereby increase manifest protectionist sentiment by bringing otherwise apathetic persons, who tended to have a disproportionate number of latent protectionists among them, into the area of discourse. That would be true whether the campaign which alerted the public was conducted on behalf of protection or conducted, as by the League of Women Voters, on behalf of freer trade. The direction of the stimulus in such a situation matters little. What matters more is that the reservoir of uninformed protectionism at the bottom of the cultural ladder is apt to be tapped by any campaign sufficiently vigorous to catch the attention of the whole public.[15]

In the 1968 presidential election campaign one of the questions which intrigued observers was the extent to which "white backlash" would affect the outcome. White backlash was the journalistic expression used to denote reaction to the victories and publicity accorded to civil rights groups. What this as well as the preceding examples point to is the nature of the attitudes that tend to be triggered by the sudden activation of previously dormant sectors of the population. Evidence indicates that the objective impact of an issue on one's life does not necessarily result in activity or even in the issue's achieving a measurable degree of salience. Generally, those in the lower socioeconomic strata and with the least education are the most apathetic.[16] Characteristically, such persons have been found to lack information and the ability to relate systematically facts to more abstract levels of conceptualization and values. Their attitudes and beliefs often lack consistency, and subtle qualitative distinctions tend to be obscured by dichotomous generalizations. When aroused, their political behavior may well appear irrational. For instance, one would think that disadvantaged, low-income persons would be more concerned with the level of government goods and services, for they are the major beneficiaries of many social programs and lack the resources to acquire them individually. But when called on to express themselves on such matters through the medium of elections, they tend to abstain. And what seems more surprising yet, when activated, they tend to vote against "progressive" policies.

> There is a clear relationship between social status and progressive or "yes" voting at the local level. The better educated, higher income voters are the bedrock of support for school taxes, health facilities, parks, recreation, airports, and other community services. "No" voting for these public services is heavy among lower income, less educated, ethnic group members.[17]

Interest groups that undertake to arouse mass support on the basis of logical appeals to self-interest are likely to find that the objects of their campaigns—even if they can be aroused—do not conform to the rational ideal on which their appeals are predicated. This may explain to a large extent why so many of the successful mass propaganda campaigns have been couched in symbolic rhetoric designed to produce favorable *images* rather than in rational analysis of the issues.

Organizations using propaganda techniques often feel that they can do a more effective job if some other organization, not directly identifiable with the primary antagonist, can be persuaded to do most of the arguing. Key notes that ". . . any group that feels itself to be in the doghouse will tend to hide behind false fronts when it propagandizes the public."[18] The exact rationale for this assumption is difficult to locate. Perhaps the most readily understandable explanation is the fear that a public relations campaign might succeed in stimulating opposition which then could be transferred to the source of the propaganda. The extent to which this occurs is, like the effects of public relations activities, difficult to ascertain. However, Stokes' analysis of the 1958 right to work referendum in Ohio is suggestive of the possibilities of unanticipated consequences in propaganda campaigns. Stokes notes that the beginning of the campaign found little more than half of the electorate even familiar with the issue, with about half of this aware group in favor of adoption of a right to work law. However, as the efforts for and against the law grew more intense, awareness spread to three-quarters of the electorate. As interest spread, support for right to work held firm only in the business community. In every other segment of the population, right to work declined in popularity until, at the conclusion of the campaign, only businessmen gave majority approval. What was the basic contributing factor to this growth of opposition? Stokes offers the following explanation:

> ... the primary source of the rising tide against right to work was the connection the public drew between the issue and the recession. Responsibility for the economic distress of 1957–1958 was not at first charged to the business community. The recession *had* reinforced the public's belief that the Republicans, as the party of business, would not prevent unemployment. But it was not until right to work was brought before the public that the economic distress was given a forceful political translation. To many people in Ohio, placing right to work on the ballot looked like an effort by business to kick the working man when he was down. With this idea planted in the public's mind, labor was able to rally the opposition to the issue successfully, leaving business isolated in support of the law.[19]

The Ohio experience suggests that the more business propagandized, the more it became identified with circumstances over which it had no control. Perhaps, then, there is wisdom in the use of "front groups."

The American Bar Association has stated that ". . . the most effective way to tell the lawyer's story is to have someone else tell it."[20] In this case, the lawyers have a ready-made proponent in insurance companies and related financial institutions. Lawyers, as the ABA observes, "are in a position to control the appointment of many fiduciaries—executors, trustees, escrow agents and the like [and] are in a position to advise a client that he should have more insurance because of estate and inheritance tax problems, and may even recommend an insurance company if requested to do so by a client."[21]

Whether or not as a result of this none too subtle suggestion, the organized bar has enjoyed the cooperation of banks and insurance companies ranging from the very large, such as John Hancock and the Guaranty Trust Company of New York, to the smaller local institutions of considerable regional prestige. Other groups are less fortunate and have to resort to the deliberate creation of auxiliary organizations. The railroad interests in Pennsylvania, in opposing a law to raise the long haul truck weight limit, not only used established associations like the Pennsylvania State Grange to disseminate their literature, but also relied on some very obvious artificial fronts. One of the public relations specialists directing the railroads program was quoted as saying: "Of course we release some stories under direct attribution, but they will be of less propaganda value than those we can generate from motorists, property owners, tax payers, farmers or women's groups. In sum, we not only have to create publicity ideas; we also have to go out into the field and create the groups and occasions so that these ideas will become realities."[22]

Not all groups that function as front organizations are the result of conscious design. Nor are they all geared toward specific issues such as pending legislation or election campaigns. Front organizations may just as likely be vehicles for the dissemination of propaganda designed to create or reinforce diffuse attitudes among the public in order to build a favorable support orientation among the masses. One such organization is the prestigious Advertising Council, which Nicholas von Hoffman has described as "a nonprofit media–business–propaganda consortium founded during World War II to 'put the skills and faculties of the advertising industry in the service of a nation at war.' "[23] The council continued its efforts "in the public interest" following the war. It conducts extensive advertising campaigns in both printed and electronic media. Few Americans have escaped being exposed to what has been estimated at over four billion dollars' worth of free advertising on television, radio, newspapers, magazines, and billboards. Many of the twenty or so campaigns conducted per year are uncontroversial. They have promoted the Presidential Physical Fitness Program, mental retardation programs, fire prevention, Zip Code, and Smokey the Bear, among other causes. Others, von Hoffman contends, instill a particular bias in public opinion over controversial political, social, or economic matters.

> Other campaigns which appear to be in the public interest grow suspect when you stop and think about them and who's connected with the council. Every litter bit does prevent America from being beautiful, but it isn't picnic trash that's causing our worst trouble: it's big industry, a fact that isn't mentioned in ads. Since the council's industries advisory committee

includes the presidents or board chairmen of U. S. Steel, Bethlehem Steel, Ford Motors, Aluminum Company of America, Scott Paper Company and Union Carbide, it's to be expected that the pollution problem is defined as obscure, unnamed citizens throwing kleenex out of car windows in national parks.

This is the same as telling people they're pigs to buy cars and TV's because they're causing inflation while omitting mention of Mr. Melvin Laird's rockets.

For years, the council has plugged the national safety council's line on automobile accidents, telling people that the carnage on the road is all owing to careless and drunken drivers. Undoubtedly these are the cause of many accidents, but Ralph Nader demonstrated that many other accidents are caused by carelessly designed and badly manufactured automobiles.

Have you ever seen an ad on television urging the automobile and tire manufacturers to stop making unsafe products?

A strong case could be made that much of this advertising is not pro bono publico but is actually in the immediate economic interest of the individuals and corporations connected with the council.[24]

We do not propose to involve ourselves in the debate concerning the existence of a tightly knit "power elite" ruling America, nor is it our intention to charge the Advertising Council with Machiavellian intent in some of its advertising. Similarity in background and outlook among the council's members no doubt accounts for much of what might be construed as conscious bias. Nevertheless, von Hoffman's charge that certain campaigns have the practical effect of obscuring facts which would negatively affect business interests is not without merit. To the extent that it is valid, regardless of the conscious intent of the Advertising Council, the council has functioned as a front organization which has propagandized the public on behalf of special interests.

The use of a front organization is a different technique from the alliance formation operations often indulged in by groups with similar aspirations, such as the American Jewish Congress and the National Association for the Advancement of Colored People.[25] It also differs from the more direct infiltration methods of the John Birch Society. The Society does seek to establish fronts, but also hopes to infiltrate established community organizations without incurring overt identification. This semisecret association would be less inclined to rely on the shotgun-type propaganda effort in the expectation that it would be able to exert a more subtle influence on opinion leaders within a community. Most of its activity is local, although coordinated from its national headquarters. Loss of the

element of secrecy—the ability to catch an opponent by surprise—
might also mean public disapproval and loss of support.[26]

PRESSURE GROUPS AND ELECTIONS: MYTHS AND
REALITIES OF GROUP VOTING

Many of the propaganda activities of organized groups become
most intense during election campaigns. This is the time when nonmember opinion is more easily accessible to the pleadings of organizations, and it is also the time when membership opinion might be
more readily unified. Interest groups also reason that, if the "right"
man can be elected, their task of persuasion will be simplified.
Finally, we cannot neglect the most widely publicized aspect of
electoral activity by interest groups—the threat of retaliation against
a candidate for public office whose record is displeasing. When the
NAM declares '"we have endeavored . . . to elect congressmen whom
we have known to possess the courage of their convictions . . . and
who fearlessly oppose the legislation we have been opposing" and
countless other organizations inform legislators that their record will
be remembered in November, the student of group politics might
indeed tremble at such awesome displays of power.[27] However, as in
the case of public relations campaigns, the hard facts of political life
do not coincide with a simplified model of human motivations.

It is beyond the abilities of an organized group to guarantee, with
any degree of certainty, that its members will automatically respond
to the suggestions of the leaders. It is, however, true that group affiliations are an important variable in the reaching of an electoral
decision. We earlier noted the seeming lack of control that group
leaders exert over the votes of their members. This is not to say that
discernible preference patterns within organization memberships do
not develop, for the same common values and interests that produce
groups frequently result in common political behavior among members. But group voting phenomena in most cases are the products
of like minds independently arriving at the same conclusion, rather
than the results of rigid controlling techniques by group leaders. As
Stokes has observed, ". . . wheat farmers may respond in unison to a
drop in the price of their crop, without needing a farm organization
to tell them that their pocketbook nerve has been touched."[28] Individual values, to the extent that they reflect group norms, are
sufficiently established to resist any sudden or capricious reversal of
position by a formal organization. It would be absurd to suppose, for
instance, that the American Jewish Congress, if for some reason it

chose to do so, could hope to accomplish even the slightest modification in the liberal tendencies of the Jewish community. Perhaps as a result of their religious values or their shared social experiences, "no matter what criteria have been used to define liberalism and conservatism, Jews have invariably been rated overwhelmingly more liberal than Christians."[29]

A fair assessment of the influence of groups over their members' votes is that it is zero at worst and only minimal at best, for organizations are not wholly impotent in such matters. Although it is doubtful that they can change their members' political values, they can publicize particular issues and candidates in an attempt to make them more visible. By playing on the basic political orientations of members, groups can have a positive effect on their voting turnout or even cause them to reevaluate candidates and issues. But such results are only marginal, for underlying political values are not called into question. Campbell et al. commented on the paradoxical situation of many organization leaders:

> When political events cause a group leadership to switch official support to the opposing party, the strong party loyalties that it has helped to create and reinforce may be reversed only with great difficulty. We can imagine that these loyalties...gain some functional autonomy as they grow stronger. They come to have a force of their own....[30]

Regardless of the problems inherent in mobilizing electoral support, attempts to do so are common election year occurrences among interest groups. Success rates vary from group to group within the limits we have outlined. Likewise, tactics vary depending on group size. The very large organizations, such as the AFL–CIO, that like to think they have substantial strength at the polls, engage heavily in the publication of voting records and personal solicitation of votes among their members. But the smaller organizations, such as business or professional groups, can make no claims of a deliverable body of voters and can only offer their services as proselytizers of a larger public. However, while the target of the efforts of the two types of groups varies, their techniques are similar. There is general recognition of the very basic fact that, while the nonpersonal appeals of mass communication should not be neglected, success will depend more on informal and personal contacts. Examples drawn from divergent sources will illustrate this technique.

Studies of United Automobile Workers Unions in Detroit and Chicago note that the leadership of both unions is actively engaged in the support of Democratic candidates through personal contacts with members. In Chicago, the local union president spent considerable amounts of time in supplementing an organizational postcard campaign. Each member of the union was given one of these cards by leadership within the place of employment and "if you got one of these Poles or Bohunks who couldn't read or write, we'd get somebody to do it for them and make them sign their X [indicating a pledge of support] on it."[31] In Detroit, similar efforts were more coordinated. The membership of the union was divided according to congressional district, and neighborhood meetings were sponsored, giving workers the opportunity to discuss the issues. At the plants, "lists of endorsed slates are passed out to the workers, and lunch hour and coffee breaks at election time are punctuated with political discussion."[32] Although both unions were equally vociferous in their efforts, the results were not the same. The majority of Detroit union members "trust the voting recommendations of labor groups," but in Chicago there is greater distrust and apathy.[33] What explains this difference? We know that the more active members of an organization tend to conform more readily to group norms.[34] The Detroit union has developed an elaborate plan of formal endorsement of candidates in which the individual member, while not participating directly, does not necessarily feel that a candidate is being "shoved down his throat." Further, there is very close collaboration between the union and the state Democratic party. This proximity between the union and the political process enables the organization to establish a "natural" connection with politics. The establishing of union membership is frequently an automatic process, and since there is an inclination of union members to view political activity as a secondary aspect of the union's proper sphere of activities, the methods of the Detroit union are a good remedy for this situation. However, the Detroit case is hardly typical.

What of the smaller organization that must work with nonmember opinions? Even if their own members are ready and willing to toe the mark, this is of little consequence. However, if the organization or its members enjoy considerable community prestige, a candidate may believe that his campaign will be augmented by the group's participation. In political contests in which the issue of compulsory health insurance is being debated, various "medical arts committees" have arranged for doctors to write personal letters urging their patients' opposition to "forces at work in this nation today which replace the health and medical care you have always enjoyed under the truly American system of private medicine."[35] In most cases, such letters urged the patient to vote for lists of endorsed candidates who, according to the physicians, could be expected to vote "right" if elected.

In Ohio, a small group of trade association executives, using virtually no publicity, worked on behalf of the candidacy of Senator Robert Taft by singling out opinion leaders in every county of the state. Each of these local influentials was urged to arrange meetings, to register Taft supporters and get them to the polls, and to have voters visited by members of their professions.[36] These programs roughly parallel the standard political party operations. To attribute unusual success to them would be to overlook the many other variables contributing to victory or defeat. In Ohio, for example, the substitution of the office-block for the party column ballot was estimated by Taft to have been responsible for more than one-fourth of his majority.[37] That physicians in Florida supported George Smathers in his successful attempt to unseat Senator Claude Pepper in the 1950 Democratic primaries can hardly be regarded as any sort of first cause. An organization's threat to punish politicians for poor voting records simply cannot be made good.[38]

Another means by which groups try to exert influence over electoral processes is that of financial contributions to campaign funds. Authorities differ in their evaluation of the importance of contributions as a technique of influencing political allocations. Some have suggested that the technique is relatively unimportant; indeed, if one concentrates on the net effects of interest group contributions on election outcomes, perhaps such a conclusion is warranted. The total contributions to Democratic candidates by interest groups tends to balance the funds donated to Republicans.[39] Since contributions are roughly offsetting, it cannot be said that they alter the relative strengths of the two parties. Undoubtedly interest group contributions have the effect of changing the character of campaigns by affording candidates more resources from which to draw in their appeals to the voters. In the 1968 national election campaign, for instance, the FCC has reported that approximately $59 million was spent on radio and television advertising alone. Without the large sums contributed by labor, business, and other organizations, such coverage would have been impossible. But when one breaks down the total amount spent, it appears that neither party benefited disproportionately from media coverage.[40] Such parity makes it virtually impossible for a group to handpick a candidate and "sell" him to the public, for there is an ample supply of resources available to opposing interests to offset any such attempt.

The benefits a group receives as a result of having contributed to a successful candidacy are rarely manifested directly in policy influence. Perhaps the single most important effect of financial contributions from the standpoint of the interest group is that they make elected officials receptive to communications from group spokesmen. This is not to say that officials will necessarily be swayed by the arguments thus communicated, but at least they will listen. Milbrath quoted one lobbyist as stating,

> A political contribution is not ever likely to change a vote or get a vote from an official, but it does get you a sympathetic audience. If you have made a contribution, the fellow looks on you with favor, and he will give you a chance to be heard.[41]

Likewise, in their study of state legislator–lobbyist interactions, Zeigler and Baer found that contributions are "somewhat more effective than other techniques" in maintaining open channels of communication.[42]

Although the value of campaign contributions is generally sufficient to induce an official to grant access to contributing organizations, it is not sufficient to force his vote. Nor are threats of withholding future donations granted much weight. Not only are alternate sources of funds available to public officials, but a threat— any threat—is much more likely to create hostility toward the threatening group than an appreciation of its power. A threat is more likely to have adverse effects on previously established communication channels than it is to induce desired results. In short, threats are bad currency in political exchanges.

From the standpoint of influencing the net result of American electoral procedures, we are forced to conclude that campaign contributions by interest groups have little differential effect, for in gross terms, the donations to political contestants by opposing groups tend to cancel one another out. Thus, it cannot be said that interest groups independently elect public officials. It would be a mistake, however, to conclude from this that campaign contributions represent gratuitous offerings which do not benefit organizations. It must be remembered that the groups' primary concern is that of winning policy decisions—not that of winning office. From this perspective it becomes obvious that contributions represent instrumental acts which facilitate political exchange by opening communication channels with decision-makers.

Not all groups, of course, use this technique to an equal extent. Many organizations simply lack the necessary funds. Generally, those groups most free with campaign donations are organized around the immediate economic interests of their members, for such groups are able to extract proportionately larger monetary resources from their members with the promise that their dues or donations will win further economic goods when employed in political exchange. Thus, we find that labor, business, and industrial interests tend to be active campaign contributors. Most of labor's contributions go to Democratic candidates, and most corporate contributions go to Republicans, but these partisan lines are not sacrosanct. For instance, all organizations are well aware of the exorbitant power that resides in the hands of congressional committee chairmen. Regardless of his party affiliation, the chairman of a committee concerned with matters central to a group's interest can expect contributions from that group if it has funds to devote to such purposes.

It is difficult to assess the extent of organizations' involvement in campaign financing. Laws pertaining to financial reports vary from state to state, and federal laws contain enough loopholes for organizations to obscure the amount of their financial involvement in campaigns. There can be little doubt, however, that interest group contributions attain staggering proportions. It has been estimated that the total amount spent on election campaigns at all levels in 1968 was approximately $300,000,000.[43] The private fortunes of candidates, individual donations, and party fund-raising dinners (even at $1,000 per plate) could not begin to cover such expenses. There are figures available that give us some indication of the magnitude of interest group contributions. Organizations which establish campaign committees at the national level are required to file reports of their spending. Although such front committees control only a portion of the total campaign expenses incurred by organized groups, their activities are indicative of the extent to which groups are involved in financing electoral procedures. Table 1 lists the funds

TABLE 1. Financial Contributions by Type of Committee[44]

Year	Labor	Miscellaneous
1956	$1,800,000	$ 700,000
1960	2,500,000	900,000
1964	3,800,000	2,100,000
1968	7,600,000	4,900,000

contributed by labor and other groups at the national level through their respective campaign committees in the four most recent presidential elections. Labor committees are adjuncts of formal unions. Not all committees, however, can be as easily traced to particular groups. Thus, committees listed as "miscellaneous" in Table 1 are fronts for a wide range of organizations. They include business, industrial, and professional interests as well as some noneconomic interests. The titles of some, such as the American Medical Political Action Committee and the Shoe Manufacturers Good Government Committee, reflect the organizations they serve. Others, such as the Committee for Action—East, West, South, and Midwest; The 1968 Campaign Fund; and the Non-Partisan Committee to Elect the Best Man, are not so obvious. It is apparent from Table 1 that the level of spending by national committees is high. Moreover, the rate of increase over the twelve years covered indicates that the importance of this type of activity is not likely to wane in the future.

There are additional ways by which interest groups attempt to in-fluence election procedures. A variety of nonfinancial contributions including personnel, equipment, and information serve the same purpose from the organization's standpoint as outright monetary con-tributions. Candidates value such resources highly and tend to look favorably on those who are in a position to supply them. Communi-cation channels thus established are just as effective as those resulting from financial contributions. Two congressmen were quoted by *Congressional Quarterly* not long after the 1968 elections concerning the types of nonfinancial aid candidates receive:

Rep. Bertram L. Podell (D, N.Y.) said that many large corporations loan "a plane and a pilot to the candidate of their choice." Podell also said corporations often "make available to a candidate . . . a fleet of automo-biles, plus the use of their public relations staff."

Rep. Bob Eckhardt (D, Texas) said that the aggregate amount of a cor-poration's indirect aid to a political candidate "by reassigning personnel and the use of mechanical equipment may exceed . . . the amount given by direct contributors."

As an example of such indirect aid, Eckhardt said, "A company which ordinarily advertises on billboards may give them up a little early . . . some-times it is an outright loan." Other examples were "the use of mailing lists of a company and the use of their reproduction equipment."[45]

Although data on this type of campaign assistance are scanty and difficult to find, it appears as if noneconomic aid of the types de-scribed above most frequently comes from business and industrial interests.

SUMMARY AND CONCLUSIONS

Although the ultimate political objectives of interest groups can be defined in terms of goods allocated through the political system, not all activities in which groups engage are direct interactions with authoritative decision-makers. Group leaders often deem it necessary to devote substantial portions of their resources to strategic activity to establish among the public conditions favorable for subsequent exchanges with political officials. We have examined two broad types of public involvement of interest groups.

Public opinion campaigns can be seen as attempts to increase the political resources at the disposal of organization leaders. A mass public supportive of a group and favorably disposed toward its demands constitutes a powerful resource in dealings with political authorities. Likewise, a hostile public is a liability. Therefore, groups try to create favorable images of themselves and their goals. The symbolic content of such attempts is usually very heavy. Numerically small organizations typically disseminate their propaganda outward, while large organizations are often forced to concentrate on internal consumption. Extensive propaganda efforts are not undertaken without risk, for they may trigger similar and offsetting campaigns by opposing interests. Moreover, if the basic values of sizable portions of the public are misperceived and subsequently violated, propaganda campaigns with their heavy reliance on symbol manipulation may have the reverse effect of that which was intended.

Financing and aiding candidates for political office is the second type of activity we examined. Like public opinion campaigns, resources are not expended on elections in anticipation of an immediate return in the form of public policy. Instead, they are best evaluated as investments in accessibility. An official whose election was aided by an organization will tend to listen to spokesmen for that organization. Thus, campaign assistance, while it is not in itself sufficient to consummate political exchange, does at least ensure a group entry to the marketplace. Rarely if ever are elections the focal points of group interests. The content of distributive decisions, *not* personnel decisions, is germane to the demands of interest groups. From the standpoint of the group advocate that is just as well, for apart from the communication channel aspect of organizational involvement in political campaigns, the influence that groups wield over election decisions is considerably less than overpowering. As Schattschneider has observed,

> Pressure groups are small organizations that do not have the political resources to play in the great arena for the highest stakes. The big game is the party game because in the last analysis *there is* no political substitute for victory in an election.[46]

Groups may increase their resources by mobilizing public opinion, and they may gain access to the political market by supporting political candidates, but to win the benefits they desire, they must interact in a more direct manner with political decision-makers. Such interactions must necessarily occur within the various governmental arenas.

NOTES

[1]Byron S. Miller, "A Law Is Passed—The Atomic Energy Act of 1946," *University of Chicago Law Review*, XV (Summer 1948), p. 804. See also Richard G. Hewlett and Oscar E. Anderson, Jr., *The New World, 1939/1956* (University Park, Pa.: The Pennsylvania State University Press, 1962), Vol. 1, p. 422.

[2]V. O. Key, Jr., *Public Opinion and American Democracy* (New York: Alfred A. Knopf, Inc., 1961), p. 515.

[3]Lester Milbrath, "Lobbying as a Communications Process," *Public Opinion Quarterly*, XXIV (Spring 1960), p. 45.

[4]Phillip Monypenny, "Political Science and the Study of Groups: Notes to Guide a Research Project," *Western Political Quarterly*, VII (June 1954), p. 197.

[5]Joseph G. La Palombara, "Pressure, Propaganda, and Political Action in the Election of 1950," *Journal of Politics*, XIV (May 1952), p. 305.

[6]Paul Lazarsfeld and Robert K. Merton, "Mass Communication, Popular Taste and Organized Social Action," in Lyman Bryson, ed., *The Communication of Ideas* (New York: Institute for Religious and Social Studies, 1948), pp. 113–18. See also Joseph T. Klapper, *The Effects of Mass Communication* (New York: The Free Press, 1960), pp. 12–97.

[7]Gerald Pomper, "The Public Relations of Organized Labor," *Public Opinion Quarterly*, XXIII (Winter 1960), p. 487.

[8]Milbrath, *op. cit.*, p. 45.

[9]Adapted from the suggestion of S. E. Finer in Henry W. Ehrmann, ed., *Interest Groups on Four Continents* (Pittsburgh: University of Pittsburgh Press, 1958), p. 251.

[10]Pomper, *op. cit.*, p. 488. See also AFL–CIO, Industrial Union Department, "Mr. and Mrs. America: The All Union Family," p. 3.

[11]Lee F. Johnson, "Housing: A 1950 Tragedy," *The Survey*, Dec. 1950, p. 553. See also House Select Committee on Lobbying Activities, *Hearings*, Housing Lobby, 81st Cong., 2nd Sess., 1950 (Washington, D.C.: Government Printing Office, 1950).

[12]House Select Committee on Lobbying Activities, *Hearings*, Housing Lobby, p. 370.

[13]Lazarsfeld and Merton, *op. cit.*, p. 115.

[14]See M. Kent Jennings and L. Harmon Zeigler, "Interest Representation in School Governance" (paper presented to the American Political Science Association Meeting, Sept. 1970), pp. 41–43.

[15]Raymond A. Bauer, Ithiel de Sola Pool, and Lewis Anthony Dexter, *American Business and Public Policy: The Politics of Foreign Trade* (New York: Atherton Press, 1963), p. 468.

[16]For a more complete discussion and review of relevant literature on this and subsequent related points, see Philip E. Converse, "The Nature of Belief Systems in Mass Publics," in *Ideology and Discontent*, ed. David E. Apter (New York: The Free Press, 1964), pp. 206–59; Thomas R. Dye and L. Harmon Zeigler, *The Irony of Democracy: An Uncommon Introduction to American Politics* (Belmont, Calif.: Wadsworth Pub-

lishing Company, 1970), pp. 127–74; and Herbert McClosky, "Personality and Attitude Correlates of Foreign Policy Orientation," *Domestic Sources of Foreign Policy*, ed. J. Rosenau (New York: The Free Press, 1967), pp. 51–110.

[17]Dye and Zeigler, *op. cit.*, p. 167.

[18]Key, *op. cit.*, p. 517.

[19]Donald E. Stokes, *Voting Research and the Businessman in Politics* (Ann Arbor, Mich.: The Foundation for Research on Human Behavior, 1960), p. 23. Similar examples of the negative consequences of organization support would be labor or NAACP endorsement in the South.

[20]American Bar Association, Standing Committee on Public Relations, *op. cit.*, p. 61.

[21]*Ibid.*, pp. 61–62.

[22]Robert Bendiner, "The Engineering of Consent—A Case Study," *The Reporter*, 11 August 1955, p. 17.

[23]*The Washington Post*, 12 January 1970, Sec. B, p. 1.

[24]*Ibid.*, p. 10.

[25]Senate Committee on the Judiciary, *Hearings*, Civil Rights, 86th Cong., 1st Sess., 1959 (Washington, D.C.: Government Printing Office, 1959), pp. 1527–71.

[26]Alan F. Westin, "The John Birch Society: Fundamentalism on the Right," *Commentary*, XXXII (Aug. 1961), pp. 93–106.

[27]Quoted in LaPalombara, "Pressure, Propaganda, and Political Action," p. 306.

[28]Stokes, *op. cit.*, p. 15.

[29]Lawrence Fuchs, "American Jews and the Presidential Vote," *American Political Science Review*, XLIX (June 1955), p. 392. See also Fuchs, *The Political Behavior of American Jews* (New York: The Free Press, 1956).

[30]Angus Campbell et al., *The American Voter* (abridged ed.; New York: John Wiley & Sons, Inc., 1964), pp. 182–83.

[31]Harold Wilensky, "The Labor Vote: A Local Union's Impact on the Political Conduct of Its Members," *Social Forces*, XXXV (Dec. 1956), p. 114.

[32]Nicholas A. Masters, "The Politics of Union Endorsement of Candidates in the Detroit Area," *Midwest Journal of Political Science*, I (Aug. 1957), p. 146.

[33]Harold L. Sheppard and Nicholas A. Masters, "The Political Attitudes and Preferences of Union Members: The Case of the Detroit Auto Workers," *American Political Science Review*, LIII (June 1959), p. 447. See also Arthur Kornhauser, Harold L. Sheppard, and Albert J. Mayer, *When Labor Votes: A Study of Auto Workers* (New Hyde Park, N.Y.: University Books, 1956).

[34]James G. March, "Group Norms and the Active Minority," *American Sociological Review*, XVIV (Dec. 1954), pp. 733–41. See also Campbell, Converse, Miller, and Stokes, *op. cit.*, p. 311.

[35]"New Power at the Polls," *Medical Economics* (Jan. 1951), p. 77.

[36]LaPalombara, "Pressure, Propaganda, and Political Action," pp. 303–25.

[37]V. O. Key, Jr., *Politics, Parties, and Pressure Groups* (New York: Thomas Y. Crowell Company, 1958), p. 694.

[38]V. O. Key, Jr., "The Veterans and the House of Representatives: A Study of a Pressure Group and Electoral Mortality," *Journal of Politics*, V (Feb. 1943), pp. 27–40.

[39]Alexander Heard, *The Costs of Democracy* (Chapel Hill, N.C.: University of North Carolina Press, 1960), p. 196.

[40]The Republicans spent $27,860,093 on electronic media coverage as opposed to $27,865,649 for the Democrats.

[41]Milbrath, *The Washington Lobbyists*, p. 283.

[42]Zeigler and Baer, *Lobbying*, p. 190.

[43]The source of this estimate is Herbert E. Alexander, Director of the Citizens Research Foundation, as reported in "Nixon Broadcast Costs Are Twice Those for Humphrey," *Congressional Quarterly Weekly Report*, XXVII (5 December 1969), p. 2441.

[44]"Record $70.1 Million Reported Spent in 1964 Elections," *ibid.*, p. 2435.

[45]*Ibid.*, p. 2439.

[46]Schattschneider, *The Semi-Sovereign People*, p. 58.

six

The Representation of Interests through Legislation

In examining the legislative process we need at the outset some understanding of the role of the legislature and legislators in establishing a basic pattern of order for the society.[1] It would hardly be plausible to assume that the group conflict inherent in a changing society can resolve itself automatically. Recalling for the moment Easton's idea that politics constitutes the "authoritative allocation of values," we can assign to the legislature the function of providing competitive demands with a tentative decision of victory or defeat.[2] The conflicting demands of groups will gravitate toward the formal institutions of government, for only within such institutions can demands be transformed into legally binding mandates. The legislature, however, is not the sole arbiter of disputes. Other governmental institutions—administrative agencies and courts—perform the same function; indeed some would say that these institutions have gradually assumed more responsibility in the formation of public policy, while the legislature's role in this area has diminished in significance. It is not our task to assess the relative importance of legislative bodies in the overall policy formation process. Suffice it to say that they remain active and important organs of government. The vicissitudes of political systems are such that the power of any element therein tends to be in a state of flux. Thus, if the legislature appears to be losing power today, tomorrow it may well regain all that it has lost and then some. There is little likelihood that legislatures in American political systems will atrophy to the point of becoming vestigial institutions of government.

LEGISLATIVE OUTPUTS: TANGIBLE AND SYMBOLIC GOODS

One of the foremost reasons for the assumption that legislatures have been losing power is a growing awareness of the symbolic nature of many legislative acts. That this awareness is a relatively recent development is a result of the rigid formalism that long characterized political thought. The emphasis on forms in institutional analysis led to an understanding of legislatures as bodies of men who, while representing distinct sets of conflicting interests, were vested by society with the authority to resolve such conflicts. Democratic values prescribed that clashes between interests should be resolved according to the principle of majoritarianism. Republicanism dictated that decision-making authority was delegated from the citizenry at large to the legislators who represented their interests. Therefore, the picture of legislatures as the only legitimate policy-making agent of government was not only consonant with formal institutional arrangements, but it also carried with it the moral sanction of normative theory. This view was reinforced by intellectual formalism which equated policy with de jure rules and formally enacted laws.

Not until the twentieth century did scholars begin to approach social and political phenomena from a pragmatic perspective rather than a formal one. Formal, legal interpretation of policies gave way to analysis based on their practical effects on people. This, in turn, focused attention on the administration of laws, for it was readily apparent once one looked at the practical effect of laws that there were frequently disparities between the formal intent of statutory provisions and their observable results. The seeming inability of legislatures to execute the moral and structural function presumed for them by democratic theorists led to an overreaction on the part of some scholars who have tended to relegate them to the role of impotent figurehead bodies that do little more than manipulate symbols to lend legitimacy to the "real" decisions made elsewhere.

That we have only recently become aware of the symbolic aspect of legislative activity should not lead us to deduce erroneously that it is itself a recent phenomenon or that it is unimportant merely because it does not fit our previous notions of what legislatures should do. We too frequently tend to equate importance with instrumentality or tangibility while failing to recognize fully the significance of evocative and symbolic goods. Whether one argues from the government position or from the interest group position, symbolic goods should not be discounted as worthless. From the former perspective, the symbolic acts performed by legislatures legitimate a host of other actions performed by governmental actors and make them acceptable to the people. In listing the various functions performed by legislatures, Wahlke et al. observed,

> Above all they ordinarily have a great deal to do with "legitimizing," or making authoritative, important classes of decisions, wherever those decisions might be made in the particular system. This involves in almost all cases a process and function of "representation" of important political groups and interests in the community. It usually involves also a high degree of ritualistic "symbol manipulation" which provides cues to political publics for responding to legislative actions. Legislatures may facilitate catharsis of political grievances by providing a forum for the verbal expression of anxieties, resentments, and aggressive desires, thus contributing to stability in the political system.[3]

Symbolic legislative outputs may also have value for interest groups. To the weak or alienated group, a symbolic victory can mean the difference between continued existence as a group and failure, for organizations with little chance of winning immediate tangible goods must be able to show some occasional successes to their members if they are to maintain their allegiance. To such groups a symbolic victory may be just as important as a tangible one. Likewise, favored groups which receive disproportionate shares of tangible goods benefit from the enactment of symbolic legislation which either legitimizes their instrumental victories or serves as a soporific for a potentially hostile public.

> The laws may be repealed in effect by administrative policy, budgetary starvation, or other little publicized means; but the laws as symbols must stand because they satisfy interests that are very strong indeed: interests

that politicians fear will be expressed actively if a large number of voters are led to believe that their shield against a threat has been removed.

More than that, it is largely as symbols of this sort that these statutes have utility to most of the voters. If they function as reassurances that threats in the economic environment are under control, their indirect effect is to permit greater claims upon tangible resources by the organized groups concerned than would be possible if the legal symbols were absent.[4]

Legislative systems do, of course, make instrumental allocative decisions as well as symbolic ones; it would be wrong to assume otherwise. Perhaps the most accurate way of viewing any legislative act is to see it as a combination of tangible and symbolic elements. The precise balance between the two domains will vary; however, rarely will either be lacking. For, as Edelman observed, "every instance of policy formation involves a 'mix' of symbolic effect and rational reflection of interests in resources, though one or the other may be dominant in any particular case."[5] Interest group leaders as well as students of politics must appreciate both these aspects and recognize the value of each.

LEGISLATURES AS INSTITUTIONS

The exchanges which result in legislative decisions cannot be understood simply in terms of the resources at the disposal of competing interests. Certainly resources are important; however, to have a bearing on goods allocated by legislatures they must be evaluated within the context in which they are to be exchanged—namely, the legislative arena. It is as important to understand the institutional structure and norms within the legislature if one is to analyze the determinants of legislative outputs as it is to appraise the relative resource positions of competing interests. These internal patterns have been termed *folkways* by Matthews.[6] While the institutional norms of the legislature are worthy of study in their own right, they are most significant for our purpose because they interact with external pressures and thus play a part in the conversion or decision-making process. Latham has written that "the legislature referees the group struggle, ratifies the victories of the successful coalitions, and records the terms of the surrenders, compromises, and conquests in the form of statutes."[7] On the other hand, Burns once described legislators as little more than elected lobbyists.[8] How can one referee if he is committed to the values of one of the participants? One way to reconcile these opposing points of view is to avoid the use of "either–or" language. Latham does not intend to suggest that the legislature is a dormant *tabula rasa* which merely approves previously reached decisions: "the legislature does not play the inert part of cash register, ringing up additions and withdrawals of strength, a mindless balance pointing and marking the weight and distribution of power among the contending groups."[9] Still less can the legislative system be understood as being made up of philosopher-kings who distill private interest into public good.

There is no objective standard by which to measure legislative performances, and it is far more fruitful to rely on the legislator's perception of his role or "definition of the situation." Members of legislatures fill a role to which certain expectations have been attached. All of the expectations do not originate with a single source, and the role played by each legislator can be understood as a sum of the total pattern of expectations. The legislator is expected to perform in a certain way by his colleagues, his constituents, and formal organizations, to name a few. The expectations may reinforce each other or they may conflict. Each legislator is a formal or informal member of many other groups. In addition, a legislator possesses individual ecological characteristics, which, to an extent not yet totally determined, are reflected by his particular personality. All of these variables help to determine how a legislator will interpret the demands of an interest group, and the reaction of a legislator to group pressure is a critical factor in determining the influence of a group.

FORMAL STRUCTURE: THE COMMITTEES

The importance of formal structure in the legislative process is that it provides part of the framework in which group conflicts can be resolved; it has "restraining and channeling effects."[10] By far the most easily identifiable aspect of the formal structure of the American legislature is the committee system. George B. Galloway notes that the "operation of the committee system is recognized as the heart of congressional activity . . . these miniature legislatures have acquired such power and prestige over the years that they are largely autonomous in the House itself which created them and whose agents they are supposed to be."[11] Matthews says much the same about the Senate, while the Committee on American Legislatures of the American Political Science Association finds the committee system dominant in the state legislative process.[12] While the committee might not make the final decision, it is here that a potential law receives its first public scrutiny, where the compromises and subtle variations upon the quid pro quo are agreed on.

Group stakes in committee assignments

The relations between interest groups and committees may develop a certain degree of stability, as most committees are "stacked" with legislators whose constituencies are most concerned with the work of the committee. For example, both the House and Senate Agriculture Committees are manned by farmers, or legislators from constituencies with a vital interest in farming. This does not ensure that the demands of interest groups and the preferences of legislators will always be harmonious, for each particular interest will have several organizations competing for the right to speak authoritatively. Consequently, organized groups take considerable interest in the process of committee assignments. While overt participation in the assigning of committee positions is rare, organizations have clearly articulated "expectations" as to the kinds of legislators who should be appointed. Masters discovered that "Democrats attempt to placate organized labor by placing pro-labor representatives on the Education and Labor Committee, while Republicans attempt to satisfy the National Association of Manufacturers by appointing pro-business members to the same committee."[13]

In addition, the operation of the seniority system limits the rapport between interest group and committee. Seniority is particularly troublesome for organized labor. Since the seniority system works to the advantage of Southerners from safe districts, labor has had a difficult time working with the chairmen of the House Education and Labor Committee. According to Masters, the Democrats seek to appoint either Southerners or members who can afford to take a forthright pro-labor stand, while Republicans, having closer connections with management, try to appoint congressmen whose pro-management bias will not diminish their chances of reelection.[14] The makeup of this committee as a factor in the strategy of interest groups is illuminated by the case of the 1955 legislative campaign for raising the federal minimum wage. Various unions had formed the Joint Minimum Wage Committee to direct an extensive effort to achieve an increase in the minimum wage from seventy-five cents to—at the least—ninety cents. After a series of preparatory operations, the Joint Committee turned to the task of guiding a bill through Congress. The first obstacle was the House Committee on Education and Labor, chaired by Graham Barden of North Carolina. Gus Tyler, director of the Political Department of the International Ladies Garment Workers' Union, saw Barden as the "key problem" and commented that "it appeared to the press that the real struggle in Washington on minimum wages was between organized labor and Barden."[15]

Most successful lobbyists are sophisticated enough to realize that the committee hearings, and the testimony presented therein, are of doubtful value in the communication of influence. Most legislators have already made up their minds and little can be done to cause a sudden change of heart. Tyler says of Barden that his "philosophy on federal minimum-wage law was a matter of public record. In open hearings before his committee, Barden announced that 'everybody knows that minimum-wage legislation is basically counter to our democratic form of government and to our competitive economy.' This philosophy was not something invented in 1955. Barden had espoused and fought for this point of view over many years in Congress, where his seniority had earned him a top post on the labor committee."[16] The significance attached to the hostility of a committee chairman is not exaggerated. The chairman has the authority to call hearings, or not to call hearings and thus kill a bill; he controls the committee's agenda and appoints subcommittee chairmen and most staff members. Interest groups whose values conflict with those of committee chairmen had better devise a scheme whereby the chairman can be circumvented.

Committee power and group strategy

The bicameral nature of the legislature can be of great advantage in overcoming the influence of a hostile chairman. Since legislation must clear both houses of Congress, it is possible in some cases for an interest group to generate or mobilize enough support in the corresponding committee of the opposite house so that the bill is at least given some measure of momentum to start it on its legislative history. The proponents of the 1955 minimum-wage law thus sought to get the bill moving in the Senate in the hope that "if the Senate passed the bill, this would favorably influence the behavior of the House and its key committee."[17] In a similar fashion, the atomic scientists who lobbied for civilian control of atomic energy in 1945 were given relief from the determined opposition of Congressman May, chairman of the House Military Affairs Committee, when the Senate voted to establish a Special Committee on Atomic Energy. Whereas the House Military Affairs Committee had opened and closed hearings on a bill to establish military control in one day, the Senate Committee spent four weeks taking testimony, thus giving the scientists critically needed time to evaluate their position.[18]

What, then, is the function of the committee hearing? If the decisions have been or will be made elsewhere (whether in the executive sessions of committees or perhaps outside the formal boundaries of the legislature), why is so much attention given to the hearings? There are many speculations, each of which may contribute something to our understanding of the problem. Truman suggests that the hearings serve as "safety valves" for the release of tension built up during the period prior to the opening of the formal hearings."[19] This idea has some merit, for it is true that crystallization, or "choosing up sides," is facilitated during the hearings. Legislators and lobbyists have the opportunity to arrive at a rough estimate of the intensity of support or opposition and to locate the various coalitions which have invariably been formed. In addition, if the hearings are given good press coverage, there is the opportunity for an interest group to pick up some inexpensive publicity. While this is of limited value in influencing the outcome of the legislation, widely publicized testimony at least gives the lobbyist the opportunity to demonstrate to his organization that he is doing his job properly. Finally, it is possible that the lobbyist can "prove his worth" during hearings. If he displays familiarity with the issues, presents his testimony without seeking to evade difficult questions, and appears willing to listen to the suggestions and comments of legislators, he may be able to establish contact with one or more of these legislators on a more personal basis and thus improve his chances of influence in the future. Hearings are a ritual—a "large verbal orchestration" in the words of Representative Clem Miller— but the artificial nature of the hearing with regard to actual decision-making should not mask its more subtle functions.[20]

Since the members of congressional committees have life or death power over the outcome of legislation, access to these members is a key part of the strategy of the lobbyist. However, this does not necessarily mean that the point of initiative rests entirely in the committee. At the state level, Steiner and Gove have indicated that "as an independent determinant of the fate of legislative proposals, the standing committee is of scant importance."[21] In their study of the Illinois legislature, the authors argue that the committees will abide by a decision reached outside the legislature if all the groups which are concerned with the issue have been involved in this informal negotiation process. While Illinois is admittedly an exception to the rule, the significance of the resolution of group conflict *before* the commencing of the formal legislative process should not be overlooked. Here, the legislators do not referee; they ratify.

In corroboration of Steiner and Gove, the senior author investigated the conflict over the regulation of milk prices in the Florida legislature.[22] The issue was whether to amend the milk control law to allow for more flexible and discretionary setting of prices by the Florida Milk Commission. In their course through the legislature, any amendments to the law would have to be passed on by the House Public Health Committee. All participants in the struggle agreed that this committee would never report out the amendments until it was given evidence that the dominant interest group, the Florida Dairy Products Association, had given its approval. The Florida Milk Commission and its ally the Florida Dairy Farmers Federation did not have to persuade the legislative committee; they had to persuade the interested organizations. To achieve this goal, a series of meetings were arranged in the offices of the Florida Milk Commission, and, after a series of negotiations and compromises, united industry support was achieved. Only at this point did the Public Health Committee, which had simply been waiting for the verdict of the interest groups, report out the amendments; the substance of these amendments exactly paralleled the statements of the milk industry speaking through its organizations. The crucial decision was reached without the involvement of legislators. After the interest groups agreed, legislative approval was no more than a formality.

LEGISLATIVE PARTIES

Before we too hastily conclude from the Florida example that legislators merely react to extragovernmental interests, we would be well advised to examine another structural feature of legislatures—legislative parties. Political scientists have long recognized that when party competition is keen, interest group strength tends to be weak. Likewise, a sluggish party system or, as is the case in some states, a one-party system tends to create a vacuum which will be filled by vigorous interest groups. The Florida Milk Commission study illustrates the type of situation that occurs within legislatures dominated by a single party. Within the legislature, the Public Health Committee's action was crucial for the resolution of the milk price issue. This must not be obscured by the fact that the committee based its decision on the will of the interests involved rather than on some other interpretation of the public good.

A second point to be made from some of the preceding examples pertains to the role of the legislature in developing policy. It is exceedingly difficult to trace a specific policy back to its origin, and most studies which attempt to do so actually begin when the demands become visible. Blaisdell has touched on this point very nicely in his analysis of the origins of public policy. He argues that "the laws which Congress enacts originate in most cases with the informal agencies, that is, the outside pressure groups." While this would seem to be a clear-cut answer to the question, Blaisdell is careful to explain that these "informal agencies" may be both primary and secondary originators of policy. By the time an issue reaches the level of visibility, there will be an array of interest groups distributed on both sides of the question. However, "we can never be certain that our research has produced the real originator."[23] Where did the pressure for a civil rights act begin? Perhaps it began with the Emancipation Proclamation, perhaps earlier.

Although we may not be able to trace policies back to the precise point at which they originate, it is reasonable to conclude that they generally develop outside the legislature. We can identify with somewhat greater reliability the mechanisms through which demands are processed once they become visible. With respect to the federal government, the initiation of policy has largely become the province of the executive.

> The Congress no longer expects to originate measures but to pass, veto, or modify laws proposed by the Chief Executive. It is the President, not the Congress, who determines the content and substance of the legislation with which Congress deals. The President is now the motor in the system; the Congress applies the brakes. The President gives what forward movement there is to the system; his is the force of thrust and innovation. The Congress is the force of inertia—a force, it should be said, that means not only restraint but also stability in policies.[24]

We have seen that when demands become stated in formal terms before legislative bodies, the institutional framework of these assemblies channels or distorts the flow of pressure. The committee system can thus be understood as part of an institutional framework which can, to some extent, control the success of particular sets of demands. A second part of the institutional framework which should be considered is the party system. Parties function less as formulators of public policy and more as recruitment, communication, and consensus-building mechanisms. In the recruitment or electoral phase of the political process, the party outweighs the interest group in importance. The system is so constructed that the only way an electoral victory can be achieved is through the party. Similarly, once elections have decided the composition of legislative bodies, the selection of individuals to occupy offices, committee posts, and key strategic positions within the legislature usually follows party lines.

As a communication channel, the legislative party structure transmits information concerning the policy programs originating in the executive branch. As a device for building consensus, the party is a standard around which legislators can rally according to their orientations toward pending policies. Normally when the party system is competitive, legislators will tend to adhere to the party position and back the program of the executive if he is of their party or oppose it if he is not. Sorauf's analysis of legislative party cohesion is of interest in this regard.

> This executive-oriented cohesion that one finds in the Congress and also in the state legislatures reflects a number of realities of American politics. It may result from the executive's control of political sanctions—patronage in some states, his personal support in fund raising and campaigning, his support of programs for the legislator's constituency. It also results from the fact that the executive increasingly symbolizes the party and its performance. A legislator of the President's party or the governor's party knows that he hurts his party and his own political future should he help make the executive look "bad" or ineffective.[25]

PARTY INFLUENCE ON VOTING

Although we have maintained that partisan affiliation—particularly in competitive environments—exerts an independent influence on legislative decision-making, it is by no means the sole factor determining a legislator's vote. One need only compare the party discipline in an American legislature with that in a parliamentary system, say Great Britain's House of Commons, to realize the lack of control American parties have over the votes of their legislative members. It is virtually impossible for us to measure with certainty the role played by the party at the moment when a legislator votes "aye" or "nay."

Such questions can be answered only by inference. McDonald's statement that "the ideal way to assess the nature and role of party influence would be to get a machine that would look into a person's mind as he was making it up and sort out and measure all of the various considerations that went into the final result" summarizes well the inferential nature of this analysis.[26] The most frequently used technique, roll call analysis, enables us to describe the degree to which members of parties vote together and the composition of deviating blocs, but it too is limited. The casting of a vote is only the final phase of the legislative process. Heinz Eulau notes that "a legislator's conduct in the final voting provides little basis for inferences about his behavior at other stages of the legislative process."[27] While he may vote with the party, he may also have engaged in negotiations with pressure groups, argued for compromises during the committee stages of a bill, or sought to have the bill made more compatible with his personal philosophy. Nevertheless, we turn to roll call votes for some fundamental data about the importance of the party.

From the vast amount of research conducted by means of roll call analysis, there seems to be no question that party influence is discernible in voting behavior. Less clear, however, are questions of the conditions under which party influence will be strong or weak, and what kinds of legislators seem to respond more quickly to party pressures. Neither party comes very close to the ideal of some political scientists that legislators should be "responsible," that is, formulate opposing programs and vote strictly according to the dictates of the party leadership.[28] Both parties are made up of legislators whose ideological commitments range widely across a continuum from "liberal" to "conservative," no matter how these terms are defined; neither party is wholly committed to a specific set of values. However, the lack of total unanimity should not serve to conceal the fact that ". . . the ideological center of gravity of the two parties *is* different; the Democrats' is toward the 'Left' and the Republicans' is toward the 'Right' of the abbreviated American political spectrum."[29]

Support for that description of congressional parties can be gathered from Julius Turner's classic description of party and constituency pressures, Robert Dahl's study of party voting and foreign policy, and David Truman's analysis of the eighty-first Congress.[30] Dahl reports that "the Republicans were, at least until 1943, overwhelmingly the party of 'isolation,' whereas the persistent tendency of the Democrats was to support 'internationalist' efforts."[31] Dahl's conclusion is based on the examination of a single set of related issues through time and does not take into account the disunities which may have made intraparty conflict more discernible over a broader range of issues. Turner's approach anticipated Truman's in that Turner categorized issues according to the extent of party cleavage. His findings may be summarized as follows. The parties displayed sharp, consistent cleavage on questions of tariff, government action ("that is, issues involving government action in fields traditionally reserved for private institutions, such as public power, crop insurance, or disaster relief"), social welfare and labor legislation, and farm legislation. They were divided, but only moderately, on questions of government regulation, Negro rights, and immigration problems. On all other issues the parties were either divided, but inconsistent in the basis of their division, or very similar in their positions. More recent studies indicate that the findings of Dahl, Turner, and Truman remain valid today. In discussing those issue areas in which party voting is a frequent occurrence, Sorauf writes,

> ... these issues include those of labor–management relations, aids to agriculture or other sectors of the economy, programs of social security and insurance, wages and hours legislation, unemployment compensation, and relief and welfare programs. These issues involve, in the oversimplifications of American politics, the "welfare state," or the whole complex debate over government responsibilities which we sum up in the liberalism–conservatism dualism.[32]

Party versus constituency

Incompatibility between a party position on an issue and constituent demand is one of the factors which makes the power of legislative parties less than absolute. When this situation occurs the legislator faces conflicting crosspressure, for both the party leaders and the legislator's constituents have resources which can be brought to bear. Legislative party leaders may be able to control patronage, committee assignments, and a variety of subtle yet valuable resources which make life easier for other legislators. All of these forces may be employed to enforce party discipline. Constituents, on the other hand, control the ultimate sanction—the vote. In an all-out conflict between party and constituency, the constituency is bound to win, for it is recognized that one's own reelection has undisputed primacy when it is in doubt. Such instances of clear-cut conflict between party and constituents are rare, however. In the first place, few issues generate sufficient interest among "the folks back home" to affect future election support. Moreover, not all legislators need to devote the same amount of effort to courting constituent support. Those whose elections are relatively distant and those who do not anticipate a serious challenge at the polls will be somewhat less inclined to weigh constituent-support resources as heavily as will those who face an immediate campaign against a strong opponent.

The composition of the constituency also affects the levels of pressure felt by legislators. Generally speaking, the smaller and more homogeneous the district, the more constrained the legislator would appear to be, for to transgress the limits of acceptable behavior is to incur the displeasure of the entire district. Heterogeneous districts, on the other hand, encompass many opposing interests; therefore, a stand that is unacceptable to one portion of the constituency is likely to win the votes of another group. Failure to yield to pressure from a vocal segment of the heterogeneous constituency is likely to be less costly than if the district is homogeneous. In practice, however, the latitude of the legislator from a heterogeneous district is not so great nor that of the legislator from a homogeneous district so confined as it may initially appear to be. For constituents to exert influence, they must be aroused. Once stimulated, the homogeneous district may be more demanding; however, fewer issues can be expected to arouse it.

If parties are competitive, the homogeneous district will find its collective demands better represented by one party than the other.[33] It will, therefore, select its legislative representatives from the more attractive party. It follows that constituency opinion and party positions on issues in such cases will tend to agree, and there will be little or no party–district conflict for the legislator. Regardless of what interests are represented in the district or how strong the party system is, when the chips are down and the legislator is forced to vote for or against the wishes of his constituents, in all likelihood it will be the constituent demands which prevail. Such was the case in 1965, for instance, when Congress was faced with the issue of repealing the provision in the Taft–Hartley Law allowing states to adopt right to work legislation. The Democratic platform on which Lyndon Johnson had run in 1964 contained a pledge that repeal would be enacted. Following the successful Democratic elections in 1964, President Johnson sought to persuade Congress to redeem the campaign pledge. Although it was a Democratic Congress and although the party machinery favored repeal, strong constituency pressures against repeal were felt by many legislators. The repeal attempt failed, providing additional evidence that party loyalty is no match for constituent support.

LEGISLATURES AND LOBBIES

Lobbying strategy and party structure

It is sometimes argued that the fluid nature of congressional parties and their inability to develop and adhere to a specific set of legislative proposals creates a vacuum which can be filled only by "outside" sources, that is, interest groups.[34] This does not seem to be a correct assumption, since it depends for its validity on the party's being the *only* source of internal pressure, a point which has been proved false by studies of the informal patterns of interpersonal relations within legislative bodies. Interest group leaders must achieve access to decision-makers of both parties, since the informal structure of power in legislative bodies *may* cut across party lines. Generally, the informal structure of power seems to correspond to the "real" structure of power, so that formal leaders, whose position of leadership is assigned by the party, are usually the legislators considered to be most influential. While the similar ideological characteristics of lobbyists and legislators of compatible persuasion make it inevitable that some drift toward partisanship on the part of interest groups will occur, lobbyists try to avoid strong partisan attachment on the assumption that, in the House or Senate, it is necessary to cooperate with leaders of both parties no matter which is in the majority. Activity on behalf of one of the major parties is not a typical part of the career patterns of lobbyists in Washington, and most believe that political parties have little to do with the formation of public policy.[35] For example, during the 1961 controversy over enlarging the House Rules Committee to reduce the influence of southern Democrats not in sympathy with the program of the president, interest groups whose ideological preferences might be described as "Republican," such as the National Association of Manufacturers, Chamber of Commerce, American Medical Association, and American Farm Bureau Federation, were engaged in a series of strategy meetings with the Democratic chairman of the Rules Committee, Howard Smith of Virginia.[36]

Two aspects of party structure appear to be related to the development of lobbies and their activities: (1) the strength of party competition, and (2) the degree of party cohesion. The former refers to the extent to which parties compete on equal footing for popular votes. The closer they approximate a fifty–fifty split, the stronger party competition is inferred to be. Cohesion, on the other hand, refers to the extent to which party influence is manifested in legislative behavior. The long-standing assumption that party strength and interest group strength are inversely related is called into question when the preceding distinctions are employed. In their four-state study, Zeigler and Baer found that well developed, competitive two-party systems do not necessarily result in weak legislative lobbies.[37] As Table 2 indicates, the two states in which lobbies are strong (Oregon and Utah) also have competitive two-party systems. In fact, only one of the four systems studied (Massachusetts) displayed the expected relationship. A much better correlate of lobby strength appears to be party cohesion. Two states (Massachusetts and

North Carolina) display strong party cohesion with concomitantly weak lobbies. Conversely, Utah and Oregon are rated weak and

TABLE 2. Party Competition, Cohesion, and Strength of Lobbies in Four States*

	Massachusetts	North Carolina	Oregon	Utah
Party Competition	Strong	Weak	Strong	Strong
Party Cohesion	Strong	Strong	Weak	Moderate
Strength of Lobbies	Weak	Weak	Strong	Strong

*Source: L. Harmon Zeigler and Michael Baer, Lobbying: Interaction and Influence in American State Legislatures (Belmont, Calif.: Wadsworth Publishing Company, 1969).

moderate with respect to party cohesion, and both have strong legislative lobbies. Since competitive party systems usually tend to be cohesive as well, the distinction between the two attributes has been blurred.

A second feature of lobbies can be predicted from the cohesiveness of legislative parties—the scope of target legislators with whom lobbyists interact. Where party cohesion is high and the rank and file legislators tend to follow their party leaders, skilled lobbyists concentrate their attention on party leaders. Low levels of *general* legislator–lobbyist interaction result; however, interactions may be both frequent and intense between legislative elites and interest group spokesmen. Strong party–interest group ties may develop in such circumstances. Addressing himself to this point, Lockard writes,

> Farm groups on the national level have not aligned themselves with either party, but in Massachusetts they are with the Republicans. Labor nationally is more sympathetic to the Democratic party and is much more helpful to it, but it maintains cordial relations with many Republicans and does not move into the inner councils of the Democratic party to the extent that it does in Massachusetts. In some areas the Democratic party in Massachusetts will leave to labor almost the whole job of campaigning for state candidates, and in many campaigns the money labor gives is a very crucial factor in the Democratic effort.[38]

Such "built-in access" has obvious consequences for lobbying techniques. In the national legislative process, lobbyists place great emphasis on personal contacts with individual legislators and devote a substantial portion of their energy toward the goal of establishing "connections." In a strong cohesive two-party state such as Connecticut, very little time is spent by lobbyists in direct contact with legislators. Much of their efforts are aimed at influencing the decision of the party at its caucus, party leadership thus absorbing the brunt of the pressure. A strong party system does not reduce the amount of pressure, as its proponents occasionally argue; rather, it channels the pressure toward holders of formal party office. While such a system may give an interest group an advantage when its particular party is in the majority, it would have adverse consequences when the opposition gained control of the legislature.

Lobbying techniques: skillful and inept

Since lobbying techniques vary to some extent with the arena in which the pressure activity is to be conducted, it will suffice to describe some techniques which seem to hold true for the lobbying process in general. In lobbying, as in any other profession, there are successes and failures. In fact, it is hard to avoid making the comment that many of the droves of lobbyists swarming around Capitol Hill really accomplish little except to convince their own membership that the flow of dues should continue. Literature produced by these organizations is devoted to an internal selling job, and an ever-expanding membership is often the lobbyist's basic goal. Many of these groups have no contact with the legislative process except at formal hearings of committees, and they are treated with patient tolerance by veteran legislators who have developed a good knowledge of the relative merits of interest groups. Often the testimony of such groups is saturated with clichés and is of limited value as a source of information. Occasionally, some lobbyists will resort to a form of misrepresentation which seems to indicate a belief that legislators can be fooled rather easily. The following comment illustrates this kind of "pressure": "I believe our case opposing the extension of rent control would be helped tremendously if we could parade in a few small property owners from around the country, a little bedraggled and run-down-at-the-heels-looking, who could get their story over to Congress that the small man who owns a little property is taking one hell of a beating."[39]

On the other hand, there are a number of expert lobbyists who know the vagaries of the legislative process and are adept at getting along with politicians. Many of these lobbyists are lawyers with a background in government service. Samuel Patterson provides a cogent description of this kind of lobbyist, whom he labels a "contact man."

> He is the legislative representative who conceives his job to be that of making crucial contacts with the members of the legislative group. He devotes his time and energies to walking legislative halls, visiting legislators, collaring them in the halls, establishing relationships with administrative assistants and others of the congressman's staff, cultivating key legislators on a friendship basis, and developing contacts on the staffs of critical legislative committees.[40]

The importance of legislative sympathy

The creation of the situation in which the contact man is successful depends to some degree on his own particular skills. However, it is probable that the success of the contact man depends more on the degree to which the legislators agree with the professed ideals of the group for whom the lobbyist is speaking, and this in turn depends more on the personal ideology of the legislator rather than on the ability of the lobbyist to manipulate or persuade. If the legislator and lobbyist have similar goals, then it is very possible that the notion of "pressure" will be foreign to both. Rather than being aware that he is the object of an attempt at influence, the legislator will probably regard any personal solicitation as the "legitimate" expression of a sound point of view.[41] On the other hand, contact between lobbyist and legislator who are working toward conflicting goals will probably be defined as an attempt at pressure, hence most senators name the organizations with whom they disagree as the most powerful and influential.[42] Frequently, such organizations are presumed to have certain legislators "in their pockets," meaning that these legislators will do the bidding of the organization once its position has been clarified. The often heard phrase, "all it takes is a phone call," reflects the sinister perception of the relationship between the group identified as influential and the legislators on whom its influence can be exercised. Actually, such a relationship is not one of power, in the sense that power describes a situation in which one actor can secure compliance from another whether or not such compliance is given voluntarily. Rather, the relationship is most likely to develop when the interest group has a sufficiently broad or permanent set of objectives to keep it constantly involved in the affairs of the legislature. The "big four" interest groups, farm, labor, business, and professional, would fall into this category; and, since most American politicians come from the same groups, the development of friendship patterns should be expected to be strongest between legislators and representatives of these organizations. Teune's study of the Indiana legislature, which records the correlation between the occupational affiliation of the legislator with attitudes toward specific interest groups, finds that the clearest relationship is that of sympathetic identification between legislators and lobbyists from the same occupational category. Thus, legislators whose occupation is farming ranked the Farm Bureau first in order of agreement with organizational goals; businessmen tended to agree with the goals of business groups, and so on. In addition to the expected hostility between business and labor, an interesting finding is the degree to which professional associations are given a high rank in agreement. Of course, the professional groups provide the largest number of political decision-makers, but it is still somewhat remarkable that even labor legislative candidates are more favorably disposed toward professional groups than they are toward labor unions.[43]

The Indiana study also provides useful comparison with Matthews' description of senators' attitudes toward lobbyists, referred to earlier in the chapter. Indiana legislators showed striking agreement on the most effective interest groups, even though they differed widely on agreement with the goals of these groups. In fact, there is a definite tendency for legislators who agree with a group's goals to score that group somewhat higher in legislative effectiveness than groups with whom they disagree. Democrats ranked the AFL–CIO more effective than the Farm Bureau, while the order is reversed with the Republicans. However, the question which elicited this response was phrased so as to equate effectiveness with the group's skill in presenting its case before the legislature. When the question was phrased to include the word "powerful," a different set of rankings was obtained. In this case, members who disagreed with the policies of the group were more likely to name that group as powerful.[44]

Zeigler and Baer found similar patterns which indicate that perceptions of group power and lobby effectiveness are not necessarily related.

> For instance, educational associations are most frequently mentioned as powerful by Utah legislators and lobbyists, yet we have seen that Utah treats education with particular vengeance and that the activities of the Utah Education Association seem only to exacerbate an already hostile attitude. By the same token, religious groups receive practically no mention in heavily Mormon Utah (similarly, the Roman Catholic Church receives scant mention in Massachusetts), causing one to speculate that perhaps the most effective pressures upon the legislature are those that go unnoticed because they are so pervasive.[45]

As a final note to this section, we should take care not to drift into some form of determinism by the automatic assumption that access to sympathetic legislators is simply a function of overlapping group affiliation. Legislators need not view themselves as governmental spokesmen for interest groups whose aspirations they share. The authors of *The Legislative System* have developed a typology of legislators' role orientations toward pressure groups consisting of three categories: facilitators, neutrals, and resistors. By relating these roles with the group identification of legislators (pro-business, pro-labor, and economic neutrals), the authors were able to conclude that the role of facilitator is most apparent among the neutrals. Those legislators who are not personally involved in the attainment of interest group goals are most likely to be open to the representations of any group which they believe to have a legitimate claim. These facilitators have had longer legislative service and are more socialized toward the "legislative way of life" than younger colleagues whose basic identifications may be with external groups.[46] Bentley's famous comment that when we say a person is reasoning on a question of public policy we are actually saying that he belongs to two groups which are clashing does not necessarily mean that the "clashing groups" are formally organized interest groups.[47] The legislature itself is a group which imposes norms on its members.

Mobilization of support

Recognition of the "independent" nature of some legislators has highlighted the reciprocal nature of the influence process. Lobbyists may influence legislators but may also be influenced themselves. The influence process clearly does not involve a one-way power relationship in which the side with the greatest amount of support invariably wins; and for that matter there is no agreement on what attributes are necessary for an interest group to be classified as "powerful." Key has come to believe that the threat of electoral retaliation is not to be regarded as a source of power, yet interviews with state legislators indicate that they consider the electoral influence of interest groups as genuine.[48] As a source of power, the willingness of a group to provide helpful services, such as information and research, does not count for much. However, such nonthreatening acts as serving as a source of expert knowledge become much more crucial when the vague notion of power is put aside and the legislator is asked to give his reasons for listening to the claims of a particular group; "pressure groups are most welcome in the legislative arena when they go beyond a mere assertion of demands and interests and present information and data which help legislators work out compromises and adjustments among the most insistent demands of groups on the basis of some vague conception of the public interest against which particular claims can be judged."[49] Legislators do not like to be "pressured," and, while they operate on the assumption that interest groups are powerful, they react to specific group claims more on the basis of usefulness.

Perhaps because of these reasons many of the techniques which pressure groups regularly employ are of doubtful impact. A case in point is the stimulation by an interest group of a deluge of letters or telegrams designed to show the legislator that there is a great amount of popular interest in his decision. This technique is most favored by organizations with a large membership. Unfortunately for the groups which seek to organize letter-writing campaigns, the mark of their organizational efforts is almost invariably present in the letters. While legislators give their mail serious consideration, generally they are not receptive to letters whose actual origin may have been with a constituent but whose wording bears close resemblance to thousands of others. Dexter writes that "it is almost impossible to organize a letter writing campaign so skillfully that an experienced mail clerk does not spot it at once as simulated and even identify its source."[50] The methods whereby such letters are obtained vary considerably in subtlety. In some instances sample letters are prepared, resulting in the legislator's receiving communications whose nearly identical wording leaves no doubt as to origin. Other interest groups prefer to leave more to the imagination of the writer and emphatically urge that the letter be phrased in one's own words. Even in these cases the group must make known to the potential writer the basic facts about the particular issue, making it quite likely that the language of the letter writer and the official statements of the group will not vary appreciably. Variations on the letter-writing theme are many. Some organizations submit ballots to their members and deposit the results in the offices of legislators, offering the ballots as evidence of "genuine" as opposed to organizationally inspired sentiments. Most mail of this kind is sorted out by an administrative assistant before it ever reaches the desk of the legislator, and if it does happen to reach his desk the chances are good that its time of arrival, in addition to its origin, will make it ineffective. Frequently, mass produced mail arrives after the bill which is being supported or opposed is out of committee and scheduled for debate, when the opinions of a single legislator are diminished in importance.

Considered singly, the letter-writing campaign is probably the least effective and most relied on lobbying technique. Its extensive use results from the fact that many pressure groups simply do not have the resources necessary to engage in more elaborate techniques. Creating the impression of constituent pressure need not be attempted only through the mails. Since a legislator's view of his constituency may in reality be concentrated toward the individuals or organizations which have been unusually active in his behalf, it is frequently of greater benefit for an interest group to arrange for these politically active individuals to contact the legislator. An example of this technique is afforded by the American Cotton Manufacturers Institute in its efforts to have quotas applied to Japanese textile imports. While cotton manufacturers in New England were relatively united in their desire to reduce the effects of cheap textile imports, manufacturers in the South were not so vociferous. There had occurred some migration of the textile industry from New England to the South, but the traditional values of the "cotton bloc" were not entirely overcome. Accustomed to supporting a free trade program which would benefit cotton farmers rather than manufacturers (Japan is the largest consumer of American raw cotton), southern legislators were only gradually adopting a more protectionist position. To dramatize the necessity for strong protectionist support in the South, the American Cotton Manufacturers Institute devoted space in the *Textile World* to a southern audience. Manufacturers were urged to oppose congressmen who refused to abandon their free-trade views by appeals of which the following is typical: "If your wife comes home with an armful of Japanese textile goods at a time when your mill is running half-time, remember whom you voted for in the last election and why."[51] The first evidence of increasing awareness, whether or not it was due to the public relations activities described above, was the passage of laws by the legislatures of South Carolina and Alabama requiring retailers who sold Japanese textiles to exhibit a sign saying "Japanese textiles sold here." In the sessions following the efforts of the American Cotton Manufacturers Institute, legislation creating import quotas was repeatedly introduced, with sponsorship usually including both New England and southern congressmen. The support for quota legislation reached its peak in the eighty-fourth Congress, during which an amendment to the Mutual Security Act establishing a quota system failed by only two votes. To avoid the eventual passage of such legislation, the executive branch began negotiations with Japan for the establishment of quotas.

This example illustrates the basic effect of carefully planned lobbying, the maximization of the possibility of victory by mobilization of sympathetic legislators. Had the economic structure of the

South not shifted, the activities of those interested in limiting Japanese imports would in all probability have come to naught. As is true in most other forms of communications, conversion in the lobbying process is rare.

The techniques of interest groups in the legislative process vary not only with the situation, but with the structure of the group. In the Japanese textile quota struggle, directly contacting congressmen would have been of little use until some groundwork could be laid at the grass roots level. Much the same sort of effort was made by the AFL–CIO Joint Minimum Wage Committee in its efforts to increase the minimum wage to $1.25 in 1959; but in labor reform legislation controversy generated by the hearings of the Select Committee on Improper Practices in the Labor–Management Relations Field, the AFL–CIO relied mainly on a few experienced lobbyists whose job was to make direct contact with congressmen. Patterson reports that the strategy was based on "*rapport* with, and promises from House and Senate Democratic leaders, and particularly the effectiveness and prestige of Senator Kennedy. It hinged on congressional understanding of the problems and complexities of organized labor, without planning for a campaign to engender widespread public support for sympathetic treatment."[52] The AFL–CIO was adjusting its strategies to what it believed to be the exigencies of the situation, but many groups never vary their techniques to any appreciable degree and this seems to be a function of their structural characteristics. Cohen's study of the Japanese peace settlement indicates that two kinds of groups were observable: those which served "specific and relatively tangible interests," and those which "cater to more general and intangible interests." Cohen found that the organizations representing tangible interests used a wide variety of methods consisting of indirect and direct communication, but the organizations whose goals were intangible relied heavily on explanatory articles. Further, the more specific the goals of the organization, the more likely it was to react quickly to the changing developments in the legislative process, giving such groups a considerable advantage in timing of communications. The smaller groups with clear objectives were more maneuverable and less encumbered by the need to keep a large membership educated in its goals.[53]

CONCLUSION

Although legislatures play a significant role in the processes through which goods are allocated by American political systems, the available evidence indicates that they are not the autonomous formulators of public policy that some purveyors of democratic mythology would have us believe. Few policies originate within legislative bodies; most are developed within executive offices. Legislatures today are primarily deliberative assemblies; that is, they investigate and debate the policy proposals brought to them. In a sense they serve as devil's advocates for the political system, for positions counter to the executive's proposals will be aired and considered. Debate over issues is virtually assured in competitive two-party systems where party cohesion is strong. Legislators tend to polarize into pro-executive and anti-executive camps depending on their party affiliation and that of the chief executive. Members of the opposition party in such circumstances probe executive policy proposals in an attempt to discover their weaknesses. Ideally this results in wise, rational decision-making. Unfortunately, the ideal is rarely attained, for party prestige, special interests, and other "contaminating" influences also enter into the deliberative calculus of legislators. The fact remains, however, that legislatures perform the incremental functions of accepting, rejecting, or modifying major policy decisions which usually originate elsewhere.

Even though initiative over policy resides elsewhere, legislatures constitute an important arena for interest group activity. Groups that enjoy a confident relationship with executive decision-makers must nevertheless take care to ensure that legislative action does not jeopardize their interests. Moreover, even though demands for tangible goods may be satisfied by the allocative decisions of executive officials, legislative legitimization for those decisions is frequently necessary. And, of course, those groups which are dissatisfied with executive policies may seek satisfaction of their demands from the legislature. In general, groups that are recognized by legislators as serving a representative function for a legitimate public will be more effective than those that are not; groups whose goals do not conflict with legislators' perceptions of the public interest will be more effective than groups whose goals do conflict with such perceptions. Within this context the tactics of the lobbyist are evaluated and his degree of skill is assessed.

NOTES

[1] See Roland Young, The American Congress (New York: Harper & Row, Publishers, 1958), pp. 1–17 for a theoretical statement of the role of the legislature.

[2] David Easton, The Political System (New York: Alfred A. Knopf, Inc., 1953), pp. 129–34.

[3]John C. Wahlke, Heinz Eulau, William Buchanan, and LeRoy Ferguson, *The Legislative System: Explorations in Legislative Behavior* (New York: John Wiley & Sons, Inc., 1962), p. 6.

[4]Edelman, *The Symbolic Uses of Politics*, pp. 37–38.

[5]*Ibid.*, pp. 41–42.

[6]Donald Matthews, "The Folkways of the United States Senate: Conformity to Group Norms and Legislative Effectiveness," *American Political Science Review*, LIII (Dec. 1959), pp. 1064–89. See also Matthews, *U.S. Senators and Their World* (Chapel Hill, N.C.: University of North Carolina Press, 1960), pp. 92–117.

[7]Earl Latham, *The Group Basis of Politics* (Ithaca, N.Y.: Cornell University Press, 1952), p. 35.

[8]James Burns, *Congress on Trial* (New York: Harper & Row, Publishers, 1949), p. 18.

[9]Latham, *op. cit.*, p. 37.

[10]Norman Meller, "Legislative Behavior Research," *Western Political Quarterly*, XIII (Mar. 1960), pp. 131–53.

[11]George B. Galloway, *History of the House of Representatives* (New York: Thomas Y. Crowell Company, 1961), p. 95.

[12]Matthews, *U.S. Senators and Their World*, pp. 147–75. Belle Zeller, ed., *American State Legislatures* (New York: Thomas Y. Crowell Company, 1954), pp. 95–102. Exceptions to the conclusions reached in *American State Legislatures* will be offered later in the chapter.

[13]Nicholas A. Masters, "House Committee Assignments," *American Political Science Review*, LV (June 1961), p. 355.

[14]*Ibid.*, p. 354.

[15]Gus Tyler, *A Legislative Campaign for a Federal Minimum Wage*, Eagleton Foundation Case Studies in Practical Politics (New York: Holt, Rinehart & Winston, Inc., 1959), p. 3.

[16]*Ibid.*

[17]*Ibid.*

[18]Byron S. Miller, "A Law Is Passed—The Atomic Energy Act of 1946," *University of Chicago Law Review*, XV (1947–1948), p. 804.

[19]David Truman, *The Governmental Process* (New York: Alfred A. Knopf, Inc., 1951), p. 372.

[20]John W. Baker, ed., *Member of the House* (New York: Charles Scribner's Sons, 1962), p. 8.

[21]Gilbert Y. Steiner and Samuel K. Gove, *Legislative Politics in Illinois* (Urbana, Ill.: University of Illinois Press, 1960), p. 82.

[22]L. Harmon Zeigler, *The Florida Milk Commission Changes Minimum Prices* (New York: The Inter-University Case Program, 1963). For conclusions similar to the above, see Oliver Garceau and Corrine Silverman, "A Pressure Group and the Pressured: A Case Report," *American Political Science Review*, XLVII (Sept. 1954), p. 675.

[23]Donald C. Blaisdell, *American Democracy Under Pressure* (New York: The Ronald Press Company, 1957), pp. 218, 221.

[24]Robert A. Dahl, *Pluralist Democracy in the United States: Conflict and Dissent* (Chicago: Rand McNally, 1967), p. 136.

[25]Frank J. Sorauf, *Party Politics in America* (Boston: Little, Brown & Co., 1968), p. 343.

[26]Neil A. McDonald, *The Study of Political Parties* (Garden City, N.Y.: Doubleday & Company, Inc., 1955), p. 70.

[27]Wahlke et al., *The Legislative System*, p. 239.

[28]The most articulate statement of this position is given in Committee on Political Parties, American Political Science Association, *Toward a More Responsible Two-Party System* (New York: Holt, Rinehart & Winston, Inc., 1950). See also Austin Ranney, *The Doctrine of Responsible Party Government* (Urbana, Ill.: University of Illinois Press, 1954).

[29]Matthews, *op. cit.*, p. 119.

[30]Julius Turner, *Party and Constituency: Pressures on Congress* (Baltimore: The Johns Hopkins University Press, 1951); Robert Dahl, *Congress and Foreign Policy* (New York: Harcourt, Brace & World, 1950); David B. Truman, *The Congressional Party: A Case Study* (New York: John Wiley & Sons, Inc., 1959).

[31]Dahl, *op. cit.*, p. 190.

[32]Sorauf, *Party Politics in America*, p. 344.

[33]See Sorauf's discussion of this point, *ibid.*, pp. 344–47.

[34]See E. E. Schattschneider, *Party Government* (New York: Holt, Rinehart & Winston, Inc., 1942) and *The Struggle for Party Government* (College Park, Md.: Program in American Civilization, University of Maryland, 1948).

[35]Lester Milbrath, "The Political Party Activity of Washington Lobbyists," *Journal of Politics*, XV (May 1958), p. 345.

[36]Richard L. Lyons, "Pressure Rises as House Moves to Vote on Rules," *Washington Post*, 31 Jan. 1961. Cited in Nelson W. Polsby, "Two Strategies of Influence in the House of Representatives: Choosing a Majority Leader, 1962" (paper presented to the 1962 annual meeting of the American Political Science Association).

[37]This discussion is based on L. Harmon Zeigler and Michael Baer, *Lobbying: Interaction and Influence in American State Legislatures* (Belmont, Calif.: Wadsworth Publishing Company, 1969), pp. 23–37, 144–51.

[38]Duane Lockard, *New England State Politics* (Princeton, N.J.: Princeton University Press, 1959), p. 163. For descriptions of the role of the party in other state legislatures, see Malcolm E. Jewell, "Party Voting in American State Legislatures," *American Political Science Review*, XLIX (Sept. 1955), pp. 773–91; William J. Keefe, "Party Government and Lawmaking in the Illinois General Assembly," *Northwestern University Law Review*, XLVII (Mar.–Apr. 1952), pp. 55–71; Keefe, "Parties, Partisanship, and Public Policy in the Pennsylvania Legislature," *American Political Science Review*, XLVIII (June 1954), pp. 450–64.

[39]House Select Committee on Lobbying Activities, *General Interim Report*, 81st Cong., 2nd Sess., 1950 (Washington, D.C.: Government Printing Office, 1950).

[40]Samuel C. Patterson, "The Role of the Labor Lobbyist" (paper presented to the 1962 annual meeting of the American Political Science Association), p. 11.

[41]Frank Bonilla, "When Is Petition 'Pressure'?" *Public Opinion Quarterly*, XX (Spring 1956), pp. 46–48.

[42]Matthews, *op. cit.*, pp. 177–78.

[43]Henry Teune, "Occupational Affiliation and Attitudes Towards Interest Groups" (paper presented to the 1962 annual meeting of the American Political Science Association).

[44]Kenneth Janda, Henry Teune, Melvin Kahn, and Wayne Francis, *Legislative Politics in Indiana* (Bloomington, Ind.: Indiana University, Bureau of Government Research, n.d.), pp. 18–19.

[45]Zeigler and Baer, *Lobbying*, p. 193.

[46]Wahlke et al., *The Legislative System*, p. 341. See also Duncan MacRae, Jr., and Edith K. MacRae, "Legislators' Social Status and Their Vote," *American Journal of Sociology*, LXVI (May 1961), p. 603.

[47]Arthur Bentley, *The Process of Government* (San Antonio, Tex.: Principia Press of Trinity University, 1949).

[48]V. O. Key, Jr., "The Veterans and the House of Representatives: A Study of a Pressure Group and Electoral Mortality," *Journal of Politics*, V (Feb. 1943), pp. 27–40. See also Key, *Public Opinion and American Democracy* (New York: Alfred A. Knopf, Inc., 1961), pp. 521–24.

[49]Wahlke et al., *op. cit.*, pp. 338–39. See also Janda et al., *op. cit.*, p. 19.

[50]Lewis A. Dexter, "What Do Congressmen Hear: The Mail," *Public Opinion Quarterly*, XX (Spring 1956), p. 20.

[51]*Textile World*, Feb. 1955, p. 51.

[52]Patterson, *op. cit.*, p. 21.

[53]Bernard C. Cohen, "Political Communication on the Japanese Peace Settlement," *Public Opinion Quarterly*, XX (Spring 1956), pp. 32–33.

seven

Administrative
Policy-Making

Early students of administration were committed to the idea
that "politics" ended with the passage of legislation and that
the administrative process consisted of the automatic enforcement of the legislative mandate. Such assumptions have long
been abandoned, and administration has come to be regarded
as an extension of the struggle which began in the legislature.[1]
It is indisputable that the administrative process does have
certain differentiating features, such as alterations in techniques of influence by interest groups and perceptions of the
environment by administrators which differ from the perceptions of legislators. But it is clearly incorrect to say that
administrators differ from legislators in that the nature of
administrative tasks is so restricted that their only concerns
are with efficiency. As governments become more intensely
involved in the control or guidance of the nation's economic

system, the complex nature of the ensuing decisions requires that administrative agencies assume much of the burden. The legislatures, faced with a multiplicity of problem-solving situations, can undertake only a general statutory suggestion of the direction of public policy. Very often decisions which may be interpreted by a group as having life or death consequences are made in the relatively secretive atmosphere surrounding administrative agencies, far from the glare of public scrutiny which permeates the legislative process. Therefore, groups hoping to influence public policy often exhibit strong interest in the establishment of administrative agencies responsible for policy in the areas of the groups' concern.

How Agencies Begin

The creation of administrative agencies is primarily a legislative function. The conditions existing at the time of the establishment of a new agency may vary considerably according to the degree of controversy, the quantity of interest group activity, the organizational apparatus of the groups involved, and the intensity of the demands for or against the proposed agency. The establishment of the first clientele agencies such as the Department of Commerce and the Department of Agriculture was undertaken in an atmosphere of relative calm.[2] The agencies were originally designed to provide services to specified segments of the economic population without much regulation. Opposition was minimal and organizationally it was practically nonexistent. In contrast, the National Labor Relations Board and the Interstate Commerce Commission were created over the vigorous and organizationally articulated objections of interest groups whose economic stability was seen as threatened. These agencies were given extensive regulatory authority over economic interests which had no desire to be regulated. Under these circumstances, the job of administration was begun in an atmosphere of hostility and resistance. Administrators had to cope with organizations whose fundamental objectives were either the abolition of the agency or the reduction of its authority to the point of impotence. Administrative agencies seek to survive, and to do this they must reduce external opposition as much as possible. This frequently means the adjustment of programs to the desires of the regulated interests.[3]

The case of the Florida Milk Commission[4]

In some cases, regulatory agencies begin their activities as a result of the desires of economic groups that the government "do something" to eliminate an unsatisfactory competitive situation. This is particularly true when the entire economy, or at least a portion of the economy, is suffering from chronic depression. For example, the Florida Milk Commission was created in 1933 as a result of the youthful commercial structure of the milk industry in that state. Faced with a substantial reduction in consumer buying power, and with competition from milk imports from more established dairy states, the milk industry began to engage in price wars. A drop in prices by one distributor was met by a corresponding drop by competitors and eventually prices fell so low that below-cost selling became prevalent. The milk industry was organized into trade associations, but they were unable to negotiate a truce privately. Finally the industry urged the state government to undertake the responsibility of establishing the exact price to be paid to dairy farmers for milk and the minimum prices at which milk could be sold wholesale and retail. The legislature, in response to this request, and in the absence of any discernible opposition, established a Milk Control Board which became the independent Florida Milk Commission in 1939. The Commission was responsible for the supervision and regulation of all economic levels of the milk industry—production, transportation, delivery, and sale. To carry out its tasks, the Commission was given statutory powers not only to set prices but also to issue licenses, which were required of all dealers for the purchase, sale, or distribution of milk.

This commission, as is true of any government organization, originated because some persons believed that a new agency was necessary for the achievement of a goal. The structure of the new Milk Commission reflected accurately the desires of its advocates and the restricted nature of the interest in milk regulation. Discussion was confined to the milk industry itself and never reached the broader public level. Consequently the law placed the regulated clientele in a position to control the operations of the Milk Commission. Rather than providing compulsory regulation, the law allowed producers in various marketing districts to petition both for control and for withdrawal of control. Further, the Commission was financed by taxes on the industry rather than by legislative appropriation. Finally, its membership consisted of persons with a professional interest in the Commission.

AGENCY–CLIENTELE RELATIONSHIPS

The clientele of an agency—"groups whose interests [are] strongly affected by an agency's activities [and provide] the principal sources of political support and opposition"—may have great impact on the way the agency's programs are enforced.[5] If the clientele of the agency is large and heterogeneous, the agency will function in a climate of greater potential conflict than if the clientele is limited and relatively united. The establishment of communications will be relatively simple in the latter case. The agency, in reaching its decisions, will have access to a limited amount of information from a single point of view. The regulated interests, in presenting arguments, will not have to compete with opposing interests. Consequently, the fewer the number of interests in the clientele of an agency, the more influential each is likely to be.[6] Attention has been given by students of administration, notably Selznick and Bernstein, to the process whereby an administrative agency gradually abandons its original crusading spirit and becomes, in a sense, the captive of the clientele.[7] This situation arises either when one of the regulated groups is dominant from the beginning, or when the political support of competing groups evaporates. The agency "becomes a protector of the status quo and uses its public powers to maintain the interest of the regulated. . . . Although an agency in this situation stresses its role of mediator and judge among conflicting group interests, its actual role is that of advocate and partisan."[8]

The early history of the Interstate Commerce Commission, the first of the federal independent regulatory agencies, illustrates the tendency of these decision-making bodies to become the "economic and political instruments of the parties they regulate and benefit."[9] The ICC was established in 1887 to protect the public in general and shippers in particular against monopolistic practices of the railroads. Its independent structure was designed to free it from partisan political influences so that it could more readily employ technical expertise in solving problems "in the public interest." Initial opposition to the ICC was strong among railroad men. Yet even in its early days, there were indications that such opposition was unnecessary. A widely quoted letter written in 1892 by Richard Olney, then the attorney general, to the president of the Burlington Railroad presaged the type of relationship that was to develop between railroads and the ICC. The letter was written in reaction to the proposed abolition of the ICC. In it, Olney stated,

> The Commission . . . is, or can be made, of great use to the railroads. It satisfies the popular clamor for a government supervision of railroads, at the same time that the supervision is almost entirely nominal. Further, the older such a commission gets to be, the more inclined it will be found to take the business and railroad view of things. It thus becomes a sort of barrier between the railroad corporations and the people and a sort of

protection against hasty and crude legislation hostile to railroad interests. . . . The part of wisdom is not to destroy the Commission, but to utilize it.[10]

It did not take Olney's prediction long to be fulfilled. The ICC soon became a captive of the railroad interests in conflicts between that industry and vocal segments of the public. The confident relationship that existed between the ICC and the railroads had ramifications in areas other than those relating to shippers and carriers, for although railroading was the first large-scale transportation industry to develop in America, it soon found itself challenged by competing transportation interests. Railroads were jealous of the privileged position that their early monopoly of commercial transportation had afforded them. In contrast to their earlier demands to abolish the ICC, rail interests fought to bring their competitors under the jurisdiction of the commission with which they had "developed such a close and continuous association . . . as virtually to form a single functional group."[11] The railroads succeeded in winning their demands for broadening the ICC's scope of authority and thereby provide a perfect example of the industrial benefits that a group can win by enhancing the authority of a decision-making body which is biased in its favor. McConnell notes, for instance, that

> . . . the Interstate Commerce Commission has generally favored the railroads over the trucking firms. In particular, it has interpreted identical regulations on rate structure differently for the railroads and for the motor carriers.[12]

Hamilton, likewise, concludes that the tactic of broadening the purview of the ICC had beneficial results for railroad interests.

> It was a shrewd move on the part of the railroads to bring it about that the regulation of the river barge, the motorbus, and motor truck would be lodged with the ICC. There may have been no conscious intent on the part of this agency to favor the older instrument. But over the years a body of practice has been built up which is definitely railroad-minded. In effect—if not in purpose—these forms of transportation have been delivered into the hands of a competitor.[13]

We referred earlier to cooptation as a process whereby marginal groups adopt the values and goals of the established elites to win benefits from the institutions controlled by the elites. The same term has been used to describe the process whereby regulatory institutions come to embrace the values and goals of elite interest groups to win their support.[14] Selznick uses the relationship between the

Tennessee Valley Authority and powerful groups within the valley to illustrate this type of cooptation. In this case the clientele of the agency had values which conflicted with the stated goals of the agency. To elicit the support of local groups, the TVA abandoned its policy of using public ownership of land as a conservation measure and thus altered its goals in exchange for support.

"Automatic" cooptation

In the case of the Florida Milk Commission, the identification of interests between regulators and regulated was immediate, and cooptation was automatic. A single-interest group, the Florida Dairy Association, presented a united, industrywide front in defense of the activities of the Commission, and kept a close eye on the Commission itself to make certain that all its members were informed of industry problems. By including both dairy farmers and milk distributors within its membership the Florida Dairy Association encompassed elements of potential disunion. However, no stresses on the organization in the form of opposing interests existed. Also, the distributors were able to affect the farmers adversely through private action. The development of specialized dairy farms brought with it dependency of the farmer on the continuation of satisfactory relations with a single large distributor who could afford to handle his entire supply of milk. Since milk is a highly perishable product, needing to be marketed immediately, the contract between farmer and distributor was of crucial importance. By maintaining its role as sole spokesman for the milk industry, the Florida Dairy Association established clear access to the administrative decision-making machinery. Representatives of the industry served on the Commission and, although they were appointed by the governor, it became accepted practice for the industry to recommend a slate of acceptable appointments, leaving the governor the choice of a final selection. The Commission established a price-fixing system acceptable to the industry and continued to regard the Florida Dairy Association as its principal source of information. An officer of the organization underscored the intimacy of governmental agency and interest group by declaring, "I have had to give so much thought to the Milk Commission . . . that I possibly think I am on the Milk Commission staff."

Access and lack of access: the State Department and
American textile manufacturers

A roughly analogous situation would be the cooperation between the National Rivers and Harbors Congress and the Corps of Engineers. In these cases of almost total harmony of interests between the government organization and the interest group, the regulated clientele actually acquires a beachhead within the institutions of government. Groups enjoying this relationship have a distinct advantage over groups which face the obstacle of lack of access. The cooperation between railroads and the Interstate Commerce Commission against the interests of trucks and water carriers has left these latter groups in a difficult position. Similarly, the American Cotton Manufacturers Institute, in seeking to accomplish a reversal of the Department of State decision with regard to the importing of Japanese textiles, had to cope with an agency which did not include any portion of the business community in its clientele. The Department of State provides an example of a government organization whose responsibility cannot be traced to one or several interest groups.[15] Its function, that of conducting the foreign relations of the nation, orients its personnel more in the direction of external pressures. This is not to say that domestic interest groups are not concerned with foreign affairs, either as a result of the impact of a given policy on the economic security of a group or as a result of ideological commitment to various causes which may be furthered or retarded by Department of State decisions. However, it is quite likely that the "position of the State Department renders it immune to the influence of such pressure groups, and its contacts with these associations are of little significance in the administration of the department's work."[16]

The Department of State does have formal mechanisms for taking the views of interest groups into account. The Bureau of Public Affairs has its Public Opinion Studies Staff which analyzes the public opinions of private groups, and the Office of Public Services (a section of the Bureau of Public Affairs) has an Organizational Liaison Staff to handle relations with interest groups at more subtle levels of communication. The publications analyzed by the Public Opinion Studies Staff are the products of six broad types of interests: international relations, economic, men's, women's, veterans, and religious organizations. Included within this spectrum would be the American Farm Bureau Federation, American Legion, and the various pacifist, religious, and nationalistic groups which regularly review State Department policy.[17]

Yet while the American Farm Bureau Federation is very influential in the affairs of the Department of Agriculture, and while the American Legion has come close to total domination of the Veterans Administration, neither of these organizations can muster much influence with the Department of State. This is suggestive of Riesman's "veto groups," each group having considerable influence in its own unique area of activities, but virtually no influence when ventures into other policy areas are undertaken.[18] The American Cotton Manufacturers Institute discovered the importance of clientele relationships when it encountered a stubborn State Department commitment to the expansion of trade with Japan. State Department policy in this area was based on the following assumptions: (1) Japan is basic to the Pacific defense system and must not be allowed to drift into the communist orbit, (2) Japan's economic position requires that it rely heavily on imports, and (3) there is increasing pressure on Japanese policy makers to extend market relations with Communist China. To enable the Japanese government to resist these internal pressures, the State Department took steps to improve the international flow of Japanese goods. Largely as a result of United States pressure, Japan was admitted to the General Agreement on Tariffs and Trade in 1955 and shortly thereafter the United States and Japan entered into a bilateral agreement under which tariff concessions were granted to 286 items.[19] The American textile industry was opposed to the admission of Japan to GATT, and its anxiety that foreign competition might destroy an already depressed industry increased with the bilateral agreement.

The manner in which such agreements are negotiated left the textile interest little hope of influencing a reversal of American policy. Under the original trade agreements legislation of 1934, the president was given the authority to negotiate bilateral agreements after consulting with the major executive departments concerned. To facilitate this process, President Roosevelt organized the Trade Agreements Committee consisting of all executive departments involved with foreign trade. In fact, the Trade Agreements Committee became dominated by the State Department in the Eisenhower administration, partially as a result of President Eisenhower's inclination to delegate final authority over foreign policy to his Secretary of State, John Foster Dulles. Hence, the negotiations for the bilateral agreement with Japan had been handled exclusively by the State Department. A brief survey of the publications of textile manufacturers clearly demonstrates their belief that the State Department was not only indifferent to their problem but hostile to their interest. The attitude of indifference was inferred from the Congressional testimony of Secretary of State Dulles. Consider for example his testimony before the House Ways and Means Committee: "Let me confess . . . that I am not an expert on tariff matters. . . . I do know something about the foreign relations of the United States. Our foreign policy, as I have put it in capsule form, is to enable the people to enjoy the blessings of liberty in peace. I am convinced that this result cannot be achieved without a cooperative trade relations."[20] This statement provides a good illustration of the conflict between the textile interest and the State Department and also describes the likely result of attempts to influence an agency by organizations which are not a part of its clientele. The textile industry complained that here the State Department "can give away the whole textile market, shut down every mill in the United States. . . . They still have done their job successfully if they keep Japan away from the Communists."[21]

STRATEGIES OF INFLUENCE

Without access to administrative machinery it is very difficult for interest groups to influence decisions. Organizations which find their interests affected by the policies of administrative decision-makers, but which do not receive the benefits of a favorable bias, may seek satisfaction for their demands elsewhere within the political system. The American Cotton Manufacturers Institute, for instance, enjoyed a much more favorable relationship with the federal government during Kennedy's administration. President Kennedy was much less willing than was his predecessor to delegate authority over foreign policy matters to his Secretary of State. Moreover, he recognized the fact that he needed the support of the Southern congressional delegations if he was to succeed in getting his legislative program approved. For these and other reasons, the Kennedy administration reverted to a more protectionist position with respect to the textile industry. It fought for the voluntary restriction of Japanese and Hong Kong textile exports to the United States, and in 1962, under GATT, a special textile agreement was concluded which permitted the president to impose certain quotas and tariffs on cotton imports. Such actions won for the administration the support of many congressmen from cotton producing districts as well as the appreciation of the ACMI for what it called an "unprecedented degree of thoughtful consideration."[22] Thus, when the arena of conflict was shifted from the Department of State to a more partisan setting in which the resources of the textile industry were more highly valued by decision-makers, the ACMI was able to win the instrumental policy decisions that it desired.

Likewise, reorganization of the administrative structure may lead to an alteration in the bias of policies affecting a given interest:

"[I]t is . . . widely believed that a change in the location of an executive agency within the administrative branch will seriously affect the ability of outside groups to influence the substance of policy as administered by the agency."[23]

Often proposals for reorganization come from groups which have lost or cannot achieve access to an agency that has responsibility for policy in the area of the group's concern, and these proposals are resisted by groups which view their relationships with the agency as satisfactory. Such recommendations very often are phrased in language reflecting the standard canons of public administration, such as the reduction of overlapping functions to reduce the burden of executive control and to ensure economical operation. However, such abstract values are not without their political implications. For example, the Hoover Commission recommended that the Department of Agriculture's Soil Conservation Service be abolished and most of its functions be assigned to the Extension Service, a goal long sought by the American Farm Bureau Federation which has extremely close ties with the Extension Service.[24] Again, the proposals that the functions of the Interstate Commerce Commission be assigned to an administrator directly responsible to the president have been opposed by railroads which have benefited by the independent status of the agency. During World War II, organized medicine began to attack the Emergency Maternal and Infant Care program of the Children's Bureau and urged its transfer from the Department of Labor to the U.S. Public Health Service, "considered by the AMA to be a more 'controllable' body."[25]

Securing "good" appointments

Ideally, one sure way for an interest group to guarantee close ties with an agency is to play a part in the selection of its personnel. Generally unsuccessful in their efforts to influence the electoral process, interest groups have had more luck in the appointment of administrative personnel. The acknowledgment that the interest group and the government agency will work together in a common area of interest of less concern to a more general public perhaps establishes more credibility. At any rate, there are far fewer targets of influence than is the case in the electoral process. High-level national appointments, such as those to the positions of Secretary of Agriculture, Commerce, or Labor, are made by the president after consultation with the interest groups representing the clientele of these agencies. Of course, the degree to which the president chooses to accept their advice depends on the extent to which he agrees with their goals and the record of these groups in political support of the president's party.

Efforts to influence appointments to independent regulatory agencies have been characteristic of interest groups since the creation of the first of these bodies, the Interstate Commerce Commission, in 1887. While there was considerable disagreement among public administration specialists about the meaning of the word *independence*—some arguing for institutional guarantees against domination by the chief executive, others believing that independence should also extend to freedom from control by centers of economic or political power—interest groups have generally been accorded the right to participate in the appointment process by government decision-makers. The case of Leland Olds, former chairman of the Federal Power Commission, illustrates this point.[26] Olds was a vigorous believer in the necessity of regulation of natural gas rates, a position which created organized hostility from the oil and natural gas producers who fought steadfastly against his reappointment. These interests were supported by Senators Kerr and Johnson and other congressmen from oil and gas producing states. In contrast, Olds was defended primarily by poorly organized consumer groups, the Americans for Democratic Action, various cooperative associations, and the National Grange. Olds' appointment had to be approved by the Senate Interstate and Foreign Commerce Committee; the subcommittee which would hold the hearings was chaired by Lyndon Johnson of Texas. The appointment was inextricably intertwined in the controversy over the Kerr bill, which the gas and oil industry had been trying to steer through Congress in an effort to amend the Natural Gas Act of 1938 in such a way as to remove the possibility of federal regulation. Serving as chairman of the Federal Power Commission, Olds had been a constant opponent of the Kerr bill and similar legislation. In fact, he had testified against the legislation only three months before his reappointment was scheduled to come before the Interstate and Foreign Commerce Committee. Unable to achieve official confirmation of their point of view either through the courts or through the legislature, the natural gas interests devoted their energies to finding a commission more amenable to their suggestions: "If Mr. Olds could be rejected and a person who was sympathetic to the industry's point of view appointed, the way would be paved to secure the enactment of desired amendments to the Natural Gas Act to remove federal regulation of the field price of gas."[27] This attitude was expressed by a representative of the Ohio Oil and Gas Association when he claimed that if Olds were reappointed "we face but one destiny—full extinction. . . . We deeply feel that the retention of Mr. Olds as a member of the FPC is a full threat to the free-enterprise system of this life in these United States."[28] Although President Truman made clear his unqualified support of Olds, the committee voted against confirmation. Before the confirmation came before the Senate, Truman commenced his support of Olds by requesting that the Democratic National Chairman send telegrams to the state chairmen suggesting that they urge the senators from their states to vote for confirmation, but this effort failed. Without attributing the result directly to the removal of Olds, it is worthy of mention that the Federal Power Commission ruled two years later that the regulation of natural gas prices was beyond its jurisdiction.

In this case the victory of the regulated clientele was won over presidential opposition by means of access to the legislative body, which was required by law to approve the appointment. If the chief executive agrees with the aspirations of a group to be relieved of the burden of regulation, the task is made easier. During the Eisenhower administration, business and management groups which had been unable to gain much influence in the appointive process during the Roosevelt and Truman years found themselves in a position to offer advice on prospective appointments at the innermost circles of the government. The influence of the Farm Bureau in the Department of Agriculture has been touched on; the Chamber of Commerce and the National Association of Manufacturers appeared to have been equally successful in seeking to affect the performance of the National Labor Relations Board through the appointive process. Long smarting under what they considered the pro-labor bias of the NLRB, management groups urged the president to use his power of appointment to achieve a "good" board. A combination of expirations of terms and resignations, coupled with the business-oriented attitude of Eisenhower's advisors, made 1953 a crucial year for the NLRB. In contrast to years of urging the abolition of the NLRB or at least reduction of its powers, the NAM in 1954 seemed satisfied:

> As an over-all appraisal it can be fairly said that the Board, with few exceptions, has followed a course of administration designed to give full faith and credit to the intent of Congress when the Taft-Hartley Act was put on the statute books. `
>
> Though the language of Taft-Hartley has remained unchanged, its interpretation by the Labor Board has not. On numerous and important issues the new Board, a majority of whose members have been appointed by President Eisenhower, has overturned established rulings, and has given the Act a new, and almost always anti-labor meaning. Indeed the Eisenhower appointees seem to have taken office with that end consciously in mind. . . . They seem to have proceeded on the assumption that since they

were appointed by a new administration, they had a license to overhaul any or all of the Board's policies. They have proceeded to imbue the Board with the employer-oriented interests of the new Administration.[29]

Establishing the conditions for effective persuasion

Persuasion is the least costly type of influence that an organization can exert in pursuing its policy demands. However, as a medium of political exchange, it is not always available for groups to employ. For persuasion to be effective, a group must first have the confidence of the political decision-makers with whom it is interacting; second, those decision-makers must value the persuasive resources (information, technical expertise, and so on) that the group commands. Both these conditions tend to be met when the clientele of a given administrative agency is homogeneous and when the agency is the dominant decision-making body which processes the demands of the client group. Persuasion in such circumstances is a consequence of administrators being "thrown into a constant association with the people they are supposed to regulate."[30] In the day-by-day performance of their tasks, administrators see very little of the more general public support which accompanied the establishment of the agency. The only people who are likely to come to the attention of administrators are those whose problems are uniquely a part of the administrative environment. Consequently, there is the tendency to view others as "outsiders." Under such circumstances it is not surprising that the administrator's perception of the public interest is in reality defined by the interests of the regulated parties. Such a situation is most likely to occur when the environment of the agency is dominated by a single interest, because the administrator will not be exposed to any appreciable extent to competing sources of information. Edelman notes that "the most effective way to make a public official act as an interest wishes him to is to assure by institutional means that he will become thoroughly acquainted with its problems as the adherents of the interest see them."[31]

As we have seen, interests tend to concentrate their efforts at one or a few agencies. Within each agency, there are usually attempts to carve out subordinate units to deal with the exclusive problems of a narrow interest; this frequently confuses efforts at reorganization. Thus, the National War Labor Board, which had jurisdiction over wage stabilization for most of American industry and labor during World War II, came to be subdivided into boards to deal with stabilization problems for only a few industries. It was found that these smaller boards were more malleable in yielding to demands for wage increases than the national board because these industry boards were able to give undivided attention to the concerns of particular industries in a manner that the larger national board could not duplicate. The intimate relationships between the industry-specific boards and their clientele led not only to familiarity but also the cooptation of the boards. Edelman describes the general forces which lead to such singularities of outlook:

> The organizational and psychological embrace of the industry around the regulatory commissioners go hand in hand. To be part of the organization in the sense of incessant exposure to its problems and decisional premises is to come to share its perspectives and values. This is not "pressure"; it is absorption. It explains the inevitability of a bias in choosing value premises: a bias which has been consistently observed by students of administrative regulation.[32]

Concentration of energy

If it is true that competition among a number of interests under the cognizance of a single agency tends to diminish the chances that any one of them will enjoy a consistently favorable bias, it is also likely that groups that are unable to concentrate on any single agency, but must divide their activities among several agencies, are at a disadvantage. Consequently, most interest groups find it highly desirable to operate within the control of a single government body. Sayre and Kaufman's analysis of interest groups in New York City reveals that these groups are highly specialized in their activities, even though some have a broad range of interest. The authors discern four types of groups concerned with government activity: those with "broad interests and a record of participation in governmental decision making" (civic associations); those with a "relatively narrow scope of interest and a high rate of participation" (for example, health and medical groups); those with a "narrow range of interest and low or intermittent participation" (ad hoc groups such as anti-fluoridation associations); and those with "broad interest and low participation." There are very few groups in this final category.[33] The first two categories of groups are the only ones capable of developing close relations with government agencies, since the ad hoc groups pass from the scene when the particular issue which brought them into being has been resolved.

Civic groups, typifying the type of association with broad interests and constant participation, concern themselves primarily with the *process* of decision-making rather than with its consequences. This means that they are theoretically interested in all governmental structures irrespective of the particular area of responsibility. In fact, the civic groups find themselves involved with "overhead" agencies and the Mayor's office. Naturally, those groups with more specialized interests are able to locate the one agency with authority over their unique area of public policy. This means that all the interest groups cultivate stable interaction with one agency. As the group and the administrative agency continue to interact, each develops specialized knowledge which may be of mutual benefit. For example, retail merchants may seek the advice of the traffic engineer's office on traffic problems; in turn the traffic engineer's office may turn to the retail merchants association for support in the event one of its programs is encountering stiff opposition. Concerning this type of relationship Sayre and Kaufman write,

> In some particular segment of officialdom, leaders of each group are usually received whenever they request an audience, their advice considered seriously when offered and often incorporated in official decisions, their views canvassed when not volunteered. In a manner of speaking, many group leaders become intimate parts of the city's machinery of governmental decision in certain spheres. They are nongovernmental in the sense that they cannot *promulgate* binding orders and rules the way officeholders clothed with public authority can, but they often have as much to say about what officeholders promulgate as the officeholders themselves, let alone the parties and other contestants for political prizes. Officeholders feel compelled to cooperate with them because they have so much influence, knowledge, and interest. Out of this official acceptance grows an integration of portions of government with relevant nongovernmental groups.[34]

INDEPENDENCE OF REGULATORY AGENCIES

Questions concerning the independence of regulatory agencies are not easily answered. No political institution which purports to be responsive is wholly autonomous; therefore, the matter of independence is one of degree. Many forces constrain the actions of agencies. We have discussed certain types of direct influence which some interest groups employ in their relations with regulatory bodies. Other groups seek to satisfy their demands indirectly by interacting with political authorities who, in turn, influence administrative decision-makers. Partisan political office-holders may also initiate action designed to affect administrative policy in response to what they believe to be the sentiments of unorganized sectors of the populace. Consequently, we are led to inquire into the mechanisms whereby regulatory agencies are subject to influence from other elements within the political system.

Administrative decision-makers are almost universally appointed office-holders. Thus, the appointing authority has some degree of influence over the agency. The power of the chief executive to appoint administrative personnel certainly earmarks him as the object of group pressure. It should not be assumed, however, that the chief executive is a helpless pawn at the mercy of the most effectively organized groups. In Florida, Governor LeRoy Collins elected to use his office to resist the tendency of the Florida Milk Commission to regulate in the interests of the milk industry by appointing a chairman who did not believe in any form of regulation. The man he selected was considered by the Florida Dairy Association to be totally unfamiliar with the problems of milk marketing and even to be an enemy of the trade association itself. The Florida Dairy Association had supported Collins in his contests for Governor and were inclined to regard him as friendly. When the members of the Association heard of Collins' intention, they sought a conference in the hope of changing his mind, and were supported by the Florida Farm Bureau and the state Chamber of Commerce. A conference was arranged, but only after the appointment had been made. While the reaction of the organized clientele of the Milk Commission was extremely hostile, support for the Governor was limited to a few urban papers and some temporary and hastily organized consumer groups. Collins was sacrificing trade association support for what he believed to be a broad but unarticulated public sympathy.

At the federal level, appointments are made by the president or his staff and approved by the Senate. As we saw in the case of President Truman's unsuccessful attempt to reappoint Leland Olds to the Federal Power Commission, and more recently in the defeat of President Nixon's nomination of Dr. John Knowles to a high office in the Department of Health, Education, and Welfare, Senatorial approval is not always automatic. Nevertheless, the appointive power of the chief executive is one avenue through which he can influence the character of regulatory agencies. That power is much more pronounced in the higher executive offices of the administrative branch than it is with respect to the independent regulatory agencies, however. Executive institutions such as the departments headed by cabinet members exist by virtue of the president's having delegated his executive powers to them. Regulatory agencies, on the other hand, are creations of Congress, and their powers and functions result from a legislative delegation of authority. Whereas the presidential power of appointment over executive-branch offices includes the power of removal, the Supreme Court has held that it is not so absolute with respect to regulatory agencies. In 1933 President Roosevelt attempted to remove a commissioner of the FTC and to replace him with someone whose views were more acceptable to his own. The incident reached the Supreme Court, which ruled against the president, saying in part:

> The authority of Congress, in creating quasi-legislative or quasi-judicial agencies, to require them to act in discharge of their duties independently of executive control cannot well be doubted; and that authority includes, as an appropriate incident, power to fix the period during which they shall continue, and to forbid their removal except for cause in the meantime. For it is quite evident that one who holds office only during the pleasure of another cannot be depended upon to maintain an attitude of independence against the latter's will.[35]

The president and Congress also share the capability of influencing regulatory agencies through their respective budgetary powers. Although Congress is the final authority over financial allocations, the president is responsible for submitting budgetary requests to the legislature. As Krislov and Musolf observe,

> Occasionally agencies have become "pets" of Congress, but generally it is to be expected that Congress will appropriate less, rather than more than the President recommends.
>
> The result is that when a collision takes place between the President and his aides, or even a purely executive agency, and a commission, the executive force generally prevails sooner or later.[36]

An incident involving the Federal Communications Commission and the Nixon administration illustrates the power wielded by the executive. In the summer of 1969 the FCC was reportedly prepared to grant the Communications Satellite Corporation the exclusive right to establish and operate a satellite system for transmitting television and telephone signals throughout the United States. President Nixon requested that the decision be delayed pending a study by his staff. In January 1970 the president sent a public memo to Dean Burch, the chairman of the FCC and a Nixon appointee, suggesting that the right to maintain such a system not be made an exclusive privilege of a single firm, but that any financially able company be allowed to do so. Two months later the FCC adopted the policy suggested by the White House. Objections were raised by several congressmen to the effect that the president was "meddling" in the quasi-legislative activities of the FCC and that he was violating the principle of agency independence. Critics of the action were particularly upset that normal channels of filing an official legal brief during FCC hearings had been bypassed in favor of a more overt application of pressure. Commenting on the utility of applying such pressure, Edwin Spievak, a legal consultant to one of the FCC commissioners, said that "the Nixon Administration no doubt discovered an extremely useful fact about the regulatory structure—its vulnerability to power relationships and its propensity to transfer decisional responsibility elsewhere whenever possible."[37]

Another source of influence from within the political system stems from the fact that federal regulatory agencies are creations of Congress. This means, of course, that Congress may withdraw its delegation of authority, restructure them, or redefine their scopes of authority. Consequently, groups which command resources uniquely suited for exchanges with legislative officeholders or with executive leaders and which perceive their interests to be affected by the policies of administrative agencies may indirectly influence such agencies through interactions with other elements within the political system.[38] But whether pressures are direct or indirect, administrative decision-makers are not without certain means of counteracting them. They are not, in other words, merely passive actors who can do little more than respond to their environment. Fainsod's comments in this regard deserve inclusion at some length:

> In stressing the limits which environmental pressures impose on the uses to which these instruments [regulatory agencies] are put, there is a tendency to underestimate the independent creative force and manipulative power which the wielders of these instruments acquire by virtue of their special competence or their strategic position in the regulatory hierarchy. The strategy by which regulatory agencies develop ability to resist or guide pressures has been relatively little explored. Yet it is obvious that, within limits, such power exists. The regulatory agency itself is capable of generating a certain amount of independent power to change its environment. ... In the process of exercising their discretionary power, regulatory agencies are often in a position to create some pressures and to extinguish others, to stir dormant parties in interest into activity and to anesthetize others, to mobilize groups to come to their support and to penalize opposition. Investigation may deflate pretensions and reveal divisions and minorities within groups which are spoken for as units. The impact of the articulate may be softened by the gentle ministrations of discreet inquiry. The manipulative power of regulatory agencies may be utilized to maintain an existing equilibrium of interests; it can be used to tilt the scale and create a new equilibrium.[39]

Publicity

Publicity is one means by which agencies can often avert direct challenges to their independence. In seeking to guarantee that the continued existence of an agency will depend on alliance with clientele groups, these groups will normally seek to keep the operations of the agency as far from public awareness as possible. This, in turn, will reduce the possibility of the agency's recruiting strength from more general public support and developing alternative reservoirs of political strength. To counteract the desire for secrecy, administrative agencies may use carefully executed public relations and propaganda programs. Thus Simon notes that "community satisfaction with the services of the Forest Service, and community understanding of those services, brought about partly by the public relations activities of the district forest ranger, have created sufficient support to keep the Forest Service in the Department of Agriculture in spite of constant pressure from the conflicting interests of stock grangers and lumbermen to transfer it to the Department of the Interior where those interests have considerably more influence."[40]

The reduction of clientele homogeneity

Another hit of strategy which can be used by administrators is the reduction of monopoly in the environment. Some interests which appear to be monolithic actually contain the seeds of discontent. If the agency can create and nourish competition by contributing to the bifurcation of an interest, its independence from that interest will be enhanced. The experience of the Florida Milk Commission serves to illustrate this point. From its creation in 1934 until the early 1950s, the Commission operated beneath the level of public awareness. Although public hearings were held, little mention of its activities was made in the press. Since no public funds were involved, the state legislature tended to approve routinely any Commission recommendations. No legislation seriously altering the functions of the Commission ever reached the floor of either the senate or house of representatives, and only rarely were such bills introduced. In the early 1950s the operations of the Commission became the subject of some public controversy. Occasional complaints that the Commission was dominated by the industry trade association, the Florida Dairy Association, were expressed by temporary and hastily organized consumers' groups. The activities of the Milk Commission were brought sharply to the public attention during the 1954 primary for governor when one of the candidates campaigned on a platform calling for the abolition of the Milk Commission. This candidate, Brailey Odham, was opposed vigorously by the Florida Dairy Association and ran last in a field of three. However, he was subsequently appointed Chairman of the Milk Commission. Joined by others who believed that the Commission should not set milk prices, Odham faced the united opposition of the Florida Dairy Association which insisted that prices should be set to avoid price wars.

During this time, the Commission had agreed to abandon all price controls above the producer level for one year. This meant that, while the milk prices offered by dairies to farmers were set, prices at wholesale and retail levels were allowed to fluctuate. In this climate, differences of opinion between farmer and distributor members of the Florida Dairy Association began to appear. In the past, farmers had supported the regulation of prices at all levels. Now some of these farmers began to express the desire for an organization, independent of the dairies, which would support the efforts of the Commission to remove controls permanently. The new members of the Commission began a campaign of persuasion, both inside and outside of the Commission, designed to take advantage of the emerging industry discord. They urged farmers to think in terms of their own interests and tried to persuade them to attend Commission meetings. At the same time, farmers were assured that the Commission would never oppose price controls at the producer level. In addition to encouraging farmers, the Commission took concrete action which could be interpreted as antagonistic to dairies. It ordered price controls extended at the producer level to surplus milk, ordered a revision in the prices charged to farmers for hauling milk, and began an investigation of possible rebating practices between dairies and retailers.

The concern for producer interests enhanced a growing cleavage within the Florida Dairy Association. In its hearings, the Commission began to see a rising independence on the part of producers. In the past the testimony of dairy farmers had not deviated from that of distributors. Now local producer groups began to declare publicly in support of the program of scrutinizing the activities of dairies. While these dairies were seeking a return to controls, some producers appeared to be satisfied with the Commission's policies. Operating under a Commission which they thought was not easily influenced by the distributors, some of the younger producers began to work for the formation of a separate, statewide organization. These efforts were consummated with the creation of the Florida Dairy Farmers Federation in 1958. The new members of the Commission were delighted with this development. Now there was an interest group in existence which was in competition with the Florida Dairy Association. The environment was no longer dominated by a single organization as it had been for so long. To ensure the continued existence of the new and friendly group, the Commission passed new orders providing for a measure of economic independence for farmers. Distributors had provided for a "dues check-off plan" by which producer organization dues were automatically deducted when the farmer was paid for his milk. Producers affiliated with the new Florida Dairy Farmers Federation were being denied this convenience, so the Commission passed an order providing that any producer group meeting certain standards could qualify for dues check-off. The Commission also tried, against distributor opposition, to institute a "just cause" order providing that a contract between producer and distributor could not be terminated without Commission approval. The Commission was thus developing an alternate source of information in the expectation that the agency would no longer have to cope with united, industrywide opposition to its programs. The Florida Dairy Association, so long the defender of the Commission, now was discouraged by what it saw as a new bias. The agency had, as Fainsod suggests, created a new equilibrium.

STABILITY AND RESISTANCE TO CHANGE

Examples of administrative agencies restructuring their environments are relatively rare. The weight of evidence would seem to indicate, as we and others have suggested, that agencies and their clientele tend to develop coincident values and perceptions to the point where neither needs to manipulate the other overtly. The confident relationships that develop uniquely favor the interest groups involved. They need only exchange persuasive resources for instrumental policy benefits within administrative markets to satisfy many of their material demands. Costly resources which would otherwise have to be exchanged in legislative markets are thereby preserved, and the interests of the regulated industry are protected regardless of the content of legislative policies, for laws are not necessarily productive of the reallocation of values suggested by their language. The actual or operational meaning of statutes may be found in the day-by-day administration of these statutes; and in this process of administration, groups which appear to have lost in the legislative arena may be successful in minimizing the effects of the law.[41] Small wonder, then, that clientele groups and regulatory agencies tend to resist alterations in what they find to be mutually rewarding relationships. The inertia that results leads to what Truman calls the "inflexibility of the established web."[42]

NOTES

[1]Dwight Waldo, *The Study of Public Administration* (Garden City, N.Y.: Doubleday & Company, 1955), p. 41. See also Martin Landau, "The Concept of Decision-Making in the 'Field' of Public Administration," in Sidney Malick and Edward H. Van Ness, eds., *Concepts and Issues in Administrative Behavior* (Englewood Cliffs, N.J.: Prentice-Hall, Inc., 1962), pp. 16–18.

[2]John A. Vieg, "The Growth of Public Administration," in Fritz Morstein Marx, ed., *Elements of Public Administration* (Englewood Cliffs, N.J.: Prentice-Hall, Inc., 1961), pp. 14–15; John M. Gaus and Leon O. Wolcott, *Public Administration and the United States Department of Agriculture* (Chicago: Public Administration Service, 1940), pp. 1–87.

[3]On this topic William R. Dill notes that "as an organization begins to function, its founders and sponsors are apt to be more sensitive to environmental inputs and more anxious to seek them out than they will be at most later stages of the organization's history," See "The Impact of Environment on Organizational Development," in Malick and Van Ness, *op. cit.*, p. 101.

[4]All comments on this agency are drawn from L. Harmon Zeigler, *The Florida Milk Commission Changes Minimum Prices* (New York: The Inter-University Case Program, 1963).

[5]This definition is from Herbert A. Simon, Donald W. Smithburg, and Victor A. Thompson, *Public Administration* (New York: Alfred A. Knopf, Inc., 1950), p. 461.

[6]Murray Edelman, "Governmental Organization and Public Policy," *Public Administration Review*, XII (Autumn 1952), p. 278.

[7]Philip Selznick, *TVA and the Grass Roots* (Berkeley: University of California Press, 1949); Marver Bernstein, *Regulating Business by Independent Commission* (Princeton, N.J.: Princeton University Press, 1955).

[8]Bernstein, *op. cit.*, pp. 270–71.

[9]Murray Edelman, *The Symbolic Uses of Politics* (Urbana, Ill.: University of Illinois Press, 1964), p. 56.

[10]Quoted by Kenneth Culp Davis, *Administrative Law Text* (St. Paul, Minn.: West Publishing Co., 1960), p. 7.

[11]Walton Hamilton, *The Politics of Industry* (New York: Alfred A. Knopf, Inc., 1957), p. 59.

[12]Grant McConnell, *Private Power and American Democracy* (New York: Alfred A. Knopf, Inc., 1966), p. 286. Also see Bernard Schwartz, "Crisis in the Commissions," *The Progressive*, XXIII (Aug. 1959), pp. 10–13.

[13]Hamilton, *op. cit.*, p. 60.

[14]Selznick, *op. cit.*, p. 13.

[15]For explorations in the decision-making process within the Department of State see Robert Ellsworth Elder, *The Policy Machine* (Syracuse, N.Y.: Syracuse University Press, 1960); Bernard C. Cohen, *The Political Process and Foreign Policy* (Princeton, N.J.: Princeton University Press, 1957); and E. Pendleton Herring, *Public Administration and the Public Interest* (New York: McGraw-Hill Book Company, Inc., 1936), pp. 69–88.

[16]Herring, op. cit., p. 77.

[17]Elder, op. cit., pp. 140–44.

[18]David Riesman, The Lonely Crowd (Garden City, N.Y.: Doubleday & Company, 1955), pp. 244–51.

[19]U.S. Department of State, "Analysis of Protocol for Accession of Japanese— General Agreements on Tariffs and Trade," Commercial Policy Series No. 150 (Washington, D.C.: Government Printing Office, 1955).

[20]House Ways and Means Committee, Hearings on H.R. 1, 84th Cong., 2nd Sess., 1956 (Washington, D.C.: Government Printing Office, 1956), p. 114.

[21]Textile World, Feb. 1955, p. 65.

[22]Quoted in Raymond A. Bauer, Ithiel de Sola Pool, and Lewis Anthony Dexter, American Business and Public Policy: The Politics of Foreign Trade (New York: Atherton Press, 1963), p. 362.

[23]Francis E. Rourke, "The Politics of Administrative Organization: A Case History," Journal of Politics, XIX (Aug. 1957), p. 461.

[24]Grant McConnell, The Decline of Agrarian Democracy (Berkeley: University of California Press, 1959), p. 136.

[25]E. Drexel Godfrey, Jr., The Transfer of the Children's Bureau (Committee on Public Administration Cases, 1949, mimeograph), p. 5.

[26]This account is drawn from Joseph P. Harris, "The Senatorial Rejection of Leland Olds: A Case Study," American Political Science Review, XLV (Sept. 1951), pp. 674–92.

[27]Ibid., p. 680.

[28]Statement of Russell B. Brown, General Counsel of the Independent Petroleum Association of America, quoted ibid., p. 686.

[29]N.A.M. Law Digest, Dec. 1954, p. 1, quoted in Seymour Scher, "Regulatory Agency Control through Appointments: The Case of the Eisenhower Administration and the NLRB," Journal of Politics, XXIII (Nov. 1961), p. 687.

[30]Statement of Senator Aiken of Vermont before the Senate Committee on Labor and Public Welfare, Hearings, Establishment of a Commission on Ethics in Government, 82nd Cong., 1st Sess., 1951, p. 213. Cited in Bernstein, Regulating Business by Independent Commission, p. 158.

[31]Edelman, "Governmental Regulation," p. 279.

[32]Edelman, The Symbolic Uses of Politics, p. 66.

[33]Wallace S. Sayre and Herbert Kaufman, Governing New York City (New York: Russell Sage Foundation, 1960), pp. 77, 481–82.

[34]Ibid., p. 511.

[35]Humphrey's Executor v. United States, 295 U. S. 602 (1935).

[36]Samuel Krislov and Lloyd D. Musolf, eds., The Politics of Regulation (Boston: Houghton Mifflin Company, 1964), p. 94.

[37]Quoted in The Wall Street Journal, 21 July 1970, p. 21.

[38]For an illuminating discussion of how several influential United States senators view their roles as intermediary between powerful constituents and federal regulatory agencies, see Charlotte P. Murphy, "Legislative Interests in Administrative Procedure during the 86th Congress: Some Notes, Quotes, and Comments," Administrative Law Bulletin, XII (Winter 1959–60), pp. 128–43.

[39]Merle Fainsod, "Some Reflections on the Nature of the Regulatory Process," in C. J. Friedrich and Edward S. Mason, eds., *Public Policy* (Cambridge, Mass.: Harvard University Press, 1940), pp. 299–320.

[40]Simon et al., *Public Administration*, pp. 415–16.

[41]Murray Edelman, "Symbols and Political Quiescence," *American Political Science Review*, LIV (Sept. 1960), pp. 695–704.

[42]David Truman, *The Governmental Process* (New York: Alfred A. Knopf, Inc., 1951), p. 467.

eight

The Judicial Process: Conflict under Carefully Defined Rules*

The study of politics as a process whereby authoritative decisions are made which operate to the advantage of some groups
and to the disadvantage of others runs into a stubborn road-
block in the form of the judicial branch of government. The
gradual abandonment of formal or legalistic approaches in
studies of legislation and, to a lesser extent, of administration,
has come much slower with respect to judicial policy-
making.[1] The traditional reluctance of scholars to place judicial policy-making within the general political process is
perhaps more a reflection of a popular belief system than the
result of inadequate methodology or inaccessibility of mate-
rials. While it is true that the courts deliberate and make
decisions in an atmosphere more secretive than other governmental bodies, recent research has demonstrated that this

184

seclusion is no real handicap. However, the judiciary branch and especially the United States Supreme Court occupies a position in our belief structure unlike that of any other agency of government. Lerner comments upon this unique status:

> Talk to the men on the street, the men in the mines, and factories and steel mills and real-estate offices and filling stations, dig into their minds and even below the threshold of their consciousness, and you will find in the main that the Constitution and Supreme Court are symbols of an ancient sureness and comforting stability.[2]

JUDGES AND POLITICS

What Lerner suggests is that the judiciary is not viewed as "political" but is somehow regarded as a purely "legal" body which functions to discover permanent truths. It is indeed paradoxical that America with its doctrine of judicial review has placed the court at the center of the policy-making process while persisting in the belief that judges are above politics.[3] Since the courts can refuse to uphold legislation which they construe to be unconstitutional, interests which cannot achieve their goals in one arena are given another chance. In such a situation, it is impossible for judges to be "above politics" simply because the decisions they reach are political. The decisions confirm benefits on some groups of people while impeding the aspirations of others.[4] Thus, the political nature of the judiciary is not solely a function of the biases or group affiliations of judges but is rather inherent in the structure of the governmental system. Coupled with the clearly supportable assumption that the values of judges are a fundamental ingredient in the process of judicial decision-making, the institutional role of courts in the governmental system makes these bodies central to the political process. The neutrality of judges is part of our myth system, but has never been characteristic of the actual decision-making process.

Arthur Bentley correctly assessed the nature of judicial politics:

> It is possible to take a Supreme Court decision, in which nothing appears on the surface but finespun points of law, and cut through all the dialectic till we get down to the actual groups of men underlying the decisions and producing the decisions through the differentiated activity of the justices.[5]

The activity of the Supreme Court in outlawing segregation in public schools brought home to many people the role of interest groups in the formulation of judicial policy. Perhaps, as Dahl suggests, the intense criticism leveled at the Court as a result of these decisions arises from dismay that the Court had forsaken its role as infallible finder of truth and gotten involved in "politics."[6] Of course, one does not have to look only at the recent history of the Court to find examples to support Bentley's thesis. Scholars skilled at tracing periods in the development of the Supreme Court's interpretation of the Constitution have little trouble refuting the myth of neutrality. For example, Miller and Howell have noted three distinct eras of constitutional interpretation: (1) from the establishment of the Supreme Court until the Civil War, when the Court sought to create and maintain a strong national union; (2) from about 1870 to 1937, when the basic drive of the Court was toward establishing a favorable climate for business by protecting it against governmental interference; (3) from 1937 until the present, when individual liberties and personal freedoms assumed more prominence than they had in either of the two previous periods.[7] In each of these periods the judges were required to choose among competing alternative choices of public policy without recourse to precedent. Even in the interpretation of precedent there can be no neutrality, for the values of the judge will color and shape what he reads.[8] It is useful also to realize that the precedents were established by prior courts, each with its own particular combination of values. Some of the leading decisions of the first part of the nineteenth century, which were woven by future justices into the fabric of the law, are primarily essays in political philosophy with only peripheral reference to the actual legal issue before the Court. John Marshall's opinion in *McCulloch* v. *Maryland* is a clear example of this technique.[9]

It is not surprising that Supreme Court decisions are frequently colored by a particular philosophical or ideological view, for "perhaps no other qualification for the Supreme Court bench is so important as political involvement."[10] It is, as Jacob states, "an unwritten qualification for the bench."[11] Nor is political experience a unique characteristic of Supreme Court justices or of federal judges in general. A 1963 survey of the backgrounds of American judges found that over half the incumbents of state and federal judgeships had held public office prior to attaining their current positions.[12] Moreover, of the judges serving on appellate and general trial courts, approximately 25% were former legislators. The implication of these facts is inescapable. Judicial decision-makers tend to be sensitive to the practical allocative results of their decisions as well as to the formal legal principles of the cases brought before them.[13]

Judicial response to criticism

In view of this evidence, it is instructive to consider what is perhaps the most articulate cornerstone of the myth that judges merely "discover" law. In *U.S.* v. *Butler* former Justice Owen J. Roberts defined the duty of the Court: "When an act of Congress is appropriately challenged in the Courts as not conforming to the constitutional mandate, the judicial branch of the government has only one duty; to lay the Article of the Constitution which is invoked beside the statute which is challenged and to decide whether the latter squares with the former."[14] Roberts was thus suggesting that the Supreme Court justice is capable of absolute detachment and objectivity and is totally uninfluenced by his social background, his identification with social or economic interests. One of Roberts' colleagues, Justice George Sutherland, defined his function similarly by saying that "the meaning of the Constitution does not change with the ebb and flow of economic events."[15] In this case, *Adkins* v. *Children's Hospital*, Sutherland held the Minimum Wage Act of 1918 to be a violation of the Fifth Amendment which he held to be protective of "freedom of contract." However, the Fifth Amendment makes no mention of such a freedom. The idea of freedom of contract was first given explicit notice in *Allgeyer* v. *Louisiana*, a Fourteenth Amendment case in which the Court held that a Louisiana statute placing restrictions on insurance companies was a violation of the "liberty contained in that amendment."[16] The reading of this new liberty into the Fourteenth Amendment had been continued in *Lochner* v. *New York* but had not become a part of litigation involving the Fifth Amendment.[17] Nevertheless, Sutherland, citing the *Allgeyer* case but ignoring several other cases which might have had a bearing on the subject, declared that "the right to contract about one's affairs as a part of the liberty of the individual protected by this clause is settled by the decisions of this court and is no longer open to question."[18]

This determination to protect the rights of property, or as Sutherland phrased it, "the good of society as a whole," characterized the second period of the Supreme Court's history according to the Miller–Howell scheme, and persisted as late as 1936. During the 1930s, a conservative bloc consisting of Justices McReynolds, Butler, Van Devanter, and Sutherland voted consistently against the New Deal legislation of President Franklin Roosevelt. Generally in support of the president were Justices Stone, Cardozo, and Brandeis. Somewhat in the middle, but with greater identification with the anti–New Deal faction, were Justice Roberts and Chief Justice Charles Evans Hughes.[19] It was in this situation that Roosevelt's "Court-packing" plan was proposed. The Hughes Court had invalidated twelve New Deal laws within four years and three presidential acts within a period of six months. Arguing that "the Court has been acting not as a judicial body, but as a policy-making body," Roosevelt proposed to Congress that whenever a federal judge who had served ten years or more failed to retire within six months after reaching his seventieth birthday, the president would be allowed to appoint an additional judge to serve on that court.[20] Interests which were disadvantaged by the New Deal and protected by the Court opposed the president's plan, but, before the issue became joined, the business community's plea of "hands off the Supreme Court" was settled by the sudden reversal of the Court's position on several key pieces of New Deal legislation. The change in the posture of the Court was accomplished by the switching of Hughes and Roberts from the "right" bloc to the "left" bloc, which thus created a majority in support of the New Deal. Roberts' concept of mechanical jurisprudence was not borne out in his voting behavior.[21]

The period during which Earl Warren was chief justice, 1953 to 1969, has been described as being "probably . . . the most activist and controversial one in the nation's history."[22] Decisions bearing on the issues of race relations, congressional powers, subversive activities, and states' rights stimulated criticism of the Court from many sources.[23] In 1954 the Warren Court issued the first, and certainly one of the most important, of its highly controversial decisions. It declared that racially segregated schools were "inherently unequal" and were therefore unconstitutional according to the equal protection clause of the Fourteenth Amendment.[24] Southern opponents of the decision referred to May 17, the day it was announced, as "Black Monday." Three years later there occurred what has become known as "Red Monday." On June 17, 1957, the Court announced four separate decisions supporting the position of individuals who had been accused of undermining national security and of subversive activities.[25] In addition to the fact that each of these decisions "was interpreted as affronting the internal security by freeing alleged 'Communist conspirators,'"[26] the decisions also challenged the authority of congressional investigating committees and imposed severe limitations on state and federal prosecution of those accused of subversive activities. Whereas initial opposition to the Warren Court was largely confined to southern legislators and proponents of school segregation, the Red Monday decisions served as a rallying point for broadening the range of anti-Court interests. Interest groups of the radical right, such as the John Birch Society and Rev. Billy James Hargis' Christian Crusade, conducted extensive propaganda campaigns against the Court. The Birch Society even demanded the impeachment of Earl Warren. Less radical conservative organizations in varying degrees of intensity also turned on the Court. Among them were the American Legion, the Daughters of the American Revolution, the National Association of Manufacturers, the Chamber of Commerce, and the American Farm Bureau Federation.

Faced with such widespread opposition from organized interests as well as from Congress, the Court adopted a somewhat more conservative posture. During the 1956 term, for instance, it had rejected civil liberties claims in only 26% of the cases decided by a full opinion, but this figure rose to nearly 49% during the 1958 term.[27] Likewise, in the area of national security withdrawal was evident. In 1959 the Court decided two cases involving the investigative powers of Congress and the states with respect to subversive activities.[28] These cases, *Barenblatt* v. *United States* and *Uphaus* v. *Wyman*, resulted in modifications of the policies enunciated in two of the Red Monday cases, *Watkins* v. *United States* and *Sweezy* v. *New Hampshire*.

The parallel between the shifting attitudes on the Warren Court and the Hughes Court of 1936 are striking. Glendon Schubert's analysis of voting patterns in the two sets of cases involving investigations of subversive activity, *Watkins*, *Sweezy*, *Barenblatt*, and *Uphaus*, reveal that a 6–1 majority in favor of the defendant in the first two cases became a 4–5 minority in the latter two. Schubert notes that there was no change in the position of a majority of the justices, and changes in the personnel of the Court could not account for the differences between the sets of cases. For the Warren bloc (Warren, Black, Douglas, and Brennan) to lose control it was necessary for two justices to switch their votes. Justices Frankfurter and Harlan, having voted for the defendants in the *Watkins* and *Sweezy* decisions of 1957, voted against the defendants' claims in the *Barenblatt* and *Uphaus* decisions of 1959.[29] In 1936, Roberts and Hughes switched, shifting the balance of power in the Court, and in 1959, Frankfurter and Harlan accomplished the same feat. In both situations the Court was under heavy attack from dissatisfied interests (including organized groups), and in both situations the Court reduced the hostility by modifying its policy decisions. Rather than being neutral observers of a political warfare being waged beneath them, courts actually assume the role of partisans in the struggle. This partisanship is not the result of a conscious evaluation of political advantages on the part of judges, but rather is a natural consequence of the position of courts in our political structure.

Personnel changes and judicial policy

Not all modifications of judicial policy are accomplished by shifting voting alignments among sitting justices. Personnel changes on the Supreme Court, as Roosevelt well knew, can have a substantial impact on the direction the Court takes. This point is illustrated by comparing the Warren Court's record on criminal due process cases with recent decisions in that area issued by the Burger Court. In a series of cases extending from 1957 through 1967, the Warren Court incurred the displeasure of a number of organizations and individuals by decisions protecting the rights of accused criminals. Law enforcement groups were particularly critical of these rulings, which they considered to be obstructions to their activities. Such cases as *Mallory* v. *United States*,[30] in which it was held that confessions obtained during an "unreasonable delay" between arrest and arraignment were inadmissible; *Escobedo* v. *Illinois*,[31] where the right of an accused criminal to legal counsel during interrogation was established; and *Miranda* v. *Arizona*,[32] in which confessions gained without first having informed the accused of his rights were invalidated, all stimulated hostile reactions from law enforcement associations. Following the *Escobedo* decision, Lytle reported:

> Garrett Byrne, President of the National Association of District Attorneys, remarked that if five men sat down to think carefully how to destroy the country they could not have done more harm to law enforcement than the present Supreme Court majority. Former New York Police Commissioner Michael Murphy criticized the Court for a "series of decisions on confessions and searches and seizures which unduly hampered law enforcement." "What the court is doing," Murphy noted, "is akin to requiring one boxer to fight by Marquis of Queensbury rules while permitting the other to butt, gouge, and bite."[33]

These decisions were particularly odious to their critics because they emanated from a closely divided Court. Both *Escobedo* and *Miranda* were decided by five-to-four splits. In the earlier of the two cases Chief Justice Warren and Justices Black, Douglas, Brennan, and Goldberg formed the majority against the opposition of White, Stewart, Harlan, and Clark. The same sides were drawn in the *Miranda* decision with the exception that Abe Fortas had replaced Goldberg in the majority coalition. Subsequent changes in Court personnel, however, have altered the delicate five-to-four balance. Prior to his retirement, President Johnson appointed Thurgood Marshall, the nation's first Negro Supreme Court justice, to succeed Clark. Marshall's appointment did not change the balance of power, for he has tended to vote with the liberals as did Clark. But President Nixon's appointments of Warren E. Burger to succeed Warren as Chief Justice and of Harry A. Blackmun to fill the vacancy left when Fortas resigned have resulted in a reorientation of the Court. On February 24, 1971, the Burger Court issued its first decision directly bearing on the *Escobedo* and *Miranda* precedents. In *Harris* v. *New York* the

Court retreated somewhat from the strict rule of inadmissibility by declaring that improperly gained evidence may be used to challenge the credibility of an accused criminal if the latter voluntarily testifies in his own defense. Commenting on the implications of the *Harris* decision, the *New York Times* reported that it "appeared to present the strongest indication to date that President Nixon's appointment of Justice Blackmun has created the conservative majority on criminal law issues that Mr. Nixon has set as his goal."[34]

The preceding example illustrates the influence over judicial policy that can be exerted by those who control selection procedures. Although the courts themselves may be relatively insulated from direct, conscious exchanges with partisan interests, the direction of judicial policy-making can be significantly affected by partisan influence over the recruitment of judicial personnel. Peltason lists this as one of the three indirect methods by which groups can attempt to control judicial policy as it bears on their immediate interests.[35] The other two strategies he notes are influencing the content of decisions and maximizing the effects of decisions as they are implemented. Let us first examine the influence groups exert over selection procedures.

SELECTING JUDICIAL PERSONNEL

The Constitution provides that federal judges are to be nominated by the president and approved by the Senate. Some of the states have provided for the election of judges by the electorate or the legislature, and some, notably California and Missouri, have sought a compromise between election and appointment. Whatever the method of selection, there has been little success in isolating judges from political influences.[36] The president, in submitting his recommendations to the Senate, will obviously select candidates whose views of the public interest are in harmony with his own, even though presidential expectations may not be borne out by the behavior of the judge once he has been appointed. In the case of a Supreme Court appointment, the president is less restricted by custom than is true when lesser federal appointments are contemplated. Inferior court appointments are subject to the rule of senatorial courtesy, meaning that the president is placed in a position of approving the decision of the Senator or local party organization in the area in which the proposed judge is to serve. However, even without the restrictions of senatorial courtesy, appointments to the Supreme Court have become the center of intense group conflict which is concentrated at the Senate Judiciary Committee. Schmidhauser writes that "a president is . . . subject to pressures which emanate from private groups which, although national in their organization attributes, may be excessively narrow and self-serving in their public policy objectives."[37]

Two frequently cited examples of interest group involvement in judicial selection procedures concern the nominations of Louis D. Brandeis and John J. Parker to the United States Supreme Court in 1916 and 1930, respectively. Brandeis, who had made a substantial reputation as a lawyer for various progressive causes such as the regulation of utilities and limitation of work hours, was opposed by groups that had been able to resist the tide of regulatory legislation by relying on a friendly court. Particularly anxious to block the nomination was the American Bar Association which argued that Brandeis did not have "judicial temperament." However, the meaning read into such a nebulous phrase varies with the values of the group using it. Brandeis had a long and active career in the practice of law, but his clients were most often those who were challenging the dominant business ideology of the time. In support of Brandeis were trade associations and other organizations conspicuous in voicing the protest. The intensity of the ideological conflict centering around the nomination of Brandeis is reflected in the absolute partisanship of the vote in the Judiciary Committee and on the Senate floor. President Wilson, who viewed his own chances for reelection as somewhat dependent on his ability to avoid an open rejection of his leadership by the Senate, worked vigorously in Brandeis' behalf and was rewarded by a straight party vote in the Judiciary (ten Democrats voting for confirmation, eight Republicans opposing) and in the Senate (forty-four Democrats and three Progressives opposed by all twenty-one Republicans and one Democrat).[38] While business-oriented groups were unsuccessful in defeating the nomination of Brandeis in 1916, the NAACP and organized labor were able to prevent the confirmation of John J. Parker in 1930. A Republican nominated by Hoover, Judge Parker was serving on the Fourth Circuit Court of Appeals. In this capacity he had written an opinion sustaining an injunction issued by a lower court to enforce a yellow-dog contract. This decision incurred the animosity of the American Federation of Labor, which did not accept Parker's reasoning that the Supreme Court decision in *Hitchman Coal and Coke Company* v. *Mitchell* left him no alternative.[39] Also, as Republican candidate for governor of North Carolina in 1920, Parker had been charged by the Democrats with intending to enfranchise Negroes. In response, Parker stated that "the participation of the Negro in politics is a source of evil and danger to both races and is not desired by the wise men in either race or by the Republican Party of North Carolina." The charges that Parker was anti-Negro and anti-labor were enough to bring about his defeat in the Senate Judiciary Committee, which voted six to ten against confirmation. The unfavorable recommendation of the Judiciary Committee was supported in the Senate by a coalition of Progressive Republicans, Republicans from states with large Negro and labor populations, and northern Democrats. The vote was thirty-nine to forty-one against confirmation with seventeen Republicans voting against the President's nominee.[40]

More recent instances of group influence on Supreme Court selection procedures occurred in 1969 and 1970 when two successive Nixon nominees failed to win Senate approval. In mid-1969, Associate Justice Abe Fortas resigned from the Court following his failure to win confirmation as chief justice. He was under threat of impeachment proceedings as a result of reputed unethical conduct stemming from his acceptance while on the Court of "a $20,000 fee from the family foundation of a man later imprisoned for illegal stock manipulation."[41] Clement F. Haynsworth was nominated to fill the position thus vacated. Like Parker nearly forty years before, Haynsworth was a Southern Republican serving on the bench of the Fourth Circuit Court of Appeals at the time of his nomination. And, like Parker, he met strong opposition from labor and civil rights organizations because of his decisions while on that court. The Senate Judiciary Committee split along party and sectional lines by recommending by a vote of ten to seven that his appointment be confirmed. During the course of the committee hearings it came to light that Haynsworth had participated in the deliberation of a case in 1963 involving a business firm with which he had a rather tenuous financial link. Although he disavowed any knowledge of the existence of that link at the time, the atmosphere created by the Fortas situation was one in which the Senate was highly sensitive to questions of judicial ethics. In such an environment, despite strong endorsements by the American Bar Association and active support by the Nixon administration, the Senate voted forty-five to fifty-five against confirmation. In general, Southern Democrats and moderate and conservative Republicans voted for Haynsworth while the remainder of the Democrats and liberal Republicans opposed him. It is impossible to say whether the influence of labor and civil rights groups would have been sufficient to defeat Haynsworth had the ethical question not arisen. But in the highly charged setting in which judicial integrity was so salient a factor, their resources were adequate to make Haynsworth the first Supreme Court nominee since Parker to be denied Senatorial approval.

Two months after the Haynsworth defeat President Nixon submitted the name of G. Harrold Carswell for approval. Carswell, like Haynsworth and Parker, was a Southern Circuit Court Justice at the time of his nomination. In the course of the subsequent committee hearings, no conflict of interest charges or implications of judicial impropriety were raised. Although the furor over ethical considerations was not directly transmitted into the Carswell situation, the liberal–conservative split within the Senate was. Moreover, the momentum generated by their success in defeating Haynsworth tended to strengthen the alliance between labor organizations and civil rights groups, both of which opposed Carswell on the basis of his record on civil rights. Additional support for the anti-Carswell forces came from within the legal profession itself. Even though the American Bar Association Committee on the Federal Judiciary found him to be qualified, many prominent lawyers and judges objected that he "lacked the legal and mental qualifications of a Supreme Court Justice."[42] Although Carswell's nomination had attracted strong opposition, President Nixon refused to withdraw it from Senate consideration. Such a move would have been construed as an admission of defeat for the administration, and since it had previously suffered a loss of prestige over Haynsworth's defeat the decision was made to fight for Carswell in the Senate. The final vote followed party lines more closely than had the Haynsworth defeat; however, the result was the same. Carswell's nomination failed to win confirmation by a margin of forty-five to fifty-one. Among the fifty-one votes cast against the appointment, thirteen were from Republican senators. Seventeen Democrats (all but one were from the South) voted for confirmation.

Examples of group conflict over confirmation are relatively rare because most presidents give consideration to the possibilities of Senate acceptance before nomination. There have been occasions of withdrawals of nominations in anticipation of rejection, but usually nominees to the Supreme Court are men whose public life is sufficiently neutral to ensure Senate approval. Such approval would seem to guarantee that Supreme Court justices will be political moderates who have not "offended powerful groups."[43] Exactly who these groups are is not a simple problem of identification since power is relative to the position of other groups. In the years following the Civil War, during which the influence of large corporations on governmental policy-making was unchallenged, the influence of railroads in Supreme Court appointments was noticeable.[44] Today, such influence is lacking. Judging from the three most recent defeats of presidential nominees, however, it would appear that labor and civil rights groups have wielded considerable influence over decisions concerning judicial personnel.

The American Bar Association's Committee on the Federal Judiciary

There is one group whose claims to legitimacy in the nomination of federal judges has been firmly established: the American Bar Association. The Association has for years been concerned with judicial appointments because "lawyers are the only group of citizens that are in daily contact with the courts, they are the only group that are really able to judge qualifications necessary for good judicial material."[45] This statement has been accepted by the federal government to a considerable degree. Although the ABA has always sought influence, in 1949 it took a step toward institutionalization of its deliberations. In that year, the Committee on the Federal Judiciary was created to "promote the nomination and confirmation of competent persons for appointments as judges of the courts of the United States and to oppose the nomination and confirmation of persons deemed by it to be not sufficiently qualified."[46]

Prior to 1949 the ABA had constituted a Special Committee on the Federal Judiciary, but this body enjoyed only limited access. There was no way it could present its recommendations until *after* the prospective judge's name had been submitted to the Senate Judiciary Committee. Although the Special Committee had established cordial relations with the Senate Committee, the organized bar sought influence *prior* to submission. The Department of Justice, which assumed the role of handling most lower federal court appointments during the Eisenhower administration, was the agency with which the ABA's Committee on the Federal Judiciary had to establish rapport. Progress in this direction was begun during the last few months of the Truman administration and by 1952 an arrangement had been made whereby all persons being considered seriously for appointments were examined by the Committee on the Federal Judiciary before actual nomination. This procedure did not apply to appointments to the Supreme Court. When a vacancy on the Court was created by the death of Chief Justice Vinson, the Committee offered its services in screening potential replacements and was told that "the appointment of a Justice to the Supreme Court was a personal appointment of the President and that if the help of the Committee was needed it would be consulted."[47]   This decision was continued with the appointment of John Marshall Harlan in 1955, but with the appointment of William J. Brennan in 1956 a new victory for the ABA was achieved.

> Deputy Attorney General Rogers, speaking in Baltimore before the regional meeting of the Association in October, 1956, said that when Mr. Justice Brennan's name was discussed with the President, he asked what the American Bar Association thought about him. When he was told that the Committee had not been asked for its opinion, he directed that the nomination be held up until the Committee could report.[48]

Such an ideal situation is recognized by the ABA as not necessarily permanent. While enjoying semiofficial status, the Committee on the Federal Judiciary is still subject to the decision of the attorney general as to the degree of participation. A case in point is President Kennedy's nomination of Arthur Goldberg to replace Felix Frankfurter. On the day the nomination was made public, Attorney General Robert Kennedy called the chairman of the Committee on the Federal Judiciary, who arranged a telephone conference with the other members of the Committee who approved Goldberg. The ABA was not consulted until the president had made an initial choice, but was called on before the Senate Judiciary Committee began its deliberations. Similarly, President Nixon initially failed to submit the names of potential Supreme Court nominees to the Committee prior to announcing his choice. Following the rejection of Carswell, however, it was announced that subsequent nominees would not be named until after the ABA had investigated their professional qualifications.

Bar associations at state and local levels also exercise influence over judicial selections. The extent of such influence, of course, varies from state to state. Generally, it can be said that influence is minimal when judges are elected.

> Bar Associations find it difficult to win great influence in the choice of nominees for judicial elections because the election itself is so obscure as to be almost invisible. When judges are selected at the general election, they occupy last place on a long ballot and few voters know much about the candidates. When judges are selected at special elections the voter turnout is usually very low. In both cases the Bar has difficulty in making its weight felt.[49]

Thus, it is not surprising that the ABA has consistently recommended that judges at the state level be appointed.

The ABA is essentially a conservative organization whose leaders have traditionally voiced laissez-faire attitudes on economic questions and have defended the ideological position normally associated with advocates of states' rights. Schmidhauser has described at length the gradual shift in emphasis from federal to state courts which accompanied the Supreme Court's assumption that economic regulation is necessary. Until the Supreme Court's basic shift in policy following the Roosevelt reorganization effort, the ABA "felt that the important economic interests and ideological values were more reliably safeguarded by the federal courts."[50] Here the ABA was throwing its support to defenders of economic conservatism. As state courts began to defend identical doctrines, the ABA became more critical of the Supreme Court and anxious to protect the integrity of the states. In a sense, the state courts have adopted the policies held by the Supreme Court prior to 1937. This idea is supported by the research of Nagel, who found that state supreme court justices tend to be "substantially more conservative than both the administrators and the legislators on the economic issues and free speech issues."[51]

Competence, then, is not to be defined entirely in terms of judicial experience and honesty, but also as a reflection of the ideology of the potential appointee. The ABA was critical of the Warren Court to the extent that Chief Justice Earl Warren decided to resign his membership. On the other hand, the criticism of the Court by the ABA was more restrained than that of nonlegal groups. The canon of ethics of the ABA declares that "[j]udges, not being wholly free to defend themselves, are peculiarly entitled to the support of the Bar against unjust criticism and clamor."[52] Thus, although the Association supported a bill to end the doctrine of preemptive federalism, it opposed the Jenner bill, which would have restricted the appellate jurisdiction of the Supreme Court. The hostility of the Association toward the content of the decisions of the Warren Court was tempered by its traditional identification with defense of the judiciary branch. Such cross-pressures are illustrated by the debate in the ABA House of Delegates concerning the Jenner bill in 1958. Walter Murphy describes this meeting:

> Meeting in February in Atlanta, the ABA's House of Delegates had before it a resolution from its Board of Governors to have the association go on record against S.646. A strange and fascinating debate ensued, with the lawyers struggling to avoid the sharp horns of an ethical and political dilemma. On the one hand, many members felt obliged to rally to the defense of the Court as an institution, if for no other reason than to appear consistent with their 1937 opposition to FDR and their later support of the constitutional amendment to freeze the size and jurisdiction of the

Supreme Court. On the other hand, a great number of lawyers, especially those from the South, were totally out of sympathy with the Warren Court's jurisprudence and, in fact, could be much harsher in their criticism of the High Bench than Jenner had ever been.[53]

The final result of this internal conflict was a resolution which, while disapproving the Jenner bill, did not provide firm support of the Court. The ABA's criticism of the Warren Court brought it into conflict with groups such as the NAACP, the American Civil Liberties Union, Americans for Democratic Action, and the AFL–CIO, all of which were defenders of the Court. Indications are that the more conservative orientation of the Burger Court will result in a more confident relationship between it and the ABA.

INFLUENCING JUDICIAL DECISIONS

Influence over judicial appointments is not automatically translated into influence over judicial decisions. As presidents have frequently discovered, their expectations at the time of appointment have not always been fulfilled in the later performance of the jurist. This, along with recognition that judicial decisions have political consequences, "has led in recent years to an exhaustive search for determinants of judges' conduct."[54] One such study was conducted by Stuart Nagel, who surveyed state and federal supreme court judges in order to determine the correspondence between their "off-the-bench" attitudes and their official policy decisions. Nagel concludes that the jurists he studied "seem to be fairly conservative" and that

... the judicial conservatism revealed in the study can probably be largely attributed to factors of class, family background, prejudicial occupations, training, age, and ethnic characteristics. And the conservative off-the-bench attitudes seem to be reflected in the decisions reached by those jurists.[55]

Others have examined the impact of party affiliation on judicial behavior,[56] but the results of these studies have been inconclusive. Schubert and Ulmer each found partisanship to be an explanatory factor in the decisions reached by the Michigan supreme court when workmen's compensation cases were brought before it.[57] Adamany, on the other hand, found overt partisanship weak in the Wisconsin supreme court. He concluded that "situational factors such as family, socio-economic group, etc., influence the development of . . . [a judge's] party identification which then becomes an important psychological factor in shaping his issue orientations."[58] Likewise Nagel, who did find an association to exist between party affiliation and judicial decisions, writes that they may "correlate with each other because they are frequently effects of the same causes," which he asserts are "personal standards of value."[59]

While there is no question that the personal biases of judges, as nurtured by their social backgrounds, play a role in the motivational activity surrounding a decision, there is the limiting factor of identification with the Court as an institution. The judicial role is more explicitly formulated than, for example, the legislative role. There is a feeling of obligation to the Court as symbol of impartiality and impersonality which has grown from the common law tradition.[60] This commitment to the abstract ideals of justice, which is presumably developed after service on the Court, can explain the failure of judges, when compared to legislators, to present a high correlation between personal values and backgrounds and the content of decisions.[61] While such factors are important, they are less satisfactory as predictive devices than is the case in the legislature. Consequently, groups which have been almost powerless at the legislative level of the political struggle are sometimes able to achieve success before the courts. Indeed, Walter Murphy has argued that wealth, status, and potential voting power, which may be decisive during conflicts over legislation, may actually be disadvantages during the judicial process.[62] The ideal of equal justice under law has clearly been a factor in the extraordinary success of the Jehovah's Witnesses, organized into the Watchtower Bible and Tract Society. A religious sect drawing most of its membership from underprivileged classes, the Witnesses have been extraordinarily successful in forty-four of fifty-five cases before the Supreme Court.[63] Expectations attached to the role of judge also help to explain the effective use of the courts by the NAACP. Neither of these groups has enjoyed much good fortune in the legislative process, but both have found in the federal courts an influential check on the power of groups which are in a position to achieve better access to the legislature.

Obstructions to organizational activity

If institutionalization of the judicial role operates to the advantage of specified types of interest groups, there is still a considerable problem to be faced in the form of technical obstructions. Individuals lack the necessary financial resources required to pursue a federal question through the lengthy process of adjudication. Krislov reports that it takes two to five years for a case to reach its culmination in a Supreme Court decision.[64] With respect to the financial resources required to undertake such lengthy proceedings, he writes,

Gordon Tiffany, Staff Director of the Commission on Civil Rights, estimated the cost of a single trial in the district court with appeal to the
court of appeals and application for certiorari at $15,000 to $18,000. In
more intricate cases the costs are steeper. A federal district court estimated
average costs to the NAACP in cases "in which the fundamental rules
governing racial problems are laid down" at $50,000 to $100,000; *Brown* v.
Board of Education cost the NAACP $200,000.[65]

While some cases are the result of the initiative of individuals,
most are supported by organizations which can provide a staff of
lawyers able to devote continuing attention to the legal problems
involved. However, to acquire "standing to sue" it is necessary to
establish that an individual is personally damaged by a statute or
some other form of official decision. Justice Frankfurter explained
the position of the Court in *Coleman* v. *Miller*: "we can only adjudi-
cate an issue as to which there is a claimant before us who has a
special, individualized stake in it. One who is merely the self-
constituted spokesman of a constitutional point of view cannot ask
us to pass on it."[66] The immediate problem of the interest group in
the judicial process is, then, to recruit a person who is willing to
undergo the strenuous ordeal of extended litigation, and who meets
the requirements stated above. There is also the additional problem
of mootness. If an individual plaintiff's standing to sue is dependent
on a particular set of circumstances, a change in these circumstances
might result in a loss of standing. For example, if the parents of a
Catholic child complain that the teaching of the Church forbids the
distribution of the King James version of the Bible in public schools,
but before the trial begins the child withdraws from school, the question is moot.[67] These problems can be overcome by the use of test
cases and by reliance on the Federal Rules of Civil Procedure which
provide for "class action." Under rule 23*a* it is possible to institute
action not only for a single individual but for all persons who are
"similarly situated":

> If persons constituting a class are so numerous as to make it impractical
> to bring them all before the court, such of them, one or more, as will fairly
> insure the adequate representation of all may, on behalf of all, sue or be
> sued.[68]

Test cases

The use of class action—which, while somewhat unclear and
subject to dispute in its application, is relied on to enjoin an official
from enforcing a statute—eliminates the problem of mootness since

a plaintiff who has lost standing can be replaced by one who has not, without suspension of the original litigation. The advantage of class action is most noticeable in the case of the NAACP, which has made the test case the foundation of its legal strategy. Rather than operating primarily to provide support for individuals already involved in legislation—a technique used frequently by the American Civil Liberties Union—the NAACP has developed a strategy designed "to secure decisions, rulings and public opinion on the broad principle instead of being devoted to merely miscellaneous cases."[69] The success of the NAACP in employing this strategy stimulates its opponents into action designed to bar the organization from entering class action suits. Southern state legislatures enacted laws prohibiting the participation in litigation of parties with no demonstrable interest and forbidding the solicitation or encouragement of unjustified litigation.[70] In defending itself against such attacks, the NAACP avoided direct confrontations with state legislatures and concentrated instead on court action. In its briefs the NAACP has argued that an interest group has a constitutional right to use the judicial process to achieve its goals and that such a group has standing to sue even though it cannot reveal the names of individual members. In *NAACP* v. *Alabama*, Justice Harlan, speaking for the Court, declared,

> The association both urges that it is constitutionally entitled to resist official inquiry into its membership lists, and that it may assert, on behalf of its members, a right personal to them to be protected from compelled disclosure by the State of their affiliation with the association as revealed by the membership lists. We think that the petitioner argues more appropriately the rights of its members, and that its nexus with them is sufficient to permit that it act as their representative before this Court. In so concluding, we reject respondent's argument that the association lacks standing to assert here constitutional rights pertaining to the members, who are not of course parties to the legislation.[71]

The deliberate creation of litigation has advantages over spontaneous action which a well-coordinated interest group can maximize. Questions of timing, for example, can be brought more readily to advantage. To illustrate, the American Jewish Congress prefers to begin its objections to Christian celebrations in public schools well in advance of holidays such as Christmas or Easter rather than during the holiday season when an unfavorable climate of opinion might be more expected.[72] Proper timing can also be determined by the group's evaluation of the attitudes of the members of a court at a particular time. Rather than face certain defeat, it might be wiser to avoid litigation and the consequent building of unfavorable precedent, until the personnel or attitudes of the court have changed. Such planning is revealed by the efforts of the NAACP to have the Supreme Court declare restrictive covenants a violation of the Fourteenth Amendment. In seeking a writ of certiorari, which requires the approval of four justices, the NAACP had been denied the writ on numerous occasions. However, in 1945 the NAACP learned that Justices Murphy and Rutledge were willing to grant a writ, and sought to provide the "leverage with which to bring two more justices to their side. . . ."[73] During this time, test cases had been initiated in various cities; and at conferences held by the NAACP, lawyers for the plaintiffs compared notes to produce a consistent trial record, since there was no certainty as to which case would be the basis of a writ. Also, attention was given to the details of each case to determine which would have the best chance for a favorable decision once a writ was granted.[74] The ultimate victory of the NAACP in the restrictive covenant cases attests to the effectiveness of organizational preparation of cases.

Scholarly journals

Newland has shown that the citation of legal periodicals by the Supreme Court is on the increase; they have been accepted by the justices as a legitimate source of information and opinion.[75] It is indeed natural for judges to consult the writings of legal scholars, published under the auspices of law schools. Consequently, a group might reason that one avenue of access to the Court is through these periodicals. When the precedents in a case are unsettled, or when the precedents run counter to the goals of a group, such sources as will give arguments some form of learned status may be valuable. To construct a body of legal opinion in support of its goal of securing a judgment against restrictive covenants, the NAACP began a campaign to have articles critical of adverse decisions and emphasizing the social and economic inequities of covenants placed in law reviews.[76] Between 1946 and 1948 more than thirty articles urging the Court to reverse the substantial body of precedents which operated to the advantage of whites and their restrictive covenants appeared in law reviews.[77] The strength of the whites lay in the opinions of previous courts; the strategy of the Negroes was thus to provide a contrasting aggregate of legal theory. The same technique was used by interests which favored the state control of offshore oil. After the Supreme Court held in *U.S. v. California* that states did not own the submerged and oil-rich land bordering their coasts, critical articles appeared in the law reviews of the affected states, encouraged by the National Association of Attorneys General. However, New-land points out that in most cases the citation of law review articles is a minor part of the written opinion.[78]

The amicus curiae brief

By far the most frequently used technique of getting the policy position of a group before the court is the *amicus curiae* brief.[79] Under the rules of the Supreme Court, organizations are permitted to file briefs in support of one of the litigants even though the organization is not an actual party to the suit. *Amicus curiae* briefs may be filed with consent of both parties or by permission of the Court if consent is denied. In most state courts, consent of the court is required. The trend before the Supreme Court, until 1949, was to pay little attention to the rule of consent; and motions for permission to file were granted as a matter of routine. The latitudinarian construction immersed the Court in a flood of briefs, many of which were of little value in that they merely parroted the position of a litigant or stated preferences without achieving much more than emotionalism. After the "Holly-wood Ten" case, involving refusal to testify before the House Un-American Activities Committee, produced forty briefs on behalf of the defendants, the Court adopted a new rule which drew careful attention to the rule of consent.[80] This tightening of the rule reduced the number of *amicus curiae* briefs substantially, especially since the United States government, as a party to about half the cases before the Court, refused consent in nearly every case. However, the stren-uous objections of Justices Black and Frankfurter led to a further modification on the part of the solicitor general of the United States. Consent is now given when the applicant has a clear interest in the decision and when the brief contains arguments or other material which would not otherwise come to the attention of the Court. This balancing between the two extremes has had an effect on the number of briefs. In 1949, the last year of the Court's failure to insist on the rule of consent, ninety-one *amicus curiae* briefs were filed, but this number had declined to nineteen by 1952. In the years following the modification of the policy of the solicitor general in 1952, an average of thirty-six briefs per session has developed.[81]

The *amicus curiae* brief represents group involvement in the judicial process even when the group has not been involved in the institution of a case and has no control over timing and other strategic considerations. According to Vose, the following organizations are most active in the use of *amicus curiae* briefs: the American Civil Liberties Union, American Jewish Congress, AFL–CIO, and the National Lawyers Guild.[82] Each of these organizations is equipped with legal talent capable of developing arguments that may have been overlooked by the parties to the litigation, and, although the specific impact of a particular brief is difficult to ascertain, evidence of the value of a carefully prepared brief is available to the extent that judicial decisions make use of the material presented or judges base a decision on an argument made in an *amicus curiae* brief. For example, in *Illinois ex rel. McCollum* v. *Board of Education*, in which the Supreme Court ruled that the use of public school facilities for religious instruction violated the establishment of religion clause of the First Amendment, the brief of the American Jewish Congress was relied on by Justice Frankfurter during the oral arguments and in his concurring opinion.[83] Frankfurter's acceptance of the arguments of the American Jewish Congress may be contrasted with Justice Jackson's reaction to a brief of the American Newspaper Publishers Association in *Craig* v. *Harney*:

> Of course it does not cite a single authority that was not available to counsel for the publisher involved and does not tell us a single new fact except this one: "This membership embraces more than 700 newspaper publishers whose publications represent in excess of eighty percent of the total daily and Sunday circulation of newspapers published in this country. The Association is vitally interested in the issue presented in this case, namely, the right of newspapers to publish news stories and editorials on cases pending in the courts."
>
> This might be a good occasion to demonstrate the fortitude of the judiciary.[84]

Justice Jackson's comments indicate the futility of an organization's attempting to apply pressure in the course of judicial proceedings. Hostility is the most likely result of such tactics. On the other hand, persuasion presented in a cogent and informative manner may serve to influence courts in a positive direction. One attorney has stated his position on the presentation of *amicus curiae* briefs as follows:

> I have always viewed the function of the *amici* to take up and emphasize those points which are novel or which if stressed in the main brief, might dilute or weaken the main forceful arguments.
>
> I never thought there was much cumulative force in the repetition of logic by eighteen briefs. Unlike good poetry, repeated it has a tendency to bore. But a weak legal argument, with a moral quality, forcefully presented by an "outsider" will not detract from the force of the main argument. . . .

The *amici* should be providing the arguments that will salvage [*sic*] the judges' consciences or square with their prepossessions should they lean toward holding for us. . . .[85]

THE CONSEQUENCES OF JUDICIAL DECISIONS

A decision by the Supreme Court does not settle a question of public policy finally and for all time. At the most visible level, the Supreme Court itself can change its mind and overturn a previous decision. Some examples of judicial retreats from earlier decisions have been presented earlier. However, explicit reversals of precedents have been accomplished on as many as seventy occasions, one of the most noteworthy being the Flag Salute cases. In *Minersville School District* v. *Gobitis* the Court ruled that public school children could be compelled to salute the flag and recite the pledge of allegiance even though the children and their parents believed that this ritual violated their religious beliefs.[86] This case involved the Jehovah's Witnesses, as did the decision three years later, in *West Virginia State Board of Education* v. *Barnette*, which specifically reversed the earlier decision.[87] Usually, the overturning of precedents can be explained by changes in the personnel of the court, as for example in *Brown* v. *Board of Education*[88] which reversed *Plessy* v. *Ferguson*.[89] However, in the Flag Salute cases, three justices who had joined in the opinion of the *Gobitis* case publicly stated their error and practically invited the witnesses to try again.[90]

Methods of circumvention

Granted that groups which have been defeated in one court decision can win in another, a more pressing question is the degree to which a Supreme Court decision, considered as the law of the land, actually has an impact on policy. On this subject, Peltason has written,

A court decision has to be enforced, the judges' opinion requires interpretation. What a decision means is determined by group conflict after a decision has been announced and the opinion read. All this activity—enforcement, postdecisional interpretation, possible reversal by some other agency or the judges themselves—which follows a judicial decision is part of the story of group conflict, the story of the political process.[91]

What are the methods whereby a Supreme Court decision can be circumvented? In addition to the obvious technique of amending the Constitution itself, a long and complex process, interests which have lost the battle in the Supreme Court can win the war by modifying the application of the decision. This process can occur either in Congress, where interests not satisfied with a decision can achieve by means of legislation what amounts to a reversal, or in the lower courts that normally are given the responsibility of interpretation and application of High Court rulings. For example, in *Federal Trade Commission* v. *Cement Institute*, the Court ruled that the basing point system of pricing, maintained under the auspices of the Cement Institute, was a combination in restraint of trade. However, the cement and steel industries were able to "rally fresh groups to their support to revise or overrule the Supreme Court decision" by legislation protecting the basing point system.[92] Another illustration of appeals to Congress by groups seeking to reduce the effects of Supreme Court decisions is the tidelands oil dispute. State control interests had been told by the Court on three occasions that the national government had title to the submerged lands. However, when Eisenhower was elected in 1952, the state control interests were afforded an ally. President Truman had vetoed legislation establishing state ownership, but Eisenhower made good a campaign promise and in 1953 signed the Submerged Lands Act, which was declared constitutional by the Supreme Court in 1954. On this subject, Lucius Barker notes that "by passing the Submerged Lands Acts in 1953, Congress and the President gave to the state-control interest that which the Court had specifically denied to them, and in effect that which the Court had given to the national-control interest."[93]

Turning to the possibility of avoiding the consequences of Supreme Court decisions through access to lower courts, we must first consider the wide discretion allowed these courts. This discretion provides initially defeated interests with the opportunity to salvage much of what they lost before the Supreme Court. The basic advantage, discretion in application of rulings by lower court judges, is gained from the right of lower court judges to raise new legal questions after the case has been returned. Once new issues are created, the process of litigation can actually be begun again, with a final result that is not necessarily consistent with the original ruling. Of 175 cases returned to state courts between 1941 and 1951, 46 involved further litigation, and in slightly less than half these cases the interests that enjoyed a favorable ruling by the Supreme Court suffered a reversal in the state courts.[94] Even without raising new issues, lower court judges have on occasion behaved in a manner that constitutes overt refusal to follow a specific Supreme Court Ruling. After *Minersville School District* v. *Gobitis*, Judge John J. Parker of the Court of Appeals for the Fourth Circuit held the ruling invalid. Parker called attention to the confession of error on the part of three of the justices in the *Gobitis* case and the retirement of two others, leaving only three justices who still supported the decision. Parker therefore reasoned that the Supreme Court would support his ruling on appeal, which it did.[95]

Such examples of resistance are perhaps of less significance than the gradual erosion of Supreme Court decisions by hostile interpretation. The behavior of the United States district judges in the segregation controversy has had precisely this result. Whereas the *Brown v. Board of Education* decision represented a clear victory for antisegregation interests, the directions of the Supreme Court concerning the methods whereby integration of public schools was to be accomplished were a concession to Southern states. After the initial decision, the Court declined to issue a decree covering all school districts and stated that all cases would be returned to district judges for the promulgation of explicit plans for integration. The instructions to the district judges made it clear that primary responsibility for integration was in the hands of the local school authorities, provided a "prompt and reasonable" effort toward compliance was made. Southern district judges, who like most Southerners felt the *Brown* decision was a mistake, were naturally responsive to local segregationist pressures and were not inclined to risk overt violation of local belief systems unless no alternative existed:

> The judge can never forget that any action of his against segregation will threaten his easy and prestigious acceptance by the community. He has become a convenient target for political leaders anxious to impress the electorate with their own soundness on segregation. The judge who delays injunctions and avoids antisegregation rules is, on the other hand, a local hero; he will hear himself referred to as one of the nation's "great constitutional scholars," a man of courage willing to risk reversal to defend the right.[96]

A final method of circumvention is simply noncompliance. A court decision is similar to any other form of governmental decree in that the extent to which it actually effects a discernible alteration in the distribution of values and forms of behavior within a political community depends on the conformity of the declaration with the interests of dominant groups within that community. Consequently, many decisions mean little since "unconstitutional" forms of behavior are continued as if no official word had been spoken. Although *Illinois ex rel. McCollum* v. *Board of Education* held that the use of public school facilities for religious instruction violated the

First Amendment prohibition against the establishment of religion, "no changes were made as a result of the decision in some of the communities which had programs of religious instruction held in school buildings during classroom time."[97] In some states, noncompliance was based on rulings by attorneys general that no changes were necessary, but in others the decision was quietly forgotten. Where the dominant coalition of interests, institutionalized in state legislatures and other state agencies responsible for the administration of public schools, opposed the decision, compliance was left in the hands of those groups and individuals who had been responsible for creating the religious instruction initially. In rare instances were adherents of the decision successful in imposing enforcement of the *McCollum* decision.

In New York City, children were released from school time to be given religious instruction off the school premises, a distinction which the Supreme Court approved in *Zorach* v. *Clauson*.[98] Having granted the legality of religious instruction off school premises, did the Court thereby reduce noncompliance? It is estimated that about one-third of the religious instruction was being held in school buildings seven years after the decision.[99] Further, the *Zorach* decision has been used to justify injection of religious instruction into school training in a manner in no way related to the specifics of the decision. Bible readings and recitations of the Lord's Prayer were justified on the basis of *Zorach* v. *Clauson* even though such actions were undertaken on school property. On the basis of this evidence, Sorauf concludes that "especially in religiously homogeneous communities where there are no dissident elements strong enough to protest or begin court action, the *McCollum* and *Zorach* rules are evaded and ignored.[100] In 1962 the Supreme Court struck down the required reading of prayers in schools.[101] One year later this policy was extended to include Bible recitations.[102] Despite these decisions, however, there is ample evidence that noncompliance is widespread. Krislov observes that "there is probably no area where there is more actual violation of Court decisions than with regard to the place of religion in our educational system."[103] The dependence of the judiciary on others for the implementation of court-made policy is amply illustrated in a statement attributed to Andrew Jackson to the effect that "John Marshall has made his decision, now let him enforce it."

These comments are not intended to suggest that the Supreme Court does not make policy, but rather that the policy which it does make is either a reflection of dominant interests or a fulcrum for values which, though separate from the dominant interests, are not in conflict with them. Although it is untenable to argue for a permanent structure of political power on a national scale, it is as untenable to maintain that all interests are represented in each government agency to the same degree. As the relative position of interests alters, the Supreme Court can both encourage rising groups to continue their efforts and provide such groups with institutional support against the attacks of other interests.[104] Groups which lack political resources or access to other political markets may find judicial decision-makers more accessible and receptive to their demands.

> Thus, unions during the 1930's, and the Negroes during the past . . . [15] years, have given vent to their felt deprivations of economic and civil justice. In these instances, the courts have acted as leaders by improving the position of minority groups who otherwise would have had little chance to be heard or to have had favorable action given their goals.[105]

Judicial leadership, however, cannot be made effective without the support of other elements within the political system as well as that of the dominant interests within society. This support need not be manifested toward each particular decision rendered, but the cumulative effect of court-made policies must not transgress the limits of acceptability. When such transgression occurs, as we have seen with regard to the United States Supreme Court, the judiciary is forced to retreat from its unpopular position.

NOTES

*This phrase is taken from Will Maslow, "The Use of the Law in the Struggle for Equality," *Social Research*, XXII (Autumn 1955), p. 308.

¹Some of the earliest and most notable departures from the traditional approach to studying the judiciary are Jack W. Peltason, *Federal Courts in the Political Process* (Garden City, N.Y.: Doubleday & Company, Inc., 1955); Glendon Schubert, *Quantitative Analysis of Judicial Behavior* (New York: The Free Press, 1959); Schubert, *Constitutional Politics* (New York: Holt, Rinehart & Winston, Inc., 1960); and John R. Schmidhauser, *The Supreme Court* (New York: Holt, Rinehart & Winston, Inc., 1960).

²Max Lerner, *Ideas for the Ice Age* (New York: The Viking Press, Inc., 1941), p. 232.

³Fred V. Cahill, Jr., *Judicial Legislation* (New York: The Ronald Press Company, 1952), p. 7.

⁴Lewis A. Froman, *People and Politics* (Englewood Cliffs, N.J.: Prentice-Hall, Inc., 1962), pp. 89–93.

⁵Arthur F. Bentley, *The Process of Government* (San Antonio, Tex.: Principia Press of Trinity University, 1949), p. 205.

[6]Robert A. Dahl, "Decision-Making in a Democracy: The Supreme Court as a National Policy-Maker," *Journal of Public Law*, VI (Fall 1957), p. 279.

[7]Arthur S. Miller and Ronald F. Howell, "The Myth of Neutrality in Constitutional Adjudication," *University of Chicago Law Review*, XXVII (Summer 1960), p. 672. Although Miller and Howell's work was published over a decade ago, even a cursory review of recent Supreme Court decisions indicates that the era of concern over the rights of individuals has not yet passed.

[8]See the following works of Stuart S. Nagel for development of this point: "Political Party Affiliation and Judges' Decisions," *American Political Science Review*, LV (Dec. 1961), pp. 843–50; "Ethnic Affiliations and Judicial Propensities," *Journal of Politics*, XXIV (Feb. 1962), pp. 92–110; and "Judicial Attitudes and Those of Legislators and Administrators" (paper presented to the 1962 annual meeting of the American Political Science Association).

[9]*McCulloch* v. *Maryland*, 46 Wheaton 316 (1819).

[10]Samuel Krislov, *The Supreme Court in the Political Process* (New York: The Macmillan Company, 1965), p. 7.

[11]Herbert Jacob, *Justice in America* (Boston: Little, Brown & Co., 1965), p. 104.

[12]The Institute of Judicial Administration at New York University, *Judicial Education in the United States: A Survey* (New York: The Institute of Judicial Administration, 1965), p. 10.

[13]For elaboration on the role of partisanship in judicial decision-making see Nagel, "Political Party Affiliation and Judges' Decisions," *op. cit.*, and David W. Adamany, "The Party Variable in Judges' Voting: Conceptual Notes and a Case Study," *American Political Science Review*, LXIII (Mar. 1969), pp. 57–73.

[14]*U.S.* v. *Butler*, 297 U.S. 1 (1936).

[15]*Adkins* v. *Children's Hospital*, 261, U.S. 525 (1923).

[16]*Allgeyer* v. *Louisiana*, 165 U.S. 578 (1897).

[17]*Lochner* v. *New York*, 198 U.S. 45 (1905).

[18]*Adkins* v. *Children's Hospital*, at 545.

[19]Schubert, *Constitutional Politics*, p. 161.

[20]Senate Report 711, 75th Cong., 1st Sess., 1937 (Washington, D.C.: Government Printing Office, 1937), pp. 41–44.

[21]For an argument maintaining no relation between Roosevelt's action and the subsequent behavior of Justice Roberts see Felix Frankfurter, "Mr. Justice Roberts," *University of Pennsylvania Law Review*, CIV (Dec. 1955), pp. 311–17.

[22]"Warren Court Record, Burger Opinions Compared," *Congressional Quarterly Almanac*, Vol. XXV (Washington, D.C.: Congressional Quarterly Service, 1969), p. 129.

[23]See Walter F. Murphy, *Congress and the Court* (Chicago: University of Chicago Press, 1962), and Clifford M. Lytle, *The Warren Court and Its Critics* (Tucson, Ariz.: The University of Arizona Press, 1968).

[24]*Brown* v. *Board of Education of Topeka*, 347 U.S. 483 (1954).

[25]*Watkins* v. *United States*, 354 U.S. 178 (1957); *Yates* v. *United States*, 354 U.S. 298 (1957); *Sweezy* v. *New Hampshire*, 354 U.S. 234 (1957); and *Service* v. *Dulles*, 354 U.S. 363 (1957).

[26]Lytle, *op. cit.,* p. 7.

[27]Murphy, *op. cit.,* p. 246.

[28]*Barenblatt* v. *United States,* 360 U.S. 109 (1959), and *Uphaus* v. *Wyman,* 360 U.S. 72 (1959).

[29]Judicial behavior during these decisions is discussed in Schubert, *Constitutional Politics,* pp. 633–38.

[30]*Mallory* v. *United States,* 354 U.S. 449 (1957).

[31]*Escobedo* v. *Illinois,* 378 U.S. 478 (1964).

[32]*Miranda* v. *Arizona,* 86 S. Ct. 1602 (1966).

[33]Lytle, *op. cit.,* p. 81, citing *Boston Evening Globe,* 14 July 1964, p. 26, and *New York Times,* 14 May 1965, p. 39. Copyright 1965 by The New York Times Company. Reprinted by permission.

[34]*New York Times,* 25 February 1971, p. 22. Copyright 1971 by The New York Times Company. Reprinted by permission.

[35]Peltason, *Federal Courts in the Political Process,* p. 29.

[36]See Henry J. Abraham, *The Judicial Process* (New York: Oxford University Press, Inc., 1962), pp. 26–88 for a description of the various methods of selecting judges.

[37]Schmidhauser, *The Supreme Court,* p. 13.

[38]Joseph P. Harris, *The Advice and Consent of the Senate* (Berkeley: University of California Press, 1953), pp. 99–114.

[39]*Hitchman Coal and Coke Company* v. *Mitchell,* 245 U.S. 229 (1917).

[40]Harris, *op. cit.,* pp. 127–32.

[41]"Justice's Resignation First Under Impeachment Threat," *Congressional Quarterly Almanac,* Vol. XXV (Washington, D.C.: Congressional Quarterly Service, 1969), p. 136.

[42]"Senate Begins Debate on Carswell Court Nomination," *Congressional Quarterly Weekly Report,* XXVII (20 March 1970), p. 776.

[43]Carl Swisher, *American Constitutional Development* (Boston: Houghton Mifflin Company, 1943), p. 113.

[44]Schmidhauser, *op. cit.,* p. 13.

[45]Edward J. Fox, Jr., "The Selection of Federal Judges: The Role of the Federal Judiciary Committee," *American Association Journal,* XLIII (Aug. 1957), p. 685. The quotation is taken from an introduction to the article by the editor.

[46]*Ibid.,* p. 685.

[47]*Ibid.,* p. 688.

[48]*Ibid.,* p. 761.

[49]Jacob, *Justice in America,* p. 99.

[50]Schmidhauser, *op. cit.,* p. 79.

[51]Nagel, "Judicial Attitudes and Those of Legislators and Administrators," *op. cit.,* p. 6.

[52]Cited in Murphy, *Congress and the Court,* p. 255.

[53]*Ibid.,* p. 164.

[54]Adamany, "The Party Variable in Judges' Voting," *op. cit.,* p. 57.

[55]Stuart S. Nagel, "Off-the-Bench Judicial Attitudes," *Judicial Decision-Making*, ed. Glendon Schubert (New York: The Free Press, 1963), p. 43. Nagel notes that the small number of federal Supreme Court judges in his sample tends to make the findings of the study primarily applicable to state supreme court judges.

[56]Schubert, *Quantitative Analysis of Judicial Behavior*, pp. 129–42; Nagel, "Political Party Affiliation and Judges' Decisions," *op. cit.*; Adamany, "The Party Variable in Judges' Voting," *op. cit.*; S. Sidney Ulmer, "The Political Party Variable on the Michigan Supreme Court," *Journal of Public Law*, XI (1962), pp. 352–62; and Sheldon Goldman, "Voting Behavior on United States Courts of Appeals," *American Political Science Review*, LX (June 1966), pp. 374–83.

[57]Schubert, *op. cit.*, pp. 132–33, and Ulmer, *op. cit.*

[58]Adamany, *op. cit.*, p. 73.

[59]Nagel, "Political Party Affiliation and Judges' Decisions," *op. cit.*, p. 847.

[60]Peltason, *Federal Courts in the Political Process*, pp. 21–22. See also Schmidhauser, "Judicial Behavior and the Sectional Crisis," *Journal of Politics*, XXIII (Nov. 1961).

[61]Nagel, "Judicial Attitudes and Those of Legislators and Administrators," *op. cit.*, p. 12.

[62]Murphy, "The South Counterattacks: The Anti-NAACP Laws," *Western Political Quarterly*, XII (June 1959), p. 372.

[63]Clement E. Vose, "Litigation as a Form of Pressure Group Activity," *Annals of the American Academy of Political and Social Science*, Sept. 1948, p. 22.

[64]Krislov, *The Supreme Court in the Political Process*, p. 41.

[65]*Ibid.*, pp. 41–42, citing *Congressional Record*, 29 January 1960, pp. 3663–64; 30 March 1964, p. 6321; and 159 Supp. 503 (E.D., Va., 1958).

[66]*Coleman* v. *Miller*, 307 U.S. 433.

[67]This possibility is explored in Will Maslow, "The Legal Defense of Religious Liberty—The Strategy and Tactics of the American Jewish Congress" (paper presented to the 1961 annual meeting of the American Political Science Association), pp. 12–13.

[68]Class Actions: A Study of Group-Interest Litigation," *Race Relations Law Reporter*, I (Oct. 1956), p. 991.

[69]Herbert Hill and Jack Greenberg, *Citizen's Guide to De-Segregation* (Boston: Beacon Press, 1955), pp. 56–57. Cited in Vose, "Litigation as a Form of Pressure Group Activity," *op. cit.*, p. 23.

[70]Murphy, "The South Counterattacks: The Anti-NAACP Laws," *op. cit.*, p. 373. See also Peltason, *58 Lonely Men* (New York: Harcourt, Brace & World, Inc., 1961), pp. 56–78; and American Jewish Congress, *Assault Upon Freedom of Association* (New York: American Jewish Congress, 1957).

[71]*NAACP* v. *Alabama*, 357 U. S. 449 (1958).

[72]Maslow, "The Legal Defense of Religious Liberty—The Strategy and Tactics of the American Jewish Congress," *op. cit.*, p. 9.

[73]Vose, "The Impact of Pressure Groups on Constitutional Interpretation" (paper presented to the 1954 annual meeting of the American Political Science Association). Cited in Schubert, *Constitutional Politics*, p. 78.

[74]Vose, *Caucasians Only* (Berkeley: University of California Press, 1959), pp. 156–57.

[75]Chester A. Newland, "Legal Periodicals and the United States Supreme Court," *Midwest Journal of Political Science,* III (Feb. 1959), pp. 58–74.

[76]Vose, *Caucasians Only,* p. 161.

[77]Peltason, *Federal Courts in the Political Process,* p. 52.

[78]Newland, *op. cit.,* p. 73. However, Newland does believe law review articles can be influential on some occasions, as in *Erie Railroad Co.* v. *Tompkins,* 304, U.S. 64 (1938). In this decision Justice Brandeis relied heavily on legal periodicals in overruling a ninety-six-year-old precedent.

[79]For a more detailed discussion of the *amicus curiae* brief see Krislov, "The *Amicus Curiae* Brief: From Friendship to Advocacy," *Yale Law Journal,* LXXII (1963), pp. 694–721.

[80]*Fowler* v. *Harper* and Edwin D. Etherington, "Lobbyists Before the Court," *University of Pennsylvania Law Review,* CI (June 1953), p. 1172.

[81]Peter H. Sonnenfeld, *Participation of* Amici Curiae *by Filing Briefs and Presenting Oral Arguments in Decisions of the Supreme Court, 1949–1957,* Michigan State University Bureau of Social and Political Research, Working Papers in Methodology, no. 2 (East Lansing, Mich.: Jan. 1957). Cited in Schubert, *Quantitative Analysis of Judicial Behavior,* p. 74.

[82]Vose, "Litigation as a Form of Pressure Group Activity," *op. cit.,* p. 30. See also "Private Attorneys-General: Group Action in the Fight for Civil Liberties," *Yale Law Journal,* LVIII (Mar. 1949), pp. 574–98.

[83]*Illinois ex rel. McCollum* v. *Board of Education,* 333 U.S. 203 (1948). See also *Harper* and Etherington, *op. cit.,* p. 1173, and Maslow, "The Legal Defense of Religious Liberty—The Strategy and Tactics of the American Jewish Congress," *op. cit.,* p. 16.

[84]*Craig* v. *Harney,* 331 U.S. 367 (1947).

[85]Vose, *Caucasians Only,* pp. 166–67.

[86]*Minersville School District* v. *Gobitis,* 310 U.S. 586 (1940).

[87]*West Virginia State Board of Education* v. *Barnette,* 319 U.S. 624 (1943).

[88]*Brown* v. *Board of Education,* 347 U.S. 483 (1954).

[89]*Plessy* v. *Ferguson,* 163 U.S. 537 (1896).

[90]In *Jones* v. *Opelika,* 316 U.S. 584 (1942), Justices Black, Douglas, and Murphy, in a joint dissenting opinion, declared "since we joined in the opinion of the Gobitis case, we think this is an appropriate occasion to state that we now believe that it also was wrongly decided."

[91]Peltason, *Federal Courts in the Political Process,* p. 55.

[92]*Federal Trade Commission* v. *Cement Institute,* 333 U.S. 683 (1948). Earl Latham, *The Group Basis of Politics* (Ithaca, N.Y.: Cornell University Press, 1952), p. 59.

[93]Lucius J. Barker, "The Supreme Court as Policy-Maker: The Tidelands Oil Controversy," *Journal of Politics,* XXIV (May 1962), p. 363.

[94]"Evasion of Supreme Court Mandates in Cases Remanded to State Courts Since 1941," *Harvard Law Review,* LXVII (May 1954), pp. 1251–59.

[95]Murphy, "Lower Court Checks on Supreme Court Power," *American Political Science Review,* LIII (Dec. 1959), p. 1026.

[96]Peltason, *58 Lonely Men,* p. 9. See also "How Southern Judges Look at Segregation," *U.S. News and World Report,* 27 Apr. 1956, pp. 48–52.

[97]Gordon Patric, "The Impact of a Court Decision: Aftermath of the McCollum Case," *Journal of Public Law*, VI (Fall 1957), pp. 455–64.

[98]*Zorach* v. *Clauson*, 343 U.S. 306 (1952).

[99]Frank J. Sorauf, "*Zorach* v. *Clauson*: The Impact of a Supreme Court Decision," *American Political Science Review*, LIII (Sept. 1959), p. 785.

[100]*Ibid.*, p. 791.

[101]*Engel et al.* v. *Vitale et al.*, 370 U.S. 421 (1962).

[102]*School District of Abington Township* v. *Schempp*, 347 U.S. 83 (1963).

[103]Krislov, *The Supreme Court in the Political Process*, p. 132.

[104]This argument is pursued in Dahl, "Decision-Making in a Democracy: The Supreme Court as National Policy-Maker," *Journal of Public Law*, VI (Fall 1957), p. 293, and Peltason, *Federal Courts in the Political Process*, pp. 55–64.

[105]William C. Mitchell, *The American Polity: A Social and Cultural Interpretation* (New York: The Free Press, 1970), p. 283.

nine

Confident Occupational Groups

Earlier we introduced the concept of support orientation toward the political system as a distinguishing element among interest groups. You will recall that groups respond to political institutions according to their perceptions of those institutions' responsiveness to the demands articulated by group spokesmen. Groups can be arrayed along a continuum ranging from those which are confident that the system's bias is such that their demands will be processed with a high probability of favorable outcome, to those which are alienated and expect little or no chance of having their demands satisfied by the system. Here we will devote our attention to a particular subset of organizations to which the system is responsive—those organized around the occupational interests of their members. We will trace their historical development, examine the internal exchanges which result in membership support, and discuss the types of external exchanges in which they participate. Specifically, we will be concerned with organizations that represent business, labor, and professional interests. We shall reserve for subsequent consideration types of organizations which are not so clearly held together by the immediate economic interests of their members, and those which are alienated from the political regime.

ORGANIZED BUSINESS

For centuries businessmen have formed organizations when it appeared to them that they had a common interest that could be furthered by collective action. The beginning of the capitalistic system in the late middle ages, attended by the growth of guilds, introduced the idea that the making of a profit is, or should be, the fundamental motive underlying a business venture. Since businessmen want to make money, it is reasonable that the achievement and maintenance of a satisfactory margin of profit is a major purpose behind the formation of associations of businessmen. In the complexities of today's economic world, this is not as simple a problem as it once may have been. In some cases a particular segment of the business community engages in "unfair" competitive practices which may threaten to disrupt the stability of a market, thus harrowing the community into subgroups and creating the necessity for protective organization. In other cases, organizations may arise to resist the encroachments of an "outside" foe, such as a militant labor union or a different type of business which seeks to win away traditional customers. Whatever the nature of the threat, business organizations have come into being to cope with change.

Businessmen are indeed a heterogeneous lot, as may be determined easily by a cursory examination of the unbelievably long list of trade associations currently extant.[1] One discovers trade associations with such diverse names and manufacturing roles as the International Association of Photo Engravers, the National Association of Box Manufacturers, the Institute of Makers of Explosives, and the American Paper and Pulp Association, to name but a few.[2] The impressive range in the diversity of economic interests within the business population might well justify bewilderment at the task of answering such unavoidable questions as (1) what organizations speak for business? (2) what are the goals of the representative organizations?

These and related questions can best be approached by examining the evolution of organized activity within the business community. Broadly speaking, two trends can be detected, one leading toward fragmentation and one toward consolidation. In the former category we will consider trade associations and industry-specific organizations which represent the particular interests of a segment of the business sector. Occasionally, as we shall see, organizational fragmentation occurs even within an industry. On the other hand, organizations predicated on the underlying unity of interests among businesses have also developed. We shall concern ourselves with tracing these two patterns of activity and analyzing the factors which explain their origin and the nature of the goods they provide to their members.

Trade associations

Olson indicates that trade associations organized around a limited set of specific tangible interests and composed of relatively few firms are uniquely suited to organizational activity.[3] The limited size of their potential memberships, their common interests, the relatively large amount of material resources that they command, and their willingness to employ their resources in pursuit of a common good all facilitate organization. Membership, furthermore, is made more attractive by providing benefits of a noncollective nature.

> ... [T]hey have not only the advantage of being composed of rather small numbers of rather substantial or well-to-do business members, but in addition all the opportunities that other organizations have to provide a noncollective good to attract members. Many trade associations distribute trade statistics, provide credit references on customers, help collect bills, provide technical research and advisory services, and so on.[4]

In fact, historical evidence seems to indicate that the original impetus to organization within the business community was based on the provision of noncollective goods. In the early days of American industrial development prior to the Civil War, organizations of businessmen were usually occasional and local. Little attention was given to public affairs. The sporadic interest of these organizations in governmental problems is the exception which proves the rule. We read, for example, of the baker guild in New York City which, in 1741, was involved in a dispute over a city ordinance fixing the price of bread. Again, in the early nineteenth century, business groupings engaged in some of the internal conflicts predating the War of

1812: "State bank advocates united to support Jackson against the combined opposition of conservative business interests and adherents of the Second Bank of the United States."[5]

These isolated examples are by no means indicative of a trend. The disturbances were brief and the organizational response temporary. One of the most conspicuous stimulants of aroused business interests, the aggressive labor union, had not yet undertaken sustained activities. Although there were cleavages between employer and employee, the close physical proximity of the parties to a dispute and the relatively small size of businesses tended to contribute to the worker's identifying himself with the success of the business venture. The country was mainly agricultural, there was no genuine labor market, and such grievances as did develop were usually resolved in an informal manner.

A hint of things to come was given with the advent of the factory system in the 1830s. Labor–management relations became less personal as the size of manufacturing establishments increased, although the old "shop" system was still dominant. Local unions sprang up in several of the larger cities and negotiated with newly formed trade associations on questions of wages. This situation was found only in areas of high population density where a fairly extensive number of workers in the same industry was concentrated and where business matters were conducted on an expanding scale.

Although there are examples of employers' associations resisting labor's demands, such as the "open shop" movement of the 1830s, the economic conditions of the next two decades contributed to a general decline in organized activity. There were periods of depression from 1838 to 1842 and from 1855 to 1856. During these periods, the existence of a large number of unemployed workers gave employers a strategic advantage. It was not unusual for workers to underbid their companions to get or retain jobs. Under these conditions employers were rarely faced with the necessity of presenting a united front.

The pre–Civil War era, then, was characterized by the following conditions: Business associations were confined to urban areas. There were no national associations comparable to those of today, since industries had not developed the complexity which would require these larger organizations. During the period just prior to the Civil War, some industries began to acquire a national basis of operations. Railroads were becoming national in scope and the iron industry was developing rapidly. Embryonic associations in these businesses sprang up under the stresses of war. It is hardly coincidence that railroads and iron manufacturers were among the first to develop elaborate and formal patterns of cooperation. In the iron industry, for example, even as late as 1863 the most likely avenue of repetitive interaction was at the regional level. Machinists' and molders' unions initiated strikes which met with the resistance of regional managerial groups, which then tried to make contact with other regional associations. One of these groups, the Iron Founders and Machine Builders Association of the Falls of the Ohio, campaigned extensively toward the goal of cooperating with major producers throughout the country. To cope with union efforts, this regional group tried to interest iron manufacturers in a national blacklist of known labor agitators. A similar effort was being undertaken in the northeastern states by the American Iron Founders Association. These efforts were continued after the war and finally resulted in a truly national organization at the turn of the century.[6]

It is impossible to assess the precise amount of impetus to industrial development that emerged as a direct result of the Civil War; however, there is little doubt that the war years fostered industrial growth. Additionally, technological growth and market expansion stimulated the American business community. Between 1850 and 1880 the amount of capital invested in manufacturing increased by more than 400%, and there was a comparable rise in the total value of products. Some selected industries exhibited astounding rates of growth. For instance, promotion of agricultural implements increased 900%, machinery nearly 700%, and pig iron slightly over 600%.[7] Natural resources were exploited greedily while the entire economy expanded with almost bewildering speed. Accompanying this growth were changes in the structure of the economy. Encouraged by technological advances, enterprises became more corporate in nature. Rather than an economy typified by bankers, merchants, and other types of small units, a shift occurred to a manufacturing economy with mass production as the key. The door was opened to large-scale enterprise.

As the economy shifted to mass production, the informal problem-solving techniques of the past were no longer adequate. No longer were workers skilled artisans who knew their employer personally and strove toward the same goal. No longer was competition largely a matter of tiny competitive units absorbing a small share of the market. The famous trust of this period undertook well planned and sometimes ruthless attempts to reduce the number of competitors. Vertical and horizontal integration, pools to regulate pricing and output, and various types of holding company operations contributed to a virtual corporate revolution.

As the numbers of competing corporations within a single industry fell, the complexity of the problems which the remaining large-scale corporations faced increased. Two problem areas common to all firms within a given industry were market control and labor relations. The tendency for industries to be dominated by a few large corporations, and the existence of common problems, created a situation uniquely suited to industrywide organization. In Olson's terms, the small pool of interested parties and the collective nature of the goods they sought facilitated associated activity.

Following the Civil War, industrial interests were increasingly beset by labor problems. The specialization of labor and the growing complexity of industrial organizations resulted in a decline in the informality of interpersonal relationships between the worker and his boss. This, in turn, allowed them to drift into the rival camps which we recognize today as management and labor.

Each group came to regard the other not as a mutual contributor to the same end but as an enemy toward whom nothing would be yielded except under compulsion. Whereas unions had formerly been ephemeral and ineffective, great strides toward cohesion provided more reliable instruments of negotiation with respect to large businesses. The year 1886 was notable for the violence of its strikes. In the years following, organized labor showed employers and the remainder of the nation that it was henceforth to be taken seriously. This was the period in which the Knights of Labor realized its largest membership and the American Federation of Labor was founded.

The "open shop" movement

The most immediate response to this surge of power was the "open shop" movement which lasted until World War I. To guide this defensive effort, most of the major industries of the country formed associations whose major (or even single) purpose was to develop a counterattack, to counterbalance the new power of labor. Organization was met with organization. The intensity with which employers shared the attitudes of hostility to labor is illustrated by an examination of the goals of the Employers Central Executive Committee, which directed the labor relations activities of the building trades: "It would be well for employers to discourage labor unions by every fair means; by insisting on their right to employ workers independent of restrictions imposed by a combination of men...."[8] Under the persistence of a threat to their security, businessmen found the common interest, so long lacking, which led to the creation of national associations. Typical of the period, many of these associations included the word *defense* in their titles. However, the relative stability of organizations begun in this period may be attributed to the fact that the threat against which a defense was necessary gave every indication of becoming a permanent part of the businessman's environment.

There is no doubt that insecurity and perhaps fear were of primary motivational significance. To select one example from many, consider the National Metal Trades Association. In July 1889, the metal pattern workers struck on a national scale. At informal meetings, employers initially agreed, without exception, that there would be no concessions, irrespective of the ultimate cost of this decision. However, as the strike continued, the employers realized that, if they were to remain committed to their position, a more formal type of arrangement to police possible deviants would be necessary. Thus, the National Metal Trades Association was born. Several manufacturers, acting on their own initiative, had negotiated agreements with the International Association of Machinists, but at the first organizational meeting of the new association all prior agreements were declared null and void. The methods of defense and attack agreed on and later carried out indicate that the newly established association did not feel constrained by the rules of "fair play" adopted by some earlier movements. The National Metal Trades Association provided its members with "labor spies" (employees who pretended to be sympathetic to labor but reported all organization attempts to management), strikebreakers, and strikebreaking funds. The association recruited a skilled corps of officers who provided guidance to members threatened with labor troubles. In exchange for these services, members surrendered all authority relating to negotiations to the association. If any member compromised or began individual negotiations he was immediately expelled. The protective aspirations of the National Metal Trades Association are well stated in one of a series of advertisements that were circulated among prospective members:

> If unopposed, the unions of metal workers will develop sufficient strength to dominate *your* shop. . . . The National Metal Trades Association . . . is the most powerful defense organization in existence and the one most feared by labor leaders. . . . *It gives its members a feeling of security obtainable in no other way* . . . the mere fact of membership has prevented many strikes.[9]

Associations and the restraint of competition

Although the initial reaction to organized labor was perhaps the most spectacular of the disturbances in the business community, the problems unique to this reaction were only a portion of the total economic life of a businessman. Equally as crucial and infinitely more complex is the problem of market control. Unrestricted competition, while idealized in the "rags to riches" myth and formalized in that rather nebulous body of thought referred to as the American business creed, is ill-suited to the economic survival of a great many types of businesses. Operating with only the most informal channels of communication, members of an industry are frequently tempted to play one competitor against another. This can be accomplished by selling below cost to drive down a business whose volume is not large enough to enable it to absorb losses, granting special concessions (usually in the form of rebates or volume discounts) to favored customers to guarantee the maintenance of a stable clientele, and any number of other elaborate devices designed to reduce the rigors of competition. These practices occur both among the members of an industry or distribution operation and between two types of businesses competing for the same market. The frequent "price wars" among gasoline distributors and milk producers illustrate the first type of practice. To use the example of milk distribution, one large dairy within an area may offer an equally large retail customer (usually a chain store) a cash discount. This discount may be met by a second dairy, which will necessitate the improving of the first dairy's original offer. Thus begins a vicious circle of price cutting. Although lower consumer prices are frequently the result of this type of competitive behavior, it can be ruinous to businesses that cannot continue to operate at a profit yet are left with no alternative but to play the deadly game.

Associations with the primary purpose of self-regulation of competitive practices are as characteristic of the period since World War I as were the anti-labor associations of the previous period. While associations of this kind were on the upswing during World War I, there was a sharp decline immediately after the war. The prosperous 1920s saw another surge, which ended in the depression. Then, with the creation of the National Recovery Administration in 1933, the number of associations again increased. Under the direct prodding of the government and with the advantage of quasi-public status, "trade associations became the *sine qua non* for every industry."[10] The movement tapered off again after the United States Supreme Court ruled the National Industrial Recovery Act unconstitutional, but trade associations helped businessmen to meet the demands of World War II. Since the end of the war, the total number of associations has remained fairly constant.

Another aspect of the development of trade associations which is striking is the active role played by the federal government. The most obvious example of the active role of the government is, of course, the National Recovery Administration of 1933. Congressional declaration of policy stated that the purpose of the National Industrial Recovery Act was ". . . to provide for the general welfare by promoting the organization of industry for the purpose of cooperative action among trade groups, to induce and maintain united action of labor and management under adequate governmental sanctions and supervision, to eliminate unfair competitive practices. . . ."[11] To achieve these goals, NRA encouraged industries to submit "codes of fair competition," which, if approved, would serve as basic law for an industry. If no code was forthcoming, the president could impose one after notice and hearing. However, the law provided for the development of codes through representative associations. This essentially "carrot and stick" approach would naturally encourage those industries which did not have associations to organize as quickly as possible.

The NRA is the most outstanding example of governmental encouragement of trade associations. However, it is far from the only example. Many agencies of the federal government, and some congressional committees, have sought to establish a working relationship with the particular portion of the population with which they are uniquely concerned, and have instigated organization efforts to facilitate the creation of clear channels of communication and influence. The Department of Commerce, the Federal Trade Commission, and the Department of Defense, to cite several examples, have encouraged the formation of associations. In some cases the active intervention of a federal agency serves as the spark to ignite organizational efforts in industries that had previously been unable to iron out factional squabbles.

The outside influence of the federal government in contributing to industrial organization can be seen in the following example involving railroad and trucking interests. During the depression years railroads experienced competition which had hitherto been unknown to them. Shippers who normally used railroads discovered that there were many advantages offered by trucks, which could not be matched by railroads. Lower rates (except for long distance hauling), door to door pick-up and delivery, and comparable inducements enabled truckers to make inroads into the freight business of railroads. The railroads, which, unlike the truckers, had exceptionally high overhead costs, could do little to meet this competition. The amount of business lost to truckers continued to soar until by 1938 it was estimated that $2 billion annually was being lost.[12] However, before the condition of the industry had reached this point, corrective action by collective means was undertaken. In 1932, railroad executives formed statewide organizations to seek legal harassment of trucking firms. In this year the trucking industry had become ready to compete with railroads for the transportation market in terms of technology and business firm organization. A few rudimentary associations among the larger trucking firms had sprung up.

The tactics of the railroads, although restricted to regional efforts, were ingenious and successful. The Iowa railroads, for example, employed Joseph Hays to undertake the task of eliminating competition from trucks. His methods were to seek rigid enforcement of weight and length laws then in existence while encouraging municipalities to enact more rigorous restrictions. Municipalities were supplied by the railroads with weighing mechanisms. In addition, Hays sought anti-trailer laws that would practically have destroyed the long-haul capabilities of trucks. The cities that were selected for this type of pressure were located at strategic points within the state which would "set up a wall of these ordinances at the Mississippi River" and thus impede long hauls.[13] In support of these goals, taxpayers' groups (composed of people not directly connected with railroads) were urged to demand legislation. The railroad employees themselves were organized into an intelligence system to discover and report violations. Courses in the estimation of weights were given to the employees, who then roamed the highways seeking violators.

Unfortunately, from the point of view of the railroads, many of the most obviously discriminatory laws were declared unconstitutional. However, the reaction to the extra-industry competition was beneficial in terms of organized activity. Such organizations as the Western Association of Railway Executives existed primarily to pursue those methods presumed to act as impediments to the continued health of the trucking industry. However, these methods were certainly not productive of long-range solutions to the problems. Railroads began to look with increasing favor at the possibility of seeking a solution through the offices of the Interstate Commerce Commission. Ironically, the truckers were experiencing problems within their industry that made many of them favor regulations by the I.C.C. Unlike railroads, entrance into the trucking market requires little capital. Consequently, businessmen who used trucks for their own purposes found it possible to hire out for extra service, charging whatever rates the market would stand. This competition from intermittent truckers, when combined with the overt hostility of railroads, led the larger trucking firms to establish the American Highway Freight Association in 1932.

The organizational efforts of truckers were given impetus with the establishment of the National Recovery Administration, while at the same time they spurned competition among rival groups for the position of legitimate representative of the industry. The American Highway Freight Association was challenged by the truck division of the National Automobile Chamber of Commerce. NRA arranged for the rival factions to meet, but rigidly adhered to its demand that a single representative association present a code of fair competition. Faced with no alternative but to merge into a single unit, the trucking industry submerged its differences and created the American Truckers Association, still a highly influential organization. Here, the role of the government was paramount: ". . . that the NRA brought the industry together into a powerful association cannot be denied."[14]

Meanwhile, compelling forces were moving the railroads toward a comparable organization, or, in the words of Earl Latham, a "more perfect union."[15] In 1933, the post of Federal Coordinator of Transportation was created to cope with, among other things, the problem of the continued loss of business by railroads. Joseph B. Eastman, who served as coordinator, lamented the fact that the railroads ". . . form a single national system, but they are separately owned and the bonds of union between them which enable them to deal with matters of common concern are rather loose and ineffective, and the question is whether they can't form a more perfect union, as the states did through the adoption of the Constitution."[16] Eastman lent further support to the unity movement in his *First Report*. In this document he mentioned the American Railway Association, which was established in 1891, and the Association of Railway Executives, created in 1914. Neither of these organizations, said Eastman, was sufficient to provide coordination on a national basis. In addition to Eastman, the Interstate Commerce Commission and even President Franklin D. Roosevelt had criticized the unnecessary confusion in the railroad industry.

While the sources of government support were clear, Latham has discovered that ". . . the specific movement that led to the formation of the Association of American Railroads was started by a group of security holders."[17] However, the specific recommendations of this group were not well received by the Association of Railway Executives, which, rather than agreeing with the security holders, made a separate set of recommendations leading to the merger of all existing associations. This plan was discussed at a joint meeting of the Association of Railway Executives and the American Railway Association, and these two organizations were subsequently merged into the Association of American Railroads in 1934. A more ambitious plan, to bring all existing regional and national associations under the same roof, was discarded, and most of the offices of the new association were filled by executives who had held positions in the two major associations prior to amalgamation.

THE UNITY OF BUSINESS

Paralleling the trend toward the proliferation of industry-specific trade associations has been the development of broader organizations designed to represent the more general interests common to the business community at large. Organizations such as the National Association of Manufacturers and the Chamber of Commerce seek to speak for the interests of every businessman irrespective of his occupation. The National Association of Manufacturers and the Chamber of Commerce of the United States are not trade associations; they are not the special advocates of the grievances of any one segment of the business population. The existence of these organizations does imply some goals common to all businessmen, some goals that transcend more narrowly perceived occupational interests. Key, while not referring specifically to these two organizations, maintains that ". . . a network of common interests pulls the business community together when its security is threatened . . . within the business community powerful factors operate to bring conformity to dominant views. Unanimity is rare, but a predominant business sentiment usually crystalizes and makes itself heard on major issues."[18]

Major issues around which the entire business community can consolidate are necessarily very broad and general in nature. Basic challenges to established economic relationships such as those presented by organized labor in the early part of the century and the change from a laissez-faire policy to governmental activism in the 1930s are sufficiently general to stimulate a unity of interests in businessmen. More specific issues, however, affect various segments of the business sector differently. Foreign trade policy, for example, splits the business community into the opposing camps of protectionists and free traders.[19] Typically, the Chamber of Commerce and the National Association of Manufacturers are reluctant to press a specific set of demands when to do so would offend a portion of their members. To maintain support from their members they are forced to confine their public policy positions to issues over which there is substantial agreement among businessmen. Since such basic issues are not consistently before the public, these organizations display tendencies to fluctuate in the activism they direct toward the political system.

The National Association of Manufacturers

The history of the NAM is indicative of the type of generalized issue necessary to stimulate organizational growth and activism. Founded in 1885, the NAM originated during a time of relative tranquility between labor and business interests which existed even though the nation was undergoing a depression. The early activities of the NAM, which were certainly inauspicious by comparison with later periods, were almost entirely concerned with the promotion of trade and commerce. The relatively innocuous nature of these activities may be determined from the first NAM program. Included in its aims were the extension of home and foreign markets, establishment of the principle of reciprocity in national legislation, restoration and completion of the merchant marine, construction of a government-owned and -operated canal to connect the Atlantic and Pacific oceans, and the improvement and extension of natural and artificial waterways.

The NAM did not flourish with these goals. In 1896 its total income was $30,748.34 and its disbursements were $39,429.80, hardly indicative of a dynamic organization. We need make no more mention of the early years of the NAM until 1903, when the goals of the association underwent such a vast change that Truman feels justified in the assertion that "1903 marked the beginning of a new organization."[20] The reorientation of NAM goals can be seen from its statements that "formal cognizance was taken of the increasing activity of organized labor."[21] This increasing activity is well reflected in the astounding increase in the membership of the American Federation of Labor from less than 350,000 in 1895 to nearly 1,750,000 in 1903. Unionism was on the move and, among the specialized trade associations, an open shop movement was gaining momentum. The "new" NAM took the role of coordinating the open shop activities of the previously unconnected associations into a consolidated open shop campaign.

From the rebirth of NAM until the 1920s, practically all its energy was expended in leading the open shop movement, lobbying against labor-approved legislation, combating strikes, and developing a public relations program to "sell" its labor policy. Compared to its meager beginnings, NAM became an organization of impressive vitality. In 1904 NAM received $153,256.61 and spent $156,138.03, nearly five times as much as it received and spent in its first year; by 1926 these totals were nearly tripled. This period of growth and expansion is described by the Senate Committee on Education and Labor:

> ... the National Association of Manufacturers has taken the leadership in mobilizing the organization and resources of corporate interests ... during the two periods prior to 1933 when labor organization acquired strength and momentum under the leadership of the American Federation of Labor.[22]

So greatly were the efforts of the NAM centered around labor problems that a post-rebirth statement attributed its beginnings not to the tariff but to labor: "Labor was already united, labor was moving as one man; labor in splendid phalanx-like precision was moving like an army to the accomplishment of its great design. Capital was disorganized, had no coherent force, had no definite, united policy to interpose against the aggressions that might be made upon its interests."[23]

During the 1920s NAM activities became more diversified, more general and, although not relegating labor to a position of unimportance, less overtly belligerent. The "normalcy" of the 1920s, during which the business community did not see itself as being immediately threatened, had a depressing effect on the support businessmen accorded the National Association of Manufacturers. After increasing in membership from 3,600 in 1913 to 5,700 in 1922, NAM membership declined to a low of 1,469 by 1933. The temporary predominance of business values, typified by the laissez-faire disposition of the Republican administrations of the era, reduced the appeal of a belligerent, ever-vigilant type of association. Having achieved some hindrance of organized labor, and with the prevailing political atmosphere more in harmony with their goals, the frantic effort to impede what had appeared an impending social upheaval became unnecessary, and the NAM seemed to relax its efforts during the years of prosperity.

The depression and the subsequent advent of the New Deal shook the complacency which had pervaded American business interests. Business values no longer appeared to be consistent with governmental policy. Accordingly businessmen adopted a more militant posture. The NAM checked its decline in membership quickly and by 1937 had recouped a substantial portion of its losses. Its new role of "whipping boy" was clearly advantageous: ". . . by its uncompromising, bitter-end battle against Franklin D. Roosevelt's New Deal, the NAM rescued itself from the grave, reunited its membership, reinforced its treasury, and established itself as the St. George of certain benighted U.S. businessmen."[24] This long-range correlation between internal strength and external threat often leads to a slackening off after a specific legislative victory. Thus, NAM membership again suffered a sharp decline after the passage of the Taft–Hartley Act in 1948.

The Chamber of Commerce

The Chamber of Commerce, like the NAM, grew out of the insecurity which pervaded the business world in the period immediately preceding World War I. Businessmen saw themselves threatened not only by labor but also by the federal government. Instances of such presumably hostile attitudes were the passage of the Sherman and Clayton Acts, the vigorous prosecution of trusts by the Theodore Roosevelt Administration, and the growing demands of disadvantaged groups for increased regulation of business.

Certainly the Chamber was not unique in assuming this defensive posture. In addition to the organizations considered in this chapter, a direct predecessor of the Chamber, the National Board of Trade, exhibited a consciousness of fear. The National Board of Trade, begun shortly after the Civil War, did not develop as a sufficiently representative organization for the purpose of reduction of anxieties; otherwise, it is unlikely that the need for a new organization would have been felt. Prior to 1912, when the Chamber of Commerce was begun, several efforts to make the National Board of Trade representative of a broad base of business opinion were unsuccessful. The National Association of Manufacturers was actually a federation of trade associations with only auxiliary connections with business interests on a localized basis. Consequently, when businessmen expressed their conviction that the government was discriminating against certain economic interests, a common response was that there was no basic agreement among these economic interests and thus no organization that could present a reliable business viewpoint except on the question of labor.

The first overt step toward a remedy was taken by an official of the national government, Secretary of Commerce and Labor Charles Nagel. He wrote that when he first assumed his duties "there was an organization in existence which I think was called the National Council, or something to that effect. . . . After one or two meetings, I concluded . . . that if commerce and industry . . . were to organize with any hope of exerting an influence, it would have to be done upon a larger basis."[25] Nagel's dissatisfaction with the current situation was shared by a considerable number of local Chambers of Commerce, and after a series of preliminary negotiations, a meeting at the offices of the Department of Commerce and Labor was arranged for February 12, 1912. The purpose of this meeting, which was attended by representatives of local Chambers and the National Association of Manufacturers, was to devise a plan whereby the Chamber of Commerce could receive its credentials as a legitimate spokesman for the business community. This was achieved partially by means of the establishment of two general types of membership: organizational and individual. Each state or local Chamber became an organizational member and the door was open to trade association affiliation. An individual member was designated as any person who is a member of an organization that belongs to the national Chamber. At a more general meeting on April 22 at which President Taft was present, these membership regulations were adopted by delegates of 2,000 local Chambers.

This classification of membership was fortunate in that it provided the opportunity for the new organization to build on the established prestige of the existing local groups. In addition to this advantage, Harwood Childs, whose *Labor and Capital in National Politics* is the authoritative account of the history of the Chamber, calls attention to fortuitous circumstances surrounding its beginnings: "The Chamber idea seems to have taken place at an opportune moment, and the wide publicity given to the undertaking, the quasi-governmental endorsement of the move, the general feeling of insecurity among a large number of business interests during the political upheaval in 1912–1913 . . . served to facilitate somewhat the early problems of recruiting."[26]

From its beginning the Chamber has maintained a stable pattern of goals and, except for the years from 1921 to 1924, has gradually increased its membership. It has avoided the more sweeping type of membership fluctuation which the NAM has experienced largely because of the selective benefits provided to members. The Chamber is essentially a federation of local organizations. Individual members receive social benefits from affiliating with local chapters over and above whatever benefits they may receive from the activities of the national organization. Moreover, many of the activities of the national organization involve providing organizational and informational services to local chapters rather than presenting precise demands to government.

Due to the heterogeneity of business interests and the size of the business community, broad umbrella organizations such as the Chamber of Commerce and the National Association of Manufacturers are unable to sustain themselves solely in the capacity of representing business interests to political decision-makers. Only when fundamental challenges to very basic values materialize can these organizations effectively function as interest groups. Typically, when demands from business are articulated to governmental authorities, it is the smaller industrial or trade association that operates as a pressure group, "for the business community as a whole is not well organized in the sense that particular industries are."[27]

TRADE ASSOCIATIONS AND REGULATION

The portions of the political system with which trade associations come into the most frequent contact are the administrative agencies charged with the task of regulating business activities. These agencies, we have seen, often tend to develop an identification with the goals of their client groups. Thus, irrespective of frequent protests that a continued expansion of regulation will lead to the demise of private enterprise, businessmen frequently support certain types of government supervision. Marver Bernstein refers to the willingness of businessmen to accept regulation as the "basic contradiction." Bernstein explains that, although businessmen deplore interference in their affairs as contributory to an upsetting of the natural order, they welcome aid that will promote the health of business even if it involves regulation: "While the businessman describes the operation of the economy in terms of absolute laissez-faire concepts, he himself does not rely exclusively on these natural forces to preserve his position in society. Instead he seeks to utilize the coercive authority of government to enhance his interests."[28] Although some types of regulatory policies were instituted to satisfy the demands of dissatisfied interests within an industry, other demands for regulation of business originated with pressure from extra-industry interests that sought a more equitable position in the total economy. In such cases, the industry to be regulated vigorously opposes any restriction on its freedom.

The initial demands for the regulation of rail transportation voiced by farmers and small merchants illustrates this point. Although the rapid expansion of railroads after the Civil War was initially a blessing, the depressions of following years produced a change in attitude. Farmers and merchants, who relied almost exclusively on railroads for the shipping of goods, complained that rates were too high and that railroads conspired to eliminate competition. This agitation for change was manifested in the Grange, the National Anti-Monopoly

League, and numerous other protest groups, and was given legislative sanction by the passage of "Granger legislation" in several mid-western states. Railroads fought against this activity but were unable to stem a tide that culminated in the passage of the Interstate Commerce Act in 1886. The movement toward regulation was begun and pursued by shippers, while the railroads, the party to be regulated, were hostile: "the burden of sponsoring regulation was . . . shouldered by shippers; the objects of the original act to regulate commerce were shippers' objectives."[29]

If the history of regulation were to remain unchanged, there is every reason to expect that a relation of hostility between the agency and the regulated party would typify most aspects of the regulatory problem. However, it frequently happens that after an initial period of hostility, the regulated businesses adopt a more cooperative attitude. Lane presents the thesis that we can characterize the attitude of business toward regulation as hostility that is gradually replaced by acceptance and eventually overt preference.[30] What are the reasons for this modification of attitude? Substantial evidence can be marshaled to indicate that the promises of regulatory statutes to distribute benefits to relatively broad and diverse interests do not materialize. Edelman's survey of the literature on the administration of regulatory statutes indicates that "there is virtually unanimous agreement among students of the anti-trust laws, the Clayton and Federal Trade Commission Acts, the Interstate Commerce Acts, the public utility statutes and the right to work laws, for example, that through much of the history of their administration these statutes have been ineffective in the sense that many of the values they have promised have not in fact been realized."[31] Few policies have been pursued unless they have been approved by the well organized groups which are being regulated.

The "life cycle" of regulatory agencies

Marver Bernstein's "life cycle" theory of regulation is in line with Edelman's conclusion. Bernstein suggests that at the time of its creation, the intentions of a regulatory agency conflict with the goals of the regulated groups. The agency operates in an environment of organized, hostile interests, which, having lost the legislative struggle, try to protect themselves from what they regard as the "onslaught" of administrators. In this atmosphere of animosity, the regulating agency frequently adopts an aggressive or crusading resolve to meet its opposition and not surrender its ambitions.[32] However, although the regulated groups have lost the first round, as borne out by the passage of the enabling legislation, they can be influential both in the operation of the agency and in the securing of "sound" men as appointees. Even at the outset, fear was expressed that the Interstate Commerce Commission, irrespective of the intentions of the legislation, would become dominated by railroad interests. Representative John Reagan of Texas, long a partisan in the movement toward regulation, feared that "the railroad interests will combine their power to control the appointment of commissioners in their own interests."[33]

It is doubtful if so simple an explanation as suggested by Reagan could explain the administrative history of the ICC. Bernstein suggests that the momentum of pressure which builds up during the "gestation" period reaches a climax with the passage of the regulatory statute and begins a decline from this point. Support reaches a peak; the combatant interests are tired and have earned a rest. It is natural that these interests would tend to regard administration as following automatically from legislation. In the case of the Interstate Commerce Commission, the support of shippers simply ceased to exist; the ICC gradually committed itself to the welfare of the railroad industry and became identified as a "railroad agency."[34] In its growing stages the ICC developed policies that were gradually modified, as, for example, in the Transportation Act of 1920. The purpose of this act was to strengthen the economic position of railroads through consolidation and merger. The guidance by the ICC of the integration into a smaller number of systems was far removed from its beginning premise of prevention of unfair rates. Not the shippers, but rather the railroads themselves were protected.

Under such circumstances it is not surprising that defense of regulation comes from the business community which was initially hostile. Under a system which permits business in its more organized aspects to pursue its interests under protection of legal sanction, it would be economically unsound to do anything but defend a regulatory agency against demands that its functions be abolished or transferred. The senior author's study of the Florida Milk Commission shows that the most formidable defenders of regulation were the larger dairies while the demands for "free enterprise" came from loosely organized and ephemeral citizens' committees whose members were aggrieved that the retail price of milk in Florida had at times been the highest in the nation.[35]

In sum, the business community as a whole through its general organizations rarely enters into political exchanges at the governmental level. The occasional instances in which the Chamber of Commerce and the National Association of Manufacturers have actively pursued common business interests have resulted from challenges to the bias of the system at the regime level. When such crises do not exist, these organizations channel their activities inward to provide selective benefits to members or they become relatively dormant until the next crisis. Smaller trade associations, on the other hand, are most active and effective in articulating specific material demands to political decision-makers. Often the values they hold are shared by government authorities and result in a favorable bias. The material resources they command coupled with the technical information at their disposal render them uniquely suited for exchanges in which issues are construed to be technical problems of implementing goals shared by the organization and the authorities. The confident relationships that exist between these groups and public officials, along with the wealth of persuasive resources commanded by them, make trade associations very powerful interest groups in contemporary America.

ORGANIZED LABOR

The history of organized labor in the United States has been marked by alternating periods of rapid growth and near stagnation. It has occasionally been remarkably violent, yet one fact above all others makes the American labor movement unique among Western industrialized nations. The labor organizations that have endured in this country have not sought a restructuring of society. To be sure, they have tried to improve the working conditions and wages of their members, but they have not attempted to challenge the basic capitalistic structure of the economy. Perhaps this can be accounted for by what historians call the optimism of the American personality, or the potential for upward mobility, to use a sociological term. What this means is that individuals in the American labor force have never developed the class consciousness typical of their counterparts in Europe because the opportunity has always existed for them or their sons to win a place within the middle class. The strength with which middle-class values have been internalized by labor activists accounts not only for the nonideological character of the labor movement, but also for much of the success that labor has enjoyed. We do not mean to imply, of course, that unionization was achieved without strife or that labor organizations universally have been nonthreatening to established elites. But by and large the threats they have posed and the violence that has resulted have involved the distribution of profits and resources, and not the more fundamental question of capitalism itself. Consequently, it is no less than ironic that a labor movement which has exerted considerable energy in divorcing itself from revolutionary leanings has nevertheless been met with calculated attempts at repression of a rather violent nature.

In Europe, where much of labor organization has been more radical, we find few examples of strikebreakers and labor spies comparable to those employed by American industry. Violent struggles such as the armed battle at Homestead in 1892 between the strikers and hundreds of Pinkerton detectives hired by Carnegie Steel; the anthracite strike of 1902; the Ludlow "massacre" of 1913, where the government of Colorado served entirely as an instrument of Colorado Fuel and Iron Corporation in breaking the strike; and the 1919 steel strike, while startling, are not obscure exceptions to the rule of violence. These examples illustrate that with respect to violence, the formative years of unionism came only to a partial end with the Roosevelt administration; customary, indeed accepted, techniques in labor–management struggles were intimidation, assault, and murder.

Although the struggles involved high economic stakes, money was hardly the only issue. Laborers were struggling for status against dominant interests. Businessmen were fighting against a subversion of the traditional social system, against "anarchism" and "socialism." The great captains of industry were self-made men of the highest degree of conformity to the American dream. In accord with the reigning values of self-interest, they did not hesitate to employ ruthlessly all weapons at their disposal for the challenger's destruction. Since the struggles involved an adjustment of property rights, employers felt themselves entitled to police protection of rights sanctioned by law. Labor therefore had to fight not only property owners but police and government officials. This situation is well illustrated by the famous reply of a coal mine operator to a minister who pleaded for some concession to striking miners during the anthracite strike of 1902: "The rights and interests of the laboring man will be protected and cared for, not by labor agitators, but by the Christian men to whom God in His infinite wisdom has given control of the property interests of the country."[36]

Continued interaction leads to a stabilization, and union-management relations have exhibited a more mature attitude on the part of both participants in recent years. For years the right of workers to bargain collectively was resisted by violence, which, though perpetrated by employers, was perhaps sanctioned by a wider segment of the public. One of the directors of the Colorado Fuel and Iron Corporation at the time of the Ludlow strike stated that the killing of people was preferable to recognizing the right of unions to represent workers for bargaining purposes, and equated his opposition to collective bargaining with the principles of the War of the Revolution. The passage of the National Labor Relations Act of 1935, which gave legal guarantee of employees' right to bargain collectively, although strenuously opposed by employers, eventually served to remove from debate one of the most emotional aspects of the problem.

A short history of the labor movement

The unusual amount of violence and less overt hostility accompanying the American labor movement helped shape the history of union organization. In addition, factors emanating from the social value system, the structure of the economy, and the characteristics of the laboring population contributed to the development of distinctive features. Robin Williams notes that the absence of traditional social ties encouraged the commercialization of labor. In an economy of promising resources but relatively meager population, labor became a "market commodity in an individualistic economy."[37] As was the case with business organizations, we can point to scattered local unions before the growth of large-scale economy after the Civil War. However, not until American industry developed its mass production techniques did the wage earner, economically and physically separated from his employer, became a "commodity" in the capitalistic market economy. As is the case with any market, the job market fluctuated and workers had to face the insecurity of losing their jobs.

Industrialization and "first generation" factory workers

Industrialization during and after the Civil War contributed not only to insecurity concerning workers' tenure, but also to the development of a large labor force as a permanent part of the economy. This rapid transformation of the economy produced a group of "first generation" factory workers. Most of the new workers did not come from working-class families since these were relatively few, but rather were the sons of farmers. Factory discipline was often demanding and constituted a severe break with former styles of life. Not only were hours long and wages low, but restraint of personal freedom was severe; working conditions were frequently unsanitary or unsafe and work rules humiliating.[38] Thus, while economic insecurity contributed to the rise of unionism, the status insecurities associated with a rapid and total break with prior life-style made economic determinism a shallow explanatory system. Although the law assumed equality in bargaining, the lone worker was not able to bargain with his employer on an equal basis. A device which would make it possible for the worker to "fight back" would allow him to improve his feeling of worth, to achieve "the erect posture of something like a human being."[39] Vincent and Mayers believe that "this is the worker's main status achieving device; without it, he is helpless before automatic machinery and forces he cannot control."[40]

The National Labor Union and the Knights of Labor

The drive toward unionism has been hampered since its inception by a heterogeneous labor population. Not only did the workers have no factory experience, but they were recruited from both European and American communities. Hence, ethnic cleavages impeded the formation of a group of people with a sufficiency of shared attitudes leading to the creation of a cohesive organization. As Robin Williams says,

> . . . the labor force was constituted mainly of heterogeneous, unorganized, relatively unskilled workers without factory experience, who hoped soon to escape from wage work. They were spread over a vast territory, often disunited in creed and language, subject to incessant shifts in the labor market and rapid technological innovations.[41]

These factors, when combined with the apparent conformity by workers to the ideals of individual responsibility and the departure from the ranks of labor through personal effort, reduced the chances of achieving a "class consciousness."

The social background of the laboring population was reflected in the failures of several serious post–Civil War efforts to form a national labor organization. In 1866 the National Labor Union, a loose confederation of local unions, a few national trade unions, and reform organizations not strictly concerned with labor problems, was organized. The National Labor Union was never able to develop a clear idea of what it sought and consequently concerned itself with a variety of "causes" such as land reform and cooperatives. Unable to develop a trade union program, it nevertheless undertook direct political action by organizing the National Labor Reform Party and making a nomination for the presidency in 1872. Most of its union members had little interest in the reformist goals of the organization and, after a series of disputes, withdrew.

The same sort of vagueness of purpose characterized the Knights of Labor. Originally a secret organization, the Knights experienced a rapid increase in membership during the decade of the 1880s. Originally made up of local labor organizations, during its period of growth it expanded into the West and diluted its membership with farmers, small businessmen, and others who had little interest in the immediate problems of the wage earner. Under its rallying slogan of "an injury to one is the concern of all," the Knights attracted 700,000 members by 1886—the equivalent of approximately 10% of the labor force.[42] The Knights experienced some success in negotiating agreements with corporations but were generally disclined to use the strike for the achievement of short-term gains. Rather than concentrating on the immediate welfare of the job-conscious worker, the leaders sought a more general and far-reaching goal: the substitution of a cooperative society for the wage system. This goal was, at least formally, based on the assumption that wage earners and other disadvantaged segments of the population could achieve a unity of interest which could be institutionalized in the common brotherhood of one union.

This ideal dictated a pattern of organization which proved to be unworkable. If they were to be one big union they had to admit everyone, but at the same time the natural trend toward occupational particularism could not be neglected. While the ideals of the union required one pattern of organization, its success depended on another. Hence, the structure of the Knights consisted of both "mixed" local assemblies and "trade" locals. The mixed local contained every type of wage earner within a particular area and was found generally in rural or semirural locations, while the trade locals were dominant in the cities. This effort to accommodate occupational groupings contributed to conflict between the skilled workers, who began to leave the mixed locals and form autonomous trade unions, and those who clung rigorously to the ideal of fundamental unity. The utopian goals of the Knights were not in harmony with the needs of its union membership, and the resultant organizational structure enhanced this ideological cleavage.[43] The quick surge in membership was followed by an equally rapid decline. Terence V. Powderly, the Grand Master, recognized the transient appeal of the organization's stated goals by remarking that, of the 700,000 members "at least 400,000 came in from curiosity and caused more damage than good." By 1893 the membership had declined to 74,635. Although the Knights of Labor continued to exist until 1917, its membership was taken over almost entirely by socialist and other reform groups.

The failures of these early organizations to sustain themselves can be explained in terms of the goals they pursued and the benefits they provided (or failed to provide) their members. To maintain a reform-ist organization members must share a common ideological commit-ment to the goals of the group. In lieu of immediate material benefits, members must be sufficiently committed to the cause to be satisfied with symbolic or expressive goods. It is obvious that such a commit-ment was lacking in these early organizations. Thus, the nature of their goals, the heterogeneous interests that they attempted to repre-sent, and their failure to provide either selective benefits or sufficient material collective benefits resulted in the failures of both the National Labor Union and the Knights of Labor.

The American Federation of Labor

In 1886, however, an organization was formed which was more limited in its immediate economic objectives and conservative in its ideology. The American Federation of Labor believed in the capital-istic system and worked to improve the lot of the worker within that system. While seeking the avoidance of more radical doctrines of class warfare or the abolition of capitalism, the AFL sought to use to their fullest advantage such short-term tactics as the strike and picketing. Further, an implicit premise on the part of the leadership was that the occupation of laborer was one of relative permanence. Accepting the status, the objectives were the improvement of that status rather than departure from it. This "business unionism," as it has come to be called, was more in harmony with the needs of the labor force. In terms of organizational response to insecurity, it offered a more tangible set of benefits than the promise of a new society. AFL goals developed not only as a response to the demands of a clientele, but also as a result of the restrictions placed on the labor movement by the environment. These goals developed in a period characterized by hostile public sentiment and antagonistic employer attitudes. The president of the United States, as well as the governors of some states, used troops against strikers. Laws were passed limiting the effect of boycotts and strikes. The Sherman Act, passed presumably to prevent illegal combinations by corporations, was applied by the courts against combinations of workers, hence against the idea of the legality of the union.

Under such circumstances it is understandable that Gompers and the other leaders tended to adopt a laissez-faire approach to the use of the government for the furtherance of the position of organized labor. While the AFL did seek to prevent the use of government agencies by corporations to the disadvantage of labor, it rarely sought governmental institutions as positive allies. Blocked on the political front, Gompers led the AFL into a strategy aimed at building union strength to the point at which a successful direct relation with the employers could be achieved. This involved building strong, financially sound unions which could bargain from a position of strength. The tactics were thus to increase the scope of unionization while at the same time disassociating labor from extremist elements, to build public support and tolerance for the time when labor would find itself engaged in a struggle with management.

In contrast to the Knights of Labor, the AFL was organized along craft lines. Each participating union had its own constitution and rules for internal government. In no case were people who were not working at the trade but sympathetic with the aims of the union permitted to join. The restricted aims and restricted membership of the AFL proved to be a durable basis for survival. In contrast to previous depression periods, the unions affiliated with the AFL held their own during the severe depression of the 1890s. These early years were not favorable to the continued existence of union organization. Unsuccessful strikes such as the Pullman, the extension of the use of the injunction by the courts, rivalry from socialist and those interested in forming a labor party, and depressed economic conditions contributing to intense employer hostility kept AFL membership stationary from 1892 to 1898. However, that membership was stable rather than declining shows the success of the AFL as contrasted with earlier experiences of unions during depressions. The return of prosperity at the beginning of the twentieth century saw AFL membership increase at a rapid rate, from less than 300,000 in 1898 to more than 1,675,000 in 1904. That the AFL's particular brand of unionism appealed to the rank and file workers can be seen not only from its membership increase of approximately 360% but also from the fact that the total membership in unions in 1904 was 2,022,300. Thus, AFL membership included all but a fraction of the unionized workers in the country.[45]

The early successes enjoyed by AFL-affiliated unions can be attributed to two factors. First, they were organized along craft lines. This meant that each local union was relatively small, and members benefited from their association with a small group having interests. Moreover, selective social benefits were more easily gained from such an association than from one with a large heterogeneous pool of members at the local level. As we shall presently see, it was necessary for larger organizations of workers to institute coercive sanctions to maintain their level of membership. Second, by focusing on areas where immediate benefits could be won, and by concentrating on economic tactics such as strikes, unions were able to win both material and symbolic benefits for their members.

From 1905 until World War I, unions met increasing resistance from employers, and they failed to make any appreciable gains in terms of overall membership. This was also a period during which organized labor was faced with internal dissension as a result of the militant and radical Industrial Workers of the World, or "wobblies," as they came to be known. Although the IWW never exceeded 50,000 members, its militant character was a direct challenge to the conservative business unionism of the AFL and to the craft basis of organization as well.[46] Shortly before World War I the AFL again began to add to its membership and to win benefits for constituent unions. During this period too, labor won two significant although largely symbolic victories in the political sphere. In 1913 the Department of Labor was formed, thereby bestowing a degree of legitimacy to organized labor that it had hitherto lacked. But not until the 1930s did labor begin to assert itself politically through this department to win material benefits. Prior to this time the department's principal activities were in the fields of immigration, naturalization, and the collection of statistics.[47] More suggestive of tangible reward, at least in intention, was the Clayton Act of 1914, which exempted unions from prosecution as conspiracies in restraint of trade and which attempted to limit the use of injunctions by federal courts. Although referred to by Gompers as labor's "Magna Charta," hostile treatment by the courts soon made it evident that the Clayton Act promised more than it was able to deliver.

During World War I, the position of the AFL was enhanced by its prompt assurance of cooperation with the government in the mobilization effort. In exchange for the removal of restrictions and suspensions that might hamper the war effort, the principle of labor representation on government agencies was accepted. Gompers became a member of the advisory commission to the Council of National Defense, and other labor leaders were appointed to most of the emergency war boards created by the government. In addition, in those industries which the government operated for the duration of the war, sanction was given to the right of workers to undertake collective bargaining. Under such favorable auspices AFL membership surged from 2,100,000 in 1915 to a peak of 4,000,000 in 1920.

Postwar reaction

Although labor, and the AFL in particular, emerged from the war in a strengthened position, these advantages were short in duration. Several major trends during the "roaring twenties" present us with the paradox of decline in membership during a period of prosperity. After the enforced truce between labor and management, active government participation in labor relations ended, releasing the unions from wartime restraints. With the continued expansion in business following the armistice, workers continued to join unions in increasing numbers until the peak year of 1920. This expansion brought renewed efforts to extend collective bargaining, which in turn produced many bitter disputes. In 1919, over four million workers were involved in strikes, many of which were to obtain or strengthen collective bargaining arrangements. Particularly significant was the union organizing campaign in the steel industry. While unionization had been successful in most of the industries connected with the war effort, industrial relations in the steel industry had not altered. At the 1918 convention of the AFL, those unions having membership in the steel industry appointed a special committee for the purpose of organizing in iron and steel factories. This campaign met with widespread success, and the employers responded with the discharge of the new union members. Led by U.S. Steel, the industry remained firm in its open shop position, and a strike involving over 350,000 workers was called. For reasons to be discussed later, the strike failed and the workers gradually returned to their jobs.

It was clear that the battle lines were being drawn over the issue of the open shop. President Wilson sought to reduce the animosity by calling a labor–management conference in October 1919, but this conference immediately split over the issue of collective bargaining and broke up with nothing achieved. However, the success of U.S. Steel encouraged an open shop movement similar to the one at the beginning of the century. Manufacturers' associations, chambers of commerce, bankers' and front-type citizens' groups, and even the National Grange united in supporting the "American plan" to prevent union organization. Open shop organizations thrived in every major industrial center in the country, conducting "patronize the open shop" campaigns, supplying employers with blacklists of union members, and furnishing money and strikebreakers to employers involved in strikes.

Unions began to lose their wartime and immediate postwar gains under the onslaught of anti-union drives and wage cuts which were introduced during the brief recession of 1921 and 1922. The larger packing companies declared themselves no longer bound by the union agreement accepted during the war, they established company unions to subvert the Amalgamated Meat Cutter and Butcher Workmen, and they restored the packing industry to the open shop. The seamen's union lost a two-month strike and was reduced to one-fifth its former size. In Chicago, the Illinois Manufacturers Association and the Chicago Chamber of Commerce were successful in maintaining open shop conditions, and even the organized building trades could not escape the anti-union drives.

What was the response of the unions? As the AFL saw its once secure position under constant and successful attack, what were the countermeasures undertaken to reduce the severity of the threat? The AFL was poorly equipped to serve as an adequate organization in this hostile environment. Following its earlier period of aggressiveness, the AFL chose now to revert to its traditional attitude. With respect to AFL doctrine, Key has noted that "dogmas, philosophies, and ideas have a strength of their own,"[48] indicating that the idea of business unionism, while not expedient under the circumstances, was rigidly adhered to beyond its period of usefulness.

Although the reluctance to go against the grain certainly contributed to the AFL's doctrine, there is a relationship between structure and ideology which cannot be overlooked. That the AFL tended to grow "old and comfortable" during the prosperous decade of the 1920s may be attributed partially to its strength among skilled craftsmen.[49] Although it included some industrial unions such as coal mining and women's garment industries, the core of its strength lay with the skilled craftsmen such as those in the building trades, certain branches of the metal industries, and the printing trades. The members of these craft unions were usually concentrated in smaller enterprises and hence did not face the problem of bargaining with giant corporations. The craft form of organization, on the other hand, could not take into account the burgeoning of semiskilled workers in the new industrial giants. In the automobile, steel, rubber, and electrical industries, for example, new machines and processes were substituting semiskilled machine tenders for skilled craftsmen working with tools. Machinery and a rigid division of labor had largely broken down craft skills. In any mass production industry a minority of skilled workers remained, often submerged in a mass of unskilled and semiskilled workers. However, this minority of skilled craftsmen included men trained in many different skills, who, under AFL organizing rules, were divided into national unions built around the particular crafts. Without legal recognition of the right to organize, and in the face of determined corporation opposition, successful organization of the mass production industries required the ability to win bitter strikes. The diffusion of power demanded by the craft system proved incapable of resisting the concentrated attack of the company.

The steel strike of 1919 is a notable example of the inability of the craft-oriented AFL to cope with the stubborn resistance of a giant corporation. Further, it is clear that the AFL failed to throw its full power behind the strike. This suggests that the AFL was less than eager to organize the mass production industries. While each union would gain if more members were added, there was the possibility that a torrent of semiskilled workers flowing into the AFL would strengthen the position of semiskilled workers already in the federation, such as the miners and garment workers, against the dominant craft union leadership. Moreover, as McConnell points out,

> . . . a very real tactical advantage accrued to organizations with small constituencies and limited objectives. Thus, a union with a relatively small number of skilled craftsmen could demand—and get—substantial economic benefits from an employer who also used the services of a large number of unskilled workers.[50]

Although AFL membership was declining, most of the craft unions, subsequent to reversals in the early postwar years, were able to maintain and in some cases increase their membership. The printing and building trades, for example, had higher memberships in 1929 than at any time in the past. These unions had always formed the dominant wing of the AFL power structure. On the other hand, the industrial unions within the AFL suffered serious losses in membership. Membership in coal mining was reduced by half; John L. Lewis of the coal miners made the only serious challenge to the reelection of Gompers in 1921. Thus, although AFL membership fell under the impact of employers' offensives and dipped below three million for most of the decade of the prosperous twenties, this occurrence strengthened the position of craft unions within the AFL. Thus, whole industries, such as automobiles and rubber, remained untouched. In these industries employers took the extra precaution of adopting programs which they hoped would make unions unnecessary. The twenties marked the peak of "company unions" whereby the need to organize was recognized but control was retained by management. Withdrawing into the industries of entrenched strength, the AFL failed to grow, proved incapable of organizing the giants of American industry, and seemed perfectly satisfied.

Industrial unionism and political action

In the mid-thirties, following depression years in which even the skilled craft unions experienced declining memberships, two developments occurred which fundamentally changed the character of the labor movement. In 1935 Congress passed the National Labor Relations Act, also known as the Wagner Act. Among its provisions was the stipulation that employers must recognize and bargain with any union selected by a majority of its employees in an open election. Thus, not only was further legitimacy bestowed on labor organizations, but that legitimacy was backed up with the authority of the federal government. Furthermore, the Wagner Act obviated the need for unions to engage in strikes to gain recognition from a company, and it specifically legalized the closed shop, resolving that point of contention between unions and employers. The second major change to occur in the thirties was the formation of the Congress of Industrial Organizations in 1938. The CIO represented a significant departure from the business unionism of the AFL, for it organized unions along industrial rather than craft lines and displayed less reluctance to engage in direct political activity than did the conservative AFL.

Stimulated by pro-labor government policy and by active organizational campaigns by both the AFL and the CIO, union membership grew dramatically in the late 1930s. By 1940 total union strength was 8,500,000, of which 4,900,000 were within the AFL and 2,800,000 were within the CIO.[51] During World War II the unions continued to flourish so that by 1945 total membership stood at 13,400,000. More important perhaps than mere numerical strength was the acceptance of unions as established organizations within society. "During the war," McConnell states, "it would have been correct to say that labor had achieved a new status in society and that unions had won their fundamental objective of legitimacy."[52] In addition, the scale of organization had changed. In spite of the craft basis of most of the AFL unions, and even though locals remained the basic building blocks of both the AFL and the CIO, the scale of organization was greatly increased. No longer were unions small groups of relatively homogeneous workers. They had become large groups, sometimes numbering a thousand or more members in a given local. Thus, the selective incentives of small group affiliation had gradually ceased to exist. Compulsory membership had replaced positive inducement as the primary factor in motivating individual workers to join. As Olson observes, "A rational worker will not voluntarily contribute to a [large] union providing a collective benefit since he alone would not perceptibly strengthen the union, and since he would get the benefits of any union achievements whether or not he supported the union."[53]

After the advantages of organizing small groups of skilled craftsmen had passed and before the federal government had established rules of organizing, strikes, picket lines, and violence had been the primary weapons of compulsion available to union leaders. It had been necessary to force individual employers to accede to closed shop demands through such means, and it had been necessary to force reluctant workers to cooperate with union policy in doing so. With the passage of the Wagner Act, however, all that changed. The legitimacy the act bestowed on unions was more than symbolic. By establishing procedural rules by which workers could be organized and by lending government sanction to compulsory membership in closed shop agreements, it profoundly altered the character of the environment in which unions operated and changed the nature of the resources union leaders needed to employ to achieve their goals. Persuasive resources replaced sanctions in exchanges with potential members. Although instances of violence still occur, they are less frequent and of lower intensity than they had been prior to the Wagner Act. Moreover, by demonstrating its willingness to enter the field of labor policy during the New Deal, the federal government not only legitimized organized labor, but also opened a new market for labor organizations to enter in pursuing their goals. The business unionism of the old AFL with its reliance on economic exchanges gave way to a more politically-oriented approach.

The CIO took the lead in departing from the old policy of political neutrality. In 1944 it formed the Political Action Committee, which had the specific aim of supporting the reelection of Roosevelt and liberal legislative candidates. The AFL remained aloof from politics until after the passage of the Taft–Hartley Act in 1947, when it too realized that political activity was necessary if labor was to retain the advantages it had won through the political system during the New Deal era. The AFL formed Labor's League for Political Education, which was similar in objectives and method to the CIO's Political Action Committee. With the merger of the AFL and the CIO in 1955, their respective political action arms were unified under the joint Committee on Political Education, or COPE.

Formal unity with continued stress

Although the 1955 merger gave the AFL–CIO a unified organizational structure, it should not be taken as an indication that there was unanimity within organized labor. Many of the antagonisms that originally led to the creation of the CIO remained. Perhaps the major area in which conciliation had occurred was the political involvement of unions. But here too consensus was not total, for objectives over specific policies did not always coincide. The conservatism of the AFL, its reluctance to be more aggressive in organizing unskilled workers along industrial lines, its emphasis on the autonomy of member unions, and its tendency to treat the CIO as an immature upstart ensured that a degree of strain would be injected into the merger.[54]

At the time the two organizations merged, George Meany of the Plumbers was president of the AFL and Walter Reuther of the United Automobile Workers was president of the CIO. Since the AFL was the stronger of the two at the time of merger, it was given a proportionate share of the offices: the president and secretary-treasurer were to come from the AFL but the Industrial Union Department, with Reuther as president, was to serve the interests of the old CIO unions. This provided an organizational basis for continuing the old craft–industrial conflict which has, in fact, grown severe. Before the 1961 AFL–CIO convention in Miami, the conflict was brought into the open by Reuther, who lamented that the "high hopes born at the time of the merger have failed to materialize."[55] While the fight does not seem to be drawn purely on the basis of a division between former CIO and AFL unions, the building trades which were an important segment of the old AFL are the source of greatest conflict with the Industrial Union Department. Unions affiliated with the Building and Construction Trades Department have joined employers in promoting "project maintenance" agreements which provide for the contracting-out of work by industrial concerns that have traditionally used their own employees for maintenance work. This induces industrial employees to disregard collective bargaining agreements with industrial unions. The IUD regards this as collusion and asserts that such agreements "have been used . . . as a union-busting and strike-breaking instrument of the employers."[56] Further examples of discord are the boycotting by craft unions of products of industrial unions and even the "raiding of industrial unions by craft unions in defiance of the orders of the AFL–CIO Executive Council." For example, the Sheet Metal Workers sought to displace the Steelworkers during a strike by the latter—the certified bargaining representative—at the Carrier Corporation. Although twice defeated in elections by Carrier employees, the Sheet Metal Workers refused to withdraw in spite of an Executive Council order, and, with the Steelworkers still picketing, finally won an NLRB election at the Carrier plant. These and other examples suggest that union strength is dissipated in what AFL–CIO president Meany calls "useless internal bickering."[57]

A comparison of the membership figures of AFL–CIO affiliates between 1955 and 1968 lends credence to the view that union strength may be on the wane. In the year of their merger the combined membership of the AFL–CIO was 16,062,000; by 1968 that figure had dropped to 15,608,000.[58] Part of the reason for this decline can be accounted for by the expulsion in 1957 of the International Brotherhood of Teamsters with its 1,500,000 members, along with two smaller unions, for corrupt practices. However, the departure of the United Auto Workers with its 1,473,000 members in the summer of 1968 is not reflected in the above figures.

The UAW pullout under Reuther is the last major change to befall the AFL–CIO as of this writing. Reuther's dissatisfaction with the conservative leadership and policies of the AFL–CIO led to his taking the UAW out of that organization and forming a rival association in conjunction with the Teamsters. The Alliance for Labor Action, as the new organization is known, numbered 3,910,000 members in 1969 and had an annual income of over $4,500,000. It remains to be seen how successful the Alliance will be. On the one hand, that the UAW and the Teamsters are the two richest and largest unions in America would seem to indicate that its chances for survival are good. However, they have historically pursued very different policies. The Teamsters, despite the charges of corruption levied against them, have made spectacular gains in membership as a result of following the principles of business unionism. In so doing they have refused to engage in political activities. McConnell describes the Teamsters as follows:

> Its leadership has always emphasized wages, hours, and working conditions. No other union has demonstrated so decisively that such a narrow range of interests is compatible with an intensive accumulation and exercise of power . . . to guard its own security the Brotherhood of Teamsters often appears more willing to collaborate with employers than with other unions. Certainly it seems true that the union is moved far less by any idea of solidarity than by the logic of its own power as an autonomous organization.[59]

The Auto Workers stand in striking contrast to the business unionism policies of the Teamsters. The UAW has been innovative and progressive in the demands it has presented and won for its members. Nor has it been reluctant to employ its resources in political exchanges. "Among the major principles of the UAW," Collins asserts, "is the traditional belief that unions should have broad social objectives that affect not only workers but all Americans."[60] The extent to which the political activism of the UAW can be accepted by the Teamsters will largely determine the ultimate success of their merger. But regardless of the longevity of the Alliance for Labor Action, there is little doubt that its two most important constituent bodies will remain healthy in their own right, for each has pursued a course which has won significant material benefits for its members, and each has continually worked to broaden its membership base.

THE POLITICAL RESOURCES OF ORGANIZED LABOR

Even a cursory examination of organized labor's involvement in politics cannot fail to uncover the tight bond between labor and the Democratic Party. Whether the focus is on campaign contributions, the endorsement of candidates, or the pro-labor policies that have emanated from government, the conclusion that labor works for and is rewarded by Democrats is inescapable. Ever since the New Deal era, when labor began to assert itself politically and when the federal government in turn began to promote the interests of organized labor, unions have concentrated almost exclusively on exchanges with Democratic officials and candidates for public office. We have discussed the extent to which labor organizations contribute financial resources in election campaigns and the general degree of voting discipline they exert over their members. While the overall impact of such activities on the composition of the political officials may be offset by counterforces from competing interests, an analysis of the distribution of labor support would indicate that by selectively investing its resources, organized labor has succeeded in establishing effective channels of communication with strategically placed public officials.

By concentrating their resources within the Democratic Party, labor unions tend to enjoy a confident relationship with members of that party who hold office. In heavily populated industrial states, where union members tend to be located, extremely close working relationships have developed between organized labor and the Democratic Party apparatus.[61] The party needs labor's support to maximize the size of its urban majority, and labor needs the party, for it has no other access to political decision-makers. In noting that labor's interest in national politics has been a fairly recent development, Masters also indicates that not until unions began to organize on an industrial basis, thereby bringing large segments of urban populations within their jurisdiction, did they develop the resources necessary for political action on a broad scale.[62] While unions maintained their craft orientation, no appreciable concentration of members of a given union within a single geographic area could develop. With the change to an industrial base, however, laborers in cities in which huge production industries existed all came under the auspices of a single union. Thus, instead of having many small organizations each with limited resources and parallel organizational structures, industrial unionism combined labor's resources under a centralized leadership. Moreover, as we have seen, the leaders of industrial unions tended to be more willing than those of craft unions to mobilize their resources and channel them into political activities.

Masters lists five categories of resources commanded by labor organizations which are suited to partisan exchange. Since party goals all pertain to winning elections, these resources bear on electoral support. First, of course, are raw votes themselves. That labor tends to vote Democratic needs no elaboration here. Nor does the fact that heavy concentrations of laborers in industrial centers assure Democratic candidates of solid support at the polls. Financial resources, Masters' second category, have also been discussed. We should add, however, that "money is a highly mobile political resource."[63] Unions cannot shift the votes of their members from one state or congressional district to another as they see fit, but they can and do send sizable financial contributions to candidates in areas where few organized laborers reside. Organization is a third resource. Extensive registration drives, get-out-the-vote campaigns, and the distribution of propaganda cannot be undertaken without an organizational structure more highly developed than that of many local parties. Labor associations are frequently in a position to supply this kind of support. Fourth, there is what Masters calls "the liberal sanction." An informal alliance is sometimes seen to unite labor organizations and other ideologically liberal interest groups. Frequently, support from such groups depends on labor's endorsement of a particular candidate. Thus, the ability to deliver the support of other organized interests can be counted among the political resources of labor unions. Finally, labor leaders are able to make available to party campaigners channels of communication which otherwise might be denied them. This is done not only through financial contributions which allow media advertising and through the use of regular union-controlled publications, but also by allowing a candidate to "cut into the network of interrelationships among community elites through labor leaders."[64]

By employing its electoral support resources judiciously, organized labor has been reasonably successful in placing a number of persons friendly to its interests in authoritative positions within the political system. In the 1970 congressional elections, for example, the AFL–CIO backed 194 winning candidates in campaigns for seats in the United States House of Representatives and nineteen winning Senatorial contestants.[65] That these individuals received labor's support in the first place indicates that they had demonstrated in varying degrees a positive orientation toward the interests of unions. The receipt of instrumental electoral support from labor organizations implies that they will be even more receptive to the demands articulated by labor leaders and lobbyists. Thus, the extent of labor organizations' current confident relationship with important officials of the political system is in large measure attributable to the effective use of resources by labor leaders in political exchanges.

LABOR'S FUTURE

In assessing the future of labor organizations in general, two areas of organizational activity emerge as crucial. First, unions must avoid the prospect of stagnation; that is, they must actively recruit new members to grow and remain dynamic. The lessons of the past indicate that a labor organization which becomes satisfied with itself and functions only to provide immediate material benefits to existing members runs the risk of losing one of its most important resources—credibility. In seeking to preserve the status quo, it is less likely to risk short-term benefits for increased benefits in the future. Thus, it tends to find itself increasingly on the defensive in bargaining situations and at a relative disadvantage compared to its bolder competitors. The conservative labor organization may continue to receive support from the privileged constituency it represents; however, as technological change results in alterations in the occupational structure of the labor force, it will find its constituency diminishing. Such changes not only bring occupational shifts within the blue-collar sector of the labor force, but also over time we can expect that sector of the population to shrink in comparison with others. Evidence indicates that America has already begun to experience just such a transformation. In 1950, for instance, 39.2% of all employed persons were in blue-collar jobs while only 37.5% were white-collar workers. By 1960 these figures had changed to 36.5% and 43.1% respectively, and in 1970 blue-collar employees accounted for only 35% while the proportion of white-collar workers had jumped to 48.6%.[66] We are led to the conclusion that labor's success in maintaining active organizations will depend, at least in part, on the extent to which it enters new occupational areas in recruiting members. In recent years we have witnessed some such activity with respect to the organization of government employees and public school teachers.

For an extant group to be attractive to a latent group, however, it must be in a position to offer that group inducements to join. This brings us to the second type of activity which will affect organized labor's future—political activity. McConnell observes that "at nearly every point in labor history at which union membership has changed markedly, the help or hindrance of government has been intimately connected."[67] To be sure, the actual material goods which labor organizations acquire for their members are attained through economic exchanges with specific employers; however, government policies have established the rules by which these exchanges are conducted. If economic benefits are to be won in markets hitherto untouched by union activity, labor must look to the political system for policies which establish the legitimacy of organizational representation and the procedural rules by which collective bargaining is to be conducted. In the long run, then, the future of organized labor appears to depend on its willingness to place a greater value on expansion than on the preservation of the status quo and on its ability to employ the political resources at its command in direct exchanges with the political system.

PROFESSIONAL ASSOCIATIONS

Of the many professional associations currently operative, the American Bar Association and the American Medical Association provide the most fruitful data for political analysis. Both have had long careers in pressure politics and the developmental pattern of both is similar. David Truman notes that medical associations appeared in the last years of the eighteenth century although the American Medical Association did not develop as a national representative organization until 1901.[68] In the same way, state associations formed the nucleus of the American Bar Association which was formally constituted in 1878 but did not achieve any appreciable degree of national coordination until it was reconstituted in 1936.[69] Additionally, each is actively involved in controlling the quality of professional training and entry into its respective occupation.

The American Bar Association

Lawyers perhaps more than physicians have suffered loss of prestige and competition from unqualified persons through the years. For many years the sole training ground for attorneys was an apprenticeship in the office of a practicing lawyer. Admission to the bar was an informal and haphazard process at best. Following the Civil War formal schooling began to gain popularity; however, as late as World War I "apprenticeships in law offices remained the dominant method of induction into the legal profession."[70] Gradually schooling gained primacy, but schools varied widely in the quality of their instruction. Many were unaccredited, profit-making ventures. The resulting quality of new lawyers ranged from near-incompetent ambulance chasers to highly skilled legal scholars and practitioners. The ABA together with the American Association of Law Schools, which the ABA had helped to organize, fought for tighter accreditation standards. Scholars who have studied the progress of the accreditation fight report that as late as the 1930s nearly ninety unaccredited institutions were still educating over one-third of the law school students, but that by the 1950s less than 10% of America's law students were in such schools. Likewise the number of unaccredited law schools had dropped to less than forty.[71]

A second area of control over the profession in which the ABA has been active is admission to the bar itself. Graduation from even an accredited law school is not sufficient demonstration of competence to entitle an individual to practice law. The same motivation that led the ABA to fight for institutional accreditation stimulated an interest in controlling admission to the bar. Jacob identifies two related reasons why tighter control over professional entry was desired:

Easy admission allowed the entry of unqualified and unscrupulous attorneys, whose work blemished the reputation of all lawyers. Moreover, easy entrance into the legal profession allowed more lawyers to compete for the available legal work and depressed the income of lawyers.[72]

The ABA, working in conjunction with the various state bar associations, was instrumental in establishing the requirement that applicants for admission to the bar demonstrate their proficiency by passing a formal bar examination. The administration of bar examinations varies from state to state. In some the state bar association itself administers the test, whereas in others an appointed board governs the examination. The net effect of the combined efforts to raise the quality of legal training and to restrict entry into the profession has been as desired. Although the legal profession today is less uniform in prestige and pay than some may desire, conditions have improved substantially over the course of the last half century.

A final area in which the bar has been active in terms of policing the legal profession concerns the deportment of practicing attorneys. In 1907 a code of professional conduct, the Canons of Ethics, was adopted and is enforced in all states. In some states in which the bar is "integrated," that is to say where membership is a precondition for practice, the state association actually administers the code. Elsewhere, the court system may do so; however, acceptance of the canons is general throughout the nation.

Although each of the programs of the organized bar which we have discussed so far relates to activities internal to the legal profession itself, they are not without ramifications on the exchanges in which the ABA participates with the political system. One of the foremost resources at the disposal of a professional interest group is its prestige, which in turn is a product of the expertise and ethics which characterize members of the profession. Thus, by policing themselves lawyers not only reduce the competition they face from unqualified individuals, but they also enhance their collective bargaining power by presenting a more attractive image to the public and to government officials. The benefits made available to attorneys are collective. Except where membership in the state association is compulsory, one need not affiliate to receive such benefits. The attractions of membership when it is voluntary must lie in nontangible selective goods such as status within the profession, social benefits, and purposive goods resulting from strongly held professional ideals. That these inducements are not sufficient for many legal professionals is attested to by the fact that in 1969 only 140,000 lawyers of over 300,000 in the United States were members of the American Bar Association.

In its external functions the ABA has tended to avoid overt conflicts involving both material and ideological issues. Instead it has maintained a certain professional aloofness which has helped to reinforce its prestige, but which also has failed to win a high degree of material benefits for its members. By far the greatest share of the ABA's political activity has been in the areas of judicial appointments and the structure and procedures of the court system. No doubt the professional detachment which the association has displayed has enhanced its persuasive resources in such areas. Apart from a concern for its professional image, another explanation for the tendency of the ABA to avoid political exchanges for more tangible goods is that lawyers are frequently politically active in their own right or through the clients and firms they represent. Therefore, the argument could be made that they do not require the pooling of their resources through a professional organization to have their demands processed by government officials. In other words, lawyers are individually politically efficacious actors. In the course of their training they become knowledgeable about important aspects of the political system; their occupation brings them into a close working relationship with political decision-makers; many, in fact, embark on political careers of their own.[73] Thus freed from the necessity to represent

the private interests of its members, the ABA has been able to cultivate its reputation as a public-regarding professional organization. As
such it enjoys a confident relationship with political authorities with
regard to the limited scope of issues in which it takes an interest.

The American Medical Association

Physicians, on the other hand, have suffered less over their collective professional prestige than have lawyers, but they also have had
fewer alternatives for organized political action from which to choose.
Consequently the American Medical Association has been more
militant than its legal counterpart in pressing for specific policy decisions from the political system. Also, it has been more successful in
attracting a higher proportion of members from within the ranks of
the profession it represents. In 1969 AMA membership stood at
approximately 220,000, which represents about two-thirds of the
nation's medical doctors.

Before we examine the external activities of the AMA, let us examine the internal aspects of its existence and discuss the goods it
provides its members in exchange for their support. Social and purposive benefits along with that of prestige within the profession no
doubt are inducements to physicians as they are to lawyers. Beyond
these nontangible benefits, however, the AMA offers its members
other selective goods. There are educational advantages by virtue of
the many technical publications and journals sponsored by the association, and much of what goes on at association meetings involves
the reading of technical papers and the exchanging of knowledge of
new developments in the field. Such informational activities have
no mean value considering the rapid advances in the field of medicine. Likewise, costs are sometimes imposed selectively on physicians
who fail to join. It is virtually impossible for an independent physician to join the staff of some hospitals. Medical association membership in such instances is a prerequisite for the use of hospital facilities.
It has also been reported that association membership decreases the
cost of malpractice insurance to physicians, because the AMA provides expert assistance to members who face malpractice suits.[74] The
net effect of these sanctions and inducements has been a relatively
high rate of membership among the medical profession.

If considerations of selective benefits and costs lead us to conclude
that the AMA's internal exchanges are conducive to high rates of
membership and stability, a shift of attention to its external activities
leads us to the opposite conclusion. The positions the AMA has
taken on public issues during the past decade and the tactics it has

employed in pursuing its goals have incurred the enmity of many laymen and physicians alike. Throughout the early 1960s and until it was passed in 1965 the AMA doggedly opposed Medicare legislation.[75] One of the favorite arguments against Medicare was that it represented a first step toward socialism. The following statement, which first appeared in the *AMA News* of March 20, 1961, illustrates this line of argument:

> The Socialist party in the United States has launched a nationwide campaign for socialized medicine in America and has made it clear it supports President Kennedy's proposal for health and medical care through the Social Security program to bring full-blown socialized medicine to this country. . . . [The Socialists] intend to use socialized medicine as the springboard to reach that bigger prize—full socialism in the United States.[76]

An extensive public relations campaign was launched by the AMA to acquaint people with what were construed to be the inadequacies of the Medicare proposal, the lack of need for it, and the desirability of alternative approaches to health care for the aged. Throughout the campaign, proponents of Medicare charged the AMA with distorting the facts that it presented. Among what he lists as the questionable tactics in which the AMA participated, Rose notes the following:

> The AMA arranged to have Blue Cross and Blue Shield and some other private insurance companies, in 1962–63, offer hospital and medical insurance to older people. Many of the state Blue Cross and Blue Shield programs either quickly withdrew these offers, after advertising them extensively, or raised their rates drastically to avoid bankruptcy. Even when available, these insurance programs were subscribed to by only one-fourth of the elderly, although it was claimed that a majority had them.[77]

In addition to its extensive public relations campaign, the AMA lobbyists were busy cultivating support among legislators in Washington. Moreover, a new political action arm of the association was established in 1961 to support congressional campaigns of legislative candidates who were acceptable to the AMA. This organization, known as the American Medical Political Action Committee, has remained very active in spite of the passage in 1965 of the Medicare program. It has been estimated that AMPAC spent close to $3.5 million during the 1968 election.[78] What is not generally known, however, is who receives AMPAC's support. AMPAC has been referred to by one of its officials as "the silent service of medicine."

The tight control over AMA policy which is reflected in the activities of AMPAC is exercised by the organization's eighteen-man board of trustees. Typically, the trustees have had a long history of activity in the association and are older men with rather conservative views. As a result they are frequently out of touch with the attitudes of younger, more liberal members of the profession. One physician summed up the goals of the association by saying, "We keep the supply of doctors low and the demand up, and the prices soar. It's as simple as that."[79] Until recently, officials of the AMA have done little to dispel such an appraisal of their organization. As late as 1967, the president of the AMA was quoted as warning that "we are faced with the concept of health care as a right rather than as a privilege."[80] Such views directly counter those held by an increasing number of physicians today. As a result, there is a growing restiveness within the organizational structure of the AMA as well as among members of the medical profession at large.

That the official positions taken by the association do not always reflect the common interest of its members is attested to by a study done by John Colombotos. Surveying the attitudes of physicians in private practice in the state of New York just before the passage of the Medicare bill, despite the prolonged war the AMA had waged against it, Colombotos found that only 54% of the physicians opposed the measure.[81] A more recent incident which indicates that sources of internal conflict have not been muted was the 1969 nomination of Dr. John Knowles as Assistant Secretary of HEW for Health and Scientific Affairs. Ostensibly, AMA opposition to Knowles was aroused because the organization had not been consulted before the public announcement of his nomination. This was considered by many within the higher echelons of the organization to be a rebuke. Although this was the public reason for opposing Knowles, there has been a good deal of conjecture that behind the procedural grievance was the fact that Knowles was considered to be "a 'hospital man,' a devotee of public health and preventive medicine likely to be out of touch with the interests of the nation's private practitioners."[82] Moreover, Knowles' earlier support of Medicare in opposition to the AMA won him no friends within the association's hierarchy. The AMA, through AMPAC, employed all the political resources at its command to see that the nomination failed to win approval in Congress. Through all of this the general membership of the association had no voice. Even members of the AMA house of delegates, the formal representative congress of the association, were unaware of steps being taken in the name of the association.

The AMA role in the affair was unclear even to some of its House of Delegates members. "In Minnesota we surely knew nothing," a delegate ruefully noted, "yet we got a lot of heat for it." And three letters from doctors to the *American Medical News*, the AMA's weekly newspaper, demanded an explanation of the organization's role.[83]

These and other instances point out that the interests on which the leaders of the AMA act in their exchanges with political authorities are inconsistent with those of a sizable portion of medical professionals. The goods they acquire are often negatively valued by members. Thus, the organization fails to win the active support that it potentially could command. Were it not for the selective costs and benefits discussed earlier one can surmise that the AMA would rapidly become moribund. Even despite such selective goods, there are indications that support for the AMA is waning. In 1960, for instance, over three-fourths of the nation's physicians were members, whereas the proportion had dropped to two-thirds by 1969.[84]

Despite its internal problems and its failure to stop Medicare, the AMA remains a highly effective interest group in its dealing with the political system. Medicare and the Knowles affair are only two of many issues in which the AMA has been active. Although these are the two which have received the most publicity in recent years, the association has lobbied for a variety of health-related matters. It is rich in resources applicable to political exchange—finances, professional reputation, and technical expertise. Moreover, through AMPAC, it is developing a store of more conventional political support resources. Its success in defeating Knowles' nomination attests to the power it can muster. But whether the AMA will continue to enjoy its confident relationship with government authorities will depend to a large extent on its success in maintaining the internal support of the profession it represents.

NOTES

[1]V. O. Key, Jr., *Politics, Parties, and Pressure Groups* (New York: Thomas Y. Crowell Company, 1958), p. 82.

[2]C. J. Judkins, *Trade and Professional Associations of the United States* (Washington, D.C.: Government Printing Office, 1952).

[3]Olson, *The Logic of Collective Action*, p. 143.

[4]*Ibid.*, p. 145.

[5]Clarence E. Bonnett, "The Evolution of Business Groupings," *Annals of the American Academy of Political and Social Science*, 179 (May 1935), p. 3.

[6]Clarence E. Bonnett, *Employers' Associations in the United States* (New York: The Macmillan Company, 1922), p. 146.

[7]Merle Fainsod, Lincoln Gordon, and Joseph C. Palamountain, Jr., *Government and the American Economy* (New York: W. W. Norton & Co., Inc., 1959), pp. 5–6.

[8]Quoted in Clarence E. Bonnett, *History of Employers' Association in the U.S.* (New York: The Vantage Press, 1956), p. 213.

[9]Senate Committee on Education and Labor, *Violations of Free Speech and Rights of Labor*, Senate Report No. 6, 76th Cong., 1st Sess., 1939 (Washington, D.C.: Government Printing Office, 1939), p. 22.

[10]Fainsod et al., *op. cit.*, p. 468.

[11]For an assessment of the NRA activities see Committee on Industrial Analysis, *The National Recovery Administration*, House Document No. 158, 75th Cong., 1st Sess., 1937 (Washington, D.C.: Government Printing Office, 1937).

[12]Senate Committee on Interstate Commerce, *Investigation of Railroads, Holding Companies, and Affiliated Companies*, Senate Report No. 26, part 2, 77th Cong., 1st Sess., 1941 (Washington, D.C.: Government Printing Office, 1941), p. 2.

[13]*Ibid.*, p. 9.

[14]Meyer H. Fishbein, "The Trucking Industry and the National Recovery Administration," *Social Forces*, XXXIV (Dec. 1955), p. 178.

[15]Earl Latham, *The Politics of Railroad Coordination: 1933–1936* (Cambridge, Mass.: Harvard University Press, 1959), p. 164.

[16]*Ibid.*, p. 165.

[17]*Ibid.*, p. 168.

[18]Key, *op. cit.*, p. 83.

[19]Bauer et al., *American Business and Public Policy*, pp. 332–40.

[20]David Truman, *The Governmental Process* (New York: Alfred A. Knopf, Inc., 1951), p. 81.

[21]Senate Committee on Education and Labor, *Hearings* (Washington, D.C.: Government Printing Office, 1939), p. 14025.

[22]Senate Committee on Education and Labor, *Violations of Free Speech and Rights of Labor* (Washington, D.C.: Government Printing Office, 1939), p. 15.

[23]Quoted in Bonnett, *op. cit.*, p. 300.

[24]"Renovation in NAM?" *Fortune*, XXXVIII (19 July 1948), p. 74.

[25]Quoted in Harwood Childs, *Labor and Capital in National Politics* (Columbus, Ohio: The Ohio State University Press, 1930), p. 10.

[26]*Ibid.*, p. 24.

[27]Olson, *op. cit.*, p. 145.

[28]Marver H. Bernstein, "Political Ideas of Selected American Business Journals," *Public Opinion Quarterly*, XVIII (Summer 1953), pp. 258–67.

[29]Fainsod et al., *op. cit.*, p. 258. See also Lee Benson, *Merchants, Farmers, and Railroads* (Cambridge, Mass.: Harvard University Press, 1955).

[30]Robert E. Lane, "Law and Opinion in the Business Community," *Public Opinion Quarterly*, XVII (Summer 1953), pp. 239–57.

[31]Murray Edelman, "Symbols and Political Quiescence," *American Political Science Review*, LIV (Sept. 1960), p. 696.

[32]Marver Bernstein, *Regulating Business by Independent Commission* (Princeton, N.J.: Princeton University Press, 1955), pp. 74–102.

[33]As early as 1878 Reagan had introduced legislation prohibiting discriminatory rates, rebates, and pools for the distribution of freight earnings.

[34]Samuel Huntington, "The Marasmus of the ICC?" *Yale Law Journal*, LXI (Apr. 1952), pp. 467–509.

[35]L. Harmon Zeigler, *The Florida Milk Commission Changes Minimum Prices* (New York: The Inter-University Case Program, 1963).

[36]Jack Barbash, *Labor Unions in Action* (New York: Harper & Row, Publishers, 1948), p. 4.

[37]Robin Williams, *American Society* (New York: Alfred A. Knopf, Inc., 1960), p. 201.

[38]See John R. Commons, *History of Labor in the United States*, 2 vols. (New York: The Macmillan Company, 1918).

[39]Clyde E. Dankert, *Introduction to Labor* (Englewood Cliffs, N.J.: Prentice-Hall, 1954), pp. 146–47.

[40]Melvin J. Vincent and Jackson Mayers, *New Foundations for Industrial Sociology* (Princeton, N.J.: D. Van Nostrand Co., Inc., 1959), p. 256.

[41]Williams, *op. cit.*, pp. 201–2.

[42]Lee Wolman, *The Growth of American Trade Unions, 1880–1923* (New York: National Bureau of Economic Research, Inc., 1924), pp. 29–32.

[43]William C. Birdsall, "The Problem of Structure in the Knights of Labor," *Industrial and Labor Relations Review*, VI (July 1953), pp. 532–46.

[44]Terence V. Powderly, *The Path I Trod* (New York: Columbia University Press, 1940), p. 60.

[45]Childs, *op. cit.*, p. 23.

[46]Philip Taft, "The I.W.W. in the Grain Belt," *Labor History*, I (Winter 1960), pp. 53–67.

[47]Grant McConnell, *Private Power and American Democracy* (New York: Alfred A. Knopf, Inc., 1966), pp. 302–3.

[48]Key, *op. cit.*, p. 67.

[49]Joel Seidman, "Efforts Toward Merger," *Industrial and Labor Relations Review*, IX (Apr. 1956), p. 353.

[50]McConnell, *op. cit.*, p. 307.

[51]Florence Peterson, *American Labor Unions* (New York: Harper & Row, Publishers, 1962), p. 43. See also Walter Galenson, *The CIO Challenge to the AFL* (Cambridge, Mass.: Harvard University Press, 1963).

[52]McConnell, *op. cit.*, p. 308.

[53]Olson, *op. cit.*, p. 88.

[54]A more complete discussion of some of the factors precipitating dissension within the AFL–CIO is contained in A. H. Raskin, "AFL–CIO: A Confederation or Federation? Which Road for the Future?" *Annals of the American Academy of Political and Social Sciences*, CCCL (Nov. 1963), pp. 37–45.

[55]"Reuther Calls for End of Strife," *I.U.D. Bulletin*, VI (Dec. 1961), p. 3.

[56]"Action on Internal Disputes," *ibid.*, p. 7.

[57]"Meany Asks End of Fights So Labor Can Go Forward," *ibid.*, p. 11.

[58]United States Bureau of the Census, *Statistical Abstract of the United States 1971*, p. 238 (Washington, D.C.: Government Printing Office, 1971).

[59]McConnell, *op. cit.*, p. 323.

[60]June M. Collins, "Labor Unions," *Large-Scale Organizations*, Vol. I of *The Emergent American Society*, ed. W. Lloyd Warner (New Haven, Conn.: Yale University Press, 1967), p. 403.

[61]See Nicholas A. Masters, "The Organized Labor Bureaucracy as a Base of Support for the Democratic Party," *Law and Contemporary Problems*, XXVII (Spring 1962), pp. 252–65, and Harry M. Scoble, *Ideology and Electoral Action* (San Francisco: Chandler Publishing Company, 1967), pp. 149–74.

[62]Masters, *op. cit.*, p. 256.

[63]Scoble, *op. cit.*, p. 173.

[64]Masters, *op. cit.*, p. 262.

[65]"Union Backed Candidates: How They Fared," *U.S. News and World Report*, 16 November 1970, p. 63.

[66]United States Bureau of the Census, *Statistical Abstract of the United States 1971*, p. 225 (Washington, D.C.: Government Printing Office, 1971).

[67]McConnell, *op. cit.*, p. 308.

[68]David Truman, *The Governmental Process* (New York: Alfred A. Knopf, Inc., 1951), p. 94.

[69]*Ibid.*, p. 95.

[70]Herbert Jacob, *Justice in America* (Boston: Little, Brown, & Company, 1965), p. 41.

[71]*Ibid.*, pp. 41–42. See also Albert J. Harno, *Legal Education in the U.S.* (San Francisco: Bancroft-Whitney, 1953); Albert P. Blaustein and Charles O. Porter, *The American Lawyer* (Chicago: University of Chicago Press, 1954), and "Modern Trends in Legal Education," *Columbia Law Review*, LXIV (1964), pp. 710–34.

[72]Jacob, *op. cit.*, p. 41.

[73]See Donald R. Matthews, *Social Background of the Political Decision Makers* (Garden City, N.Y.: Doubleday & Company, 1954).

[74]Oliver Garceau, *The Political Life of the American Medical Association* (Cambridge, Mass.: Harvard University Press, 1941), pp. 103–4, and Reuban Kessell, "Price Discrimination in Medicine," *Journal of Law and Economics*, I (Oct. 1958), pp. 2–53, both cited in Olson, *The Logic of Collective Action*, pp. 138–40.

[75]For a concise description of the AMA's fight on the Medicare issue see Arnold M. Rose, *The Power Structure: Political Processes in American Society* (New York: Oxford University Press, 1967), pp. 400–455.

[76]Quoted by Rose, p. 409.

[77]*Ibid.*, p. 425.

[78]"AMA: Doctors and Politics," *Newsweek*, 28 July 1969, p. 87.

[79]*Wall Street Journal*, 7 February 1969, p. 1.

[80]*Ibid.*

[81]John Colombotos, "Physicians and Medicine: A Before–After Study of the Effects of Legislation on Attitudes," *American Sociological Review*, XXXIV (June 1969), p. 326.

[82]"Just What the Doctor Ordered," *Newsweek*, 7 July 1969, p. 15. Copyright Newsweek, Inc.

[83]"AMA: Doctors and Politics," *Newsweek*, 28 July 1969, p. 86. Copyright Newsweek, Inc.

[84]*Wall Street Journal*, 7 February 1969, p. 1.

ten

Noneconomic
Groups

Although they are among the richest, the most powerful, and
the most studied interest groups in America, organizations
formed around the economic and occupational interests of
their members by no means constitute the total universe of
politically active interest groups in the United States. Moreover, there are indications that noneconomic interest groups
are becoming increasingly important political actors.[1]   The
activities of ethnic and religious minority groups, ideological
organizations, and single interest groups such as environ-
mentalist organizations attest to the growth of noneconomic
associations.   It would be unrealistic, however, to infer that
the interests which motivate all organizations in this category are devoid of economic content.   Certainly one of the
more important demands articulated by minority groups is

that of equal economic opportunity. Likewise, many ideological groups adopt specific positions on economic issues. What distinguishes such organizations from the more purely economic ones is not so much the type of policies they demand from the political system as it is the goals and values that bind their members together. The commonality of interests within each type of occupational or professional organization discussed in Chapter 9 results from the respective positions of the membership of each group within the nation's economic structure. Consequently, the benefits those associations provide to their members tend to be defined largely in terms of this one shared characteristic. Since individuals are composites of many roles in life, groups organized around the interests stemming from the occupational role alone can represent only a portion of their members' interests. Other types of organizations provide benefits which are beyond the scope of economic interest groups. Let us examine some of the major types of noneconomic groups active in the American political system today.

Ethnic and Religious Minority Groups

It is virtually impossible in many instances to disassociate ethnic characteristics from religion. For many ethnic groups—the Irish, Poles, Italians, and Jews, for example—a large part of the cultural heritage which sets them apart stems from common religious ties. Moreover, many of the interests which bring them into contact with the political system arise from religious issues. Not all ethnic minorities, of course, share a common religion. American Negroes are the most active minority group in the nation today, yet even though many religious leaders have arisen from within their ranks to lead civil rights groups and several unique religious organizations have developed with the Negro community, no religious homogeneity such as that which characterizes the Jewish minority exists within black America. Likewise, common religious affiliations is not a unique characteristic of American Indians, another active minority today. Other ethnic groups such as Puerto Ricans and Chicanos do share a single religious heritage; however, as a source of political demands, religion appears to be less important than social or economic factors. The generally inferior socioeconomic status of Puerto Ricans and Chicanos may account for the more economic nature of their demands than of those made by other ethnic groups which have homogeneous religious ties but which are also more fully established within the nation's economic structure. In their study of ethnic minorities in New York City, Glazer and Moynihan note "the splintering of traditional economic classes along ethnic lines, which tends to create class-ethnic combinations that have considerable significance...."[2] If socioeconomic status or class is a prominent source of minority group demands while such groups occupy identifiably inferior economic positions, then we must also conclude that as they become assimilated into society, the class character of their demands will pale in comparison to the other interests which will have developed from their shared experiences. Frequently, religion continues to bind ethnic groups long after economic factors cease to be a collective concern. As Glazer and Moynihan observe,

> ... it is a good general rule that except where color is involved as well the specifically *national* aspect of most ethnic groups rarely survives the third generation in any significant terms.... The groups do not disappear, however, because of their *religious* aspect which serves as a basis for their subcommunity, and a subculture.[3]

Thus, while economic and national interests may be important components of minority group interests during the years immediately following mass immigrations, religious and racial bases for group solidarity tend to become increasingly significant thereafter.

Racial distinctiveness, of course, is not common to all ethnic groups. When it is a factor, as the statement by Glazer and Moynihan indicates, it can appreciably complicate the procedure of assimilation. Obviously, Negroes are not new immigrants to America. They have lived in the United States in sizable numbers as long as it has been a nation, yet they remain unassimilated today. Interestingly, however, not until after World War II, when they began to migrate out of the rural South and into Northern cities in large numbers, did a sustained drive toward social and economic betterment develop. No doubt the unique conditions in the post–Civil War South effectively preempted any possibility of relieving the deprivation of Negroes there. But now that the Negro minority is becoming somewhat more dispersed and now that social, political, and economic changes are occurring in the South, it is entirely possible that assimilation will follow. In any event, it is clear that when a minority group is a racial minority as well as a national or religious minority, it is subject to forces which inhibit socioeconomic integration and strengthen group identification beyond those encountered by other ethnic minorities.

Group identification

Members of minority groups are provided with group identification on the basis of "race, religion, immigrant status, and origins in other than Anglo-Saxon countries" at an early age.[4] Studies of children of nursery school and very early primary school age indicate that identifications on the basis of racial, religious, and national differences are present. Negro and white children within this age group are aware of racial differences expressed in physical characteristics and many use racial terms which imply the perception of differences in the social roles of Negroes and whites.[5] The same findings apply to Jewish children of the same age group, as illustrated by the remarks of a second grade Jewish girl:

> I'm Jewish. . . . Jews are the best people, mother said. You know I'm a Jew. . . . I'm not allowed to go [to church]. Only synagogue. [Churches] ain't no good. Synagogue is better. Catholics don't like Jews. Make fun of Jews.[6]

Of great significance is the conclusion that the minority group children show earlier and greater identification than majority group children of the same age. Negro children show more concern with their racial characteristics than white children; Jewish children are more conscious of their own group than Protestants; and Catholics are more group conscious than Protestants but less so than Jews.

However convincing this evidence may be, it is a mistake to assume that a member of a minority group automatically desires to identify himself with the customs and traditions of his family and immediate associates. There is nothing in the personality structure of a person that makes him inclined to identify, interact, and undertake political activity on behalf of a minority group any more than there is in the personalities of members of any other broadly defined aggregate or "categoric group." Members of minority groups have overlapping affiliations with other groups, which may be easily activated while minority group affiliation remains dormant. For example, a Polish druggist could easily be motivated to support fair trade legislation through the auspices of the National Association of Retail Druggists in cooperation with other druggists of varying ethnic or religious backgrounds. There must be some reason for identification and, as is the case with all interest groups, such identification is produced by "pressure from the outside and the consequences of that pressure."[7] Whereas the outside pressure operating on other types of potential interests might be ideological or economic, the pressures imposed on a minority group may be categorized by the word "prejudice." While many definitions of prejudice may be found, one of the most useful is Allport's "an aversive or hostile attitude toward a person who belongs to a group, simply because he belongs to that group, and is therefore presumed to have the objectionable qualities ascribed to the group."[8] While it is fruitless to attempt to argue that there is perfect correlation between degree of prejudice and minority group identification, it is fairly obvious that, in the United States, opposition to majority prejudice is a strong catalyst to minority protest movements.

In some cases, group identification occurs without visible prejudice; in others the minority group is the object of prejudice, yet has ineffective group identification. In the latter case, the desire is usually to escape identity as a member of a minority by means of name changing and the avoidance of contact with other members of the group. No effective organization to protest discrimination will occur, since the only shared characteristic of the members of such a group is being identified by the majority as possessing certain undesirable qualities. The conditions under which minority groups will normally undertake political activity are described by Wirth: "The continued subordination over a long period of time of any special class in the population, when coupled with the concentration of that group in large numbers, with social visibility based on racial traits or cultural characteristics, with intense competition with the dominant group, and with rising levels of education, generally results in the emergence of group-consciousness and eventually the overt struggle for recognition."[9] The reader will have no trouble applying this description to the status of the American Negro, whom Wirth believes to be the "principal shock absorber of the antiminority sentiment of the dominant whites."[10] Hence, the persistent struggle of Negro organizations toward the attaining of "first class citizenship" has attracted more attention than the efforts of other minorities, such as Catholics and Jews.

The components of minority status

A proper comprehension of the concept of the minority is crucial to the understanding of the politics of minorities. The word refers not to numerical characteristics but rather to physical or cultural characteristics which cause a "singling out" from others and a consequent unequal treatment. Although the size of the group apparently has a direct relationship to the treatment the minority may expect from the majority, it is very possible that people whom we consider to be a minority are a numerical majority. In the southern black belt, where the population is 50% or more Negro, there is no question that Negroes are placed in the status of a minority in the sense that they are totally subordinate to the white community. Clearly, the density of minority group population increases prejudice and organizational reactions to prejudice. In the case of both the Jews and the Catholics, discrimination did not become a problem until the impetus of increased immigration was provided. If the group is small, the chances of assimilation increase while the probability of prejudice decreases (although this "law of density" cannot stand alone). Examples of this situation are the Jew in China, the Negro in Brazil, or the Hindu in America. In each of these cases, if the minority population were to increase markedly, there is little doubt that the pattern of assimilation would be reversed.[11]

The United States is liberally sprinkled with minority groups, and since the distribution of many minority groups is regional, many patterns of discrimination are localized and the protest activity is correspondingly restricted to a particular area. In addition, many of the ethnic minority groups were organized primarily for the purpose of maintaining loyalty to the "old country" and not for the pursuit of goals through participation in the domestic political process.[12] Thomas and Znaniecki describe the Polish community in America as operating through the Polish National Alliance to "turn the Polish immigrants in this country into a strong and coherent part of the Polish Nation."[13] Another instructive example is the Japanese of the West Coast. Here, the Japanese American Citizens' League grew under the guidance of the Nisei who opposed the tendency of the older generation to support the militarist activities of the Japanese government. In this case, events taking place abroad had consequences for the nationality group whose position in the host society was threatened.[14] It is natural that minority groups with foreign identifications take unusual interest in foreign policy, and there is much evidence of gradual shifts in party loyalty among such groups according to the position taken on a particular issue by one of the two major parties. Occasionally, minority activities in foreign policy take the form of direct pressure on officeholders, as illustrated by President Harry Truman's statement that, during the United Nations debate over the partitioning of Palestine, "I do not think I ever had so much pressure and propaganda aimed at the White House as I had in this instance." President Truman continued by saying that "the persistence of a few of the extreme Zionist leaders—actuated by political motives and engaging in political threats—disturbed and annoyed me. . . . The Jewish pressure on the White House did not diminish in the days following the partition vote in the U.N."[15] While other examples of internationalist-type pressure may be found, we are more interested at this point in "nationalist" organizations whose attention is largely concentrated domestically, those representing Negroes, Catholics, and Jews.

Catholics: the political socialization of religion

Catholicism is given political expression primarily through the instrument of the Church, rather than through voluntary secular associations. The reasons for this assumption of the role of political agent by the Church may be found both in the nature of the Catholic faith (and consequent structure of the Church) and in the social composition of the Catholic laity. Many of the immigrant groups are Roman Catholic and there is considerable overlapping between identification as a minority on the basis of nationality and minority religious status. To some extent, national solidarity has been transformed into religious solidarity, especially when assimilation into the larger society is impeded. Certainly there are many examples of hostility between the Catholic groups—Poles and Italians object to the domination of the Irish in the affairs of the Church—but there is still a very basic unifying function performed by the Church as an institution. The initial anti-Catholic movements in this country did not develop until the beginnings of Irish immigration and the later Italian immigration. However, as a nationality group the Irish now encounter so little prejudice that it is doubtful if they can be considered a minority. The Irish are, nevertheless, held together by their loyalty to the Catholic Church, and the extent to which they remain a minority will be on this basis rather than on that of nationality. The Italians, by way of contrast, retain the stereotype of "foreigners" and this, as well as their Catholicism, contributes to their minority status. Yet the probability of assimilation is sufficient to enable one to advance the thesis that the Italians will gradually retain minority status primarily through Catholicism.

The transfer of the tensions of prejudice to the religious area has generated a reaction which might be described as the political socialization of religious biases. Discrimination against people simply because they are Catholics is negligible, but religious conflict between the two major religions has increased. Since the Catholic Church does not acknowledge any separation between church and state, and since the Church is formally organized to promote internal unity, it is ideally suited for political activity: ". . . all acts by human beings have religious significance, and [the Church] realistically recognizes that all acts of the churches have political significance if they affect the relative power of groups."[16] Consequently, it is usually the Catholic clergy which is given the responsibility of speaking to political questions. But contrary to what most non-Catholics believe to be the case, the Roman Catholic clergy do not always speak with a single voice. The structure of the Church has been such that each bishop is responsible only to the pope. Therefore, within the area circumscribed by common theological and papal requisites, each bishop has a certain amount of freedom with respect to the particular political issues he deems important and the intensity and kinds of political activity in which he chooses to engage. The rigid hierarchical organization of the Church has resulted in Catholic bishops becoming "the last of the great autocrats."[17] Only in recent years have Catholic positions on public issues begun to be coordinated on a national level. We will return to this point shortly.

The authority wielded by the clergy over parishioners in both spiritual and temporal affairs, combined with the authoritarian organizational structure within each diocese, has created a style of political interaction unique among religious bodies. For the most part religious organizations in America avoid direct political exchanges; when they do become involved in the policy-making process, they tend to concentrate their activities in judicial arenas. Catholic political activities tend to be concentrated in legislative and administrative decision-making systems. Strong ties exist between the Democratic Party and Catholic voters—particularly in major urban areas where the Irish have tended to dominate political processes. The result is that the Catholic Church has an advantageous position with respect to partisan political leaders. The Democrats have come to rely on strong Catholic majorities in the cities to overcome the predominantly Republican vote from the suburbs. Republicans, on the other hand, seek to reduce the Democratic tendencies among Catholic voters. Since "individual priests, bishops, and cardinals are often men of considerable community-wide or national prestige" and since "they are thought to be on very special terms with the voters who are their spiritual charges," the clergy not only have access to political leaders but they also command a considerable amount of persuasive resources.[18] The style of interaction that results is not highly visible. Clerical and political elites often communicate outside the public forums. When Church spokesmen do articulate positions publicly, for example, at committee or agency hearings or in speeches and press releases, their tone tends to be muted, no doubt because of concern over triggering the latent but widespread anti-Catholic sentiment and fears of "popery" among non-Catholics.

The single most influential organization of national scope through which Catholic interests are represented is the United States Catholic Conference. Originally organized in 1917 as the National Catholic

Welfare Conference, its initial function was overseeing the religious welfare of Catholic servicemen during World War I. At the end of the war, however, the bishops decided to maintain the organization as a coordinating agency. In the mid-1960s the Vatican retreated from its position opposing the establishment of any intermediate authority between Rome and diocesan bishops. Consequently, the NCWC was reorganized in 1966 and given the new name of the United States Catholic Conference. The USCC maintains a permanent staff in Washington, D.C., which conducts most of its politically oriented activities. The Legal Department of the USCC has traditionally been the most active branch of the organization with respect to the political system. Its staff of five lawyers prepares briefs outlining the Conference's position on pending legislation, regulatory policies, and judicial cases in which the Conference takes an interest. The Legal Department also undertakes the major portion of other types of lobbying on behalf of the Conference. Murray Stedman has observed that

> [t]he bulk of contacts between the Legal Department and agencies of the federal government is, as might be imagined, informal, and the liaison is two-way. It is common practice for a government official to request the assistance of the NCWC, usually through its Legal Department, for help in the formulation of regulations.[19]

When other branches of the organization are called to present testimony before legislative committees, they receive advice and assistance in preparing their statements from the Legal Department.

In 1961 and 1962 the Conference actively opposed President Kennedy's proposals to provide federal aid to education, because parochial schools were excluded from the program. The Education Department of the NCWC, under the direction of Monsignor Frederick G. Hochwalt, was the most visible actor in the struggle. Monsignor Hochwalt testified before various executive and legislative bodies during the course of the campaign. "The staff of the Legal Department," Stedman reports, "stayed in the background, although it was responsible for the massive legal briefs relied upon by the Education Department."[20] The ultimate defeat of Kennedy's aid program, of course, cannot be attributed solely to the NCWC, for it had powerful allies including the United States Chamber of Commerce and the National Association of Manufacturers. Nor was the NCWC the only church-affiliated organization to oppose the measure. The National Catholic Education Association, composed of Catholic teachers and administrators, was also active in its opposition. It should be noted, however, that the relationship between the NCWC and the NCEA was extremely close.

The National Catholic Educational Association (14,000 teachers and administrators) is closely associated with the USCC [formerly the NCWC], and for years Monsignor Hochwalt served as its executive secretary. This interlocking directorate has made for excellent communication and coordination within the Catholic educational establishment.[21]

The Jews

The Jews stand in sharp contrast to the Catholics on two counts. First, the church and religion are not strongly emphasized in Jewish life, and second, the Jewish religion is split into orthodox, conservative, and reformed branches. These factors contribute to the weak hierarchical structure of Jewish religious life and thus make it inevitable that the expression of Jewish political values be undertaken by voluntary associations. Also, discrimination against Jews has been based not only on their status as a religious minority, but also on ethnic or racial characteristics. In fact, in contemporary American life the tendency toward anti-Semitism has been almost wholly divorced from religious objections and has rested on a stereotype built on presumed cultural characteristics. Discrimination against Jews had been both brutally direct and subtle. Social discrimination, such as the exclusion of Jews from exclusive clubs, occupational discrimination, the operation of the "quota system" in colleges and graduate schools, and occasional discrimination against Jews in the buying and selling of real estate attest to the persistence of anti-Semitism.

Anti-Semitism, like other patterns of discrimination, started slowly and reached its peak in correlation with Jewish immigration, which spurted upward in the 1880s and continued to increase until World War I, after which a policy of restriction was followed. Accordingly, World War I represents a high point in anti-Semitism. One measure of anti-Semitism may be found in A. L. Severson's study of discriminatory want ads. Ads specifically excluding Jews rose from less than 1% in 1911 to 4% in 1921 and finally to slightly over 13% in 1926.[22] During this period the first Jewish defense organization came into existence. The American Jewish Committee was a small organization of wealthy Jews who were not recent immigrants. Its goal was to resist anti-Semitism by the use of restrained and localized action. The Anti-Defamation League of B'nai B'rith came shortly after to serve as the political branch of a well-established fraternity. The ADL was more a mass organization and has been inclined toward more general exposure of discrimination. Rose believes that the ADL has been the most effective of the Jewish organizations and has increased group identification. He remarks, "When Jews meet anti-Semitism, and in so far as they look to a national organization to aid them, they probably think first of the ADL."[23] A third organization, by far the most militant, is the American Jewish Congress, begun in 1918 as a "democratically elected parliamentary assembly representing all American Jews."[24] Its membership was primarily the newer immigrants and a partial reason for its creation was opposition to the more elitist American Jewish Committee. Its militancy is expressed in its passionate defense of Zionism and its reliance on direct lobbying techniques in efforts to secure governmental prohibitions against racial and religious discrimination. Initially, the American Jewish Congress proposed to obtain treaty provisions at the Versailles conference protecting the rights of Jews in the defeated countries and to generate support for a Jewish state in Palestine, the latter goal being realized many years later. During the 1930s anti-Semitism increased after a brief drop, according to Severson's statistics, and was expanded into political forms by means of organized groups using anti-Semitism in efforts to achieve political power. Donald Strong accounted for 121 organizations disseminating anti-Jewish literature between 1933 and 1940. The growth of such organizations seemed to be related to the increasing power of Nazi Germany, for prior to 1933 only five anti-Semitic associations were in operation.[25] This new type of threat was combated under the energetic leadership of the American Jewish Congress, whose usual militant posture plunged it actively into resistance.

The initial response to organized anti-Semitism by Jewish groups was vigorous, but more enduring has been the articulation of goals designed to ensure the preservation of Jewish cultural values. While the Anti-Defamation League continues to propagandize against discrimination and anti-Semitism, the American Jewish Congress has expanded its interests particularly with respect to religious liberty. The AJC's Committee on Social Action is actively engaged in winning support for the position that "religious liberty is best preserved when government remains strictly and severely aloof from all religious affairs."[26] This belief is expressed in the AJC's resistance to the releasing of children from school for religious instruction, recitation of prayers in class, nuns teaching in their religious attire, and so on. Of course, church–state controversies are not confined to public schools, as is illustrated by the AJC's opposition to the inclusion of religious questions in the census.

The Jewish population in the United States, estimated in 1967 to be 5,721,000, is highly concentrated in urban areas. To meet the needs of this population, nearly every large city in the country has some type of Jewish organization, usually called a Jewish Community Council or Jewish Community Relations Council. The function of these organizations is "to deal with problems of anti-Semitism and community relations and to coordinate the network of Jewish charitable, religious, educational and social welfare agencies."[27] Also represented on such councils are representatives of the national organizations, which operate through the local groups primarily on questions of anti-Semitism. The initiative for action frequently begins at the local level. The local association is more directly involved in the affairs of the community and is sensitive to the problem of establishing workable relationships with majority portions of the population. For example, when a question of beginning legal action to prohibit the performance of a nativity play in the public schools is being debated, the community council may feel that, if the litigant is known to be a Jew or if his case is supported by a Jewish organization, the pattern of relationships between Jews and Christians may be upset. The American Jewish Congress, not so closely identified with a particular locale, is usually more anxious to begin action but cannot risk disruption of the Jewish community by moving without prior discussions with local leaders through the community councils. As in any political organization, a major part of the pressure process is internal. The AJC must persuade its clientele that a particular course of action will have beneficial consequences sufficient to offset the possibility that community relations will be damaged.

On national issues the same necessity for achieving minimal cohesion exists. Since none of the national organizations is in a position to attempt solidification, several "umbrella" organizations undertake the task.[28] The Synagogue Council of America is composed of the rabbinical and congregational bodies of the three branches of Judaism, and the National Community Relations Advisory Council serves as a coordinating mechanism for the national Jewish organizations and the local community councils. These two organizations include approximately 80% of the organized Jewish community. The two inclusive organizations work together through joint committees such as the Joint Advisory Committee on Religion and Public Schools. This committee, with its legal work prepared by the American Jewish Congress, advises local organizations and undertakes direct action at the national level, as, for example, the filing of an *amicus curiae* brief in the McCollum case or the testimony in Congress against a proposed constitutional amendment declaring the country Christian. Yet such formal devices will never achieve total mobilization, for there will always be internal conflicts. The Anti-Defamation League and the American Jewish Committee have withdrawn from the National Community Relations Council. These organizations have been less rigid in their approach to church–state relations and have usually favored, for example, joint Christmas–Hanukkah celebrations, a practice strenuously opposed by the American Jewish Congress. Also, local–national conflict occasionally erupts. When the American Jewish Congress challenged the New York Sunday closing law as applied to a kosher butcher shop which closed on Saturday, both the local kosher butchers' association and the kosher butchers' workers union filed briefs defending the statute. Examples of such conflict occur with such frequency that the problem of cohesion can be called crucial in the influence process. To focus on external problems, internal disunity must be reduced beneath the level of distraction, a task which occupies a substantial portion of the efforts of the leadership.[29]

Negroes

The Negro minority, which constitutes 10% of the American population, is both the oldest and most consistently discriminated against of all minority groups in this country. The visible physical characteristics and slave ancestry of Negroes might be considered two basic factors explaining why they have retained minority status for so long. From the beginning of slavery in the early seventeenth century until the defeat of the Confederate States of America, there was virtually no opportunity for group identification and protest activity. The slaves were not allowed to communicate and few were even given the opportunity to learn to read. Although there were sporadic outbursts of revolutionary fervor, the group life of the Negro was too restricted for cohesive action. As Robin Williams has suggested, "militancy, except for sporadic and short-lived uprisings, is not characteristic of the most deprived and oppressed groups, but rather of those who have gained considerable rights so that they are able realistically to hope for more."[30]

Williams states further that "a militant reaction from a minority group is most likely when (a) the group's position is rapidly improving, or (b) when it is rapidly deteriorating, especially when this follows a period of improvement."[31] Such was the situation giving birth to the first organized Negro protests. The freedom of Reconstruction gave them new opportunities for political participation, but the militant protests of the Reconstruction period were submerged by vigorous white Southern countermovements following the removal of federal troops. By the 1890s white supremacy was firmly established as a way of life. The white South believed that it was possible and desirable to return the Negroes to their original status, and with the aid of secret societies and the tacit support of the federal government, the rule of Jim Crow dominated. Protest movements could not survive such an assault and were replaced by "accommodation." Myrdal describes the leadership of Booker T. Washington as typical of the period of accommodation in that it was "realistic."[32] As leader of a conciliatory school of thought, he was willing to sacrifice social and political equality, even to the extent of accepting inequalities in justice.[33] It is doubtful that more could have been accomplished under the circumstances, and Washington did mold together a basis of support in the white community which would probably have been lost by more vigorous methods.

However, dependence on the benevolence of whites could not obliterate the fact that "every Negro has some sort of conflict with the white world."[34] It was inevitable that a reaction against Washington's leadership would occur and that this reaction would take the form of protest. Led by W. E. B. Du Bois, a small group of Negro intellectuals demanded full social and political equality and, hopefully, cultural assimilation. The "Niagara Movement" (so called because the first meeting of the leaders of the reaction met at Niagara Falls in 1905) intended not only to develop more vigorous forms of political activity, but also to replace Washington's compromising policies as the dominant mode of the Negro community. Although this movement lasted only five years, it merged with the National Association for the Advancement of Colored People four years later.

From the beginning of its organizational life, the NAACP has exhibited many of the qualities that typified it at its inception. The initiative for the organization came from white abolitionists such as Oswald Garrison Villard and, for many years, a substantial portion of the leadership positions was filled by whites. Gradually, while retaining its interracial distribution at the branch level, the NAACP national leadership has become primarily the responsibility of Negroes. However, the organization has had primary attraction not for the Negro masses, but for the "talented tenth"—the minority of upper-class, educated Negroes. The militancy of Du Bois did not appeal to this type of membership which, according to Lewin's "periphery theory," would desire to achieve status within society at large. To achieve such status, it is necessary to reduce identification with the low-status minority group. Lewin states,

> In a minority group, individual members who are economically successful, or who have distinguished themselves in their professions, usually gain a high degree of acceptance by the majority group. This places them culturally at the periphery of the underprivileged group and makes them more likely to be "marginal" persons. They frequently have a negative balance and are particularly eager to have their "good connections" not endangered by too close a contact with those sections of the underprivileged group which are not acceptable to the majority.[35]

The elitist type of NAACP membership has behaved in a manner generally within the limits of Lewin's description of the peripheral leader. Although its rank and file membership has expanded and hence shifted to some extent from the elite to the "common Negroes," it is still committed to the avoidance of any form of protest other than the pursuit of civil rights through legal action. Thus, Roy Wilkins, head of the NAACP, has said that the organization "would prefer using legal action as a last resort in the many situations which will arise in hundreds of communities."[36]

Largely avoiding participation in mass protest movements such as the March on Washington Movement (which ultimately forced President Roosevelt to establish a Fair Employment Practices Commission during World War II) has, of course, worked to the advantage of the NAACP in many instances.[37] By pursuing a persistent policy of hammering away at restrictions, the NAACP can claim such notable victories as the abolition of white primaries, restrictive covenants, and segregation in public schools. Ironically, however, its most conspicuous victory, the 1954 Supreme Court decision in *Brown* v. *Board of Education*, also resulted in the NAACP's losing its position as unchallenged leader among Negro civil rights interest groups. That decision was widely publicized, and that it represented a clear-cut victory for antisegregationists in general and for Southern Negroes in particular was inescapable. Important though it was, the benefits it bestowed were largely symbolic. The *Brown* decision gave moral sanction to the integrationist cause, but it did little to alter the material conditions of segregation.[38] Of course, this was not a foregone conclusion at the time the decision was rendered, nor was it the sole reason for the NAACP's loss of hegemony. Equally if not more important was the raising of the expectations of large numbers of Negroes. Having won one highly publicized victory, symbolic though it was, many Negroes became eager for additional benefits once they saw that the system could be made responsive to their demands. Moreover, a sense of impatience accompanied the rise in expectations. Growing numbers of Negroes were no longer willing merely to wait out the lengthy and costly process of litigation—the principal tactic employed by the NAACP. Writing in 1961, Eric Lincoln captured this sense of urgency when he observed that

> . . . to many Negroes, the way of the NAACP is too slow, too expensive and too uncertain. . . . Negroes cannot understand why they must spend time and money again and again to have the courts secure them privileges that all other Americans—and many resident aliens—take for granted.[39]

One year after the initial *Brown* decision an event occurred which was to catalyze a new type of civil rights organization, and which is also generally conceded to represent a turning point in the civil rights struggle in the South. The major civil rights organizations at the time—the NAACP, the Urban League, and the Congress of Racial Equality—were all concentrated in the North. Of these three only CORE participated in direct protest activities outside the established channels of political exchange. CORE, however, was not a well-organized association capable of sustaining a coherent program at the national or even regional level. Kenneth Clark writes,

> It is significant that CORE did not become a major civil rights organization until the civil rights movement reached a crescendo after the Brown decision of 1954. Before that, CORE seemed to be a rather constricted, dedicated, almost cult-like group of racial protestors who addressed themselves to fairly specific forms of racial abuse which could be dramatized by their particular method of direct action and personal protest.[40]

In 1955 the civil rights movement spawned its first Southern-based organization. In that year the Negroes of Montgomery, Alabama, protesting discrimination in seating on the local public bus line, formed the Montgomery Improvement Association with Rev. Martin Luther King, Jr. as its leader. King led a CORE-style direct protest boycott of the bus line. The publicity accorded the successful boycott launched King and his program of nonviolent protest into national prominence. As a direct consequence of his success in Montgomery and of the personal prestige which he commanded, a new regional association was organized in 1957 under King's leadership. This organization, the Southern Christian Leadership Conference, employed the tactics of nonviolent direct confrontation against specific discriminatory institutions and policies. "Mass demonstrations were used to challenge the legality of both legal and *de facto* segregation and to prick the conscience of white elites."[41] Such tactics, unlike those of the NAACP, gave the Negro masses in the South an opportunity to participate in the activities of the association and thereby receive the selective benefits stemming from collective purposive action. Martin Luther King's great charismatic appeal further provided benefits for those who chose to become personally involved in the various SCLC protests. But no doubt the greatest factor in attracting active participation in the protests led by the organization was success. The policy demands of the SCLC were carefully selected so that the moral resources of the SCLC were sufficient to ensure the continuous flow of what appeared to be tangible benefits. In analyzing the internal exchanges necessary to maintain an interest group which must resort to protest activities, Lipsky writes,

> The intangible rewards of assuming certain postures toward the political system may not be sufficient to sustain an organizational base. It may be necessary to renew constantly the intangible rewards of participation. And to the extent that people participate in order to achieve tangible benefits, their interest in a protest organization may depend upon the organization's relative material success. Protest leaders may have to tailor their style to present participants with tangible successes, or with the appearance of success. Leaders may have to define the issues with concern for increasing their ability to sustain organizations. The potential for protest among protest group members may have to be manipulated by leadership if the group is to be sustained.[42]

The specific segregationist policies against which the SCLC protested (particularly in its early years) tended to represent the most overt aspects of Southern racism. Consequently they were also the most vulnerable to the tactics of nonviolent moral protest and publicity which the organization employed. By selecting such targets, King and the SCLC were able to provide a more or less continuous flow of tangible victories to Southern Negroes.

In the early 1960s Negro protest underwent another transformation at least as significant as that which gave rise to the SCLC-style direct action organization. In noting this change, Moynihan observes that the earlier period was one in which "the demands of the Negro American were directed primarily to those rights associated with the idea of Liberty: the right to vote, the right to free speech, the right to free assembly," while those emerging in the sixties were more concerned with the implementation of equality.[43] Another way of construing this reorientation is in terms of a shift from concern over formal civil rights to one centered on de facto political and economic equality.[44] If the Montgomery bus boycott is seen as marking the beginning of the earlier period, then the SCLC demonstrations in Birmingham, Alabama in 1963 can be viewed as marking the commencement of the latter. Instead of concentrating its demands on the rectification of a single abuse, as it had in the past, the SCLC sought to end discrimination in the areas of housing, employment opportunities, and public accommodations. Although the SCLC and its followers remained nonviolent, the Birmingham demonstrations triggered violent reaction from segregationists, and unorganized blacks responded in kind. The immediate results of the protest were not as spectacular as many wished. Clark, for example, remarks that the major accomplishments seemed to be "negotiations leading to minimal concessions."[45] Indirectly, however, the new militancy and the broadened scope of conflict led to the enactment of the Civil Rights Act of 1964, which was "the first significant entry of Congress into the civil rights field."[46]

The Civil Rights Act, like the *Brown* decision a decade earlier, was largely a symbolic victory. It provided federal sanction against discriminatory practices in voting registration, public accommodations, public education, and employment, but the tangible results of this legislation depended on implementation. De facto discrimination and inequality remained conditions with which Negroes were forced to contend. Neither the 1964 Civil Rights Act nor the concessions won in the early sixties by the SCLC and other direct action organizations such as CORE and the new Student Nonviolent Coordinating Committee were sufficient to satisfy Negro demands for equality. These demands called for a virtual restructuring of major aspects of American social, political, and economic life and a reorientation of its bias. Such demands are never met with ease or speed, and satisfaction for them cannot be immediate. Whereas the earlier targets of protest —segregated lunch counters, for instance—were specific and primarily symptomatic manifestations of inequality, the issue of de facto equality represented a fundamental challenge to the bias of the American political regime. Demands of the former type are much more easily met than are those of the latter. Moreover, by virtue of having won desired decisions in a variety of contests involving particular liberties, the expectations of Negroes for further demand satisfaction had been raised. White society, through the political system it controlled, was simply unable or unwilling to respond to the new Negro demands as rapidly as they were being made. Thus, the violence in Birmingham signaled a new phase in the tactics of Negro protest.

The anger and frustration that had been vented in Birmingham in 1963 was released in Harlem, Chicago, Philadelphia and Rochester in 1964, Watts in 1965, Omaha, Atlanta, Dayton and dozens of other places in 1966. Finally, in 1967 there were over 100 rebellions in over 70 different cities.[47]

The tactics of nonviolence which had marked the approach taken by Martin Luther King and the Southern Christian Leadership Conference were no longer acceptable to the masses of Negroes who, ironically, had been stimulated into active participation by the successes of the very organization which they now failed to support. The SCLC could still provide solidary, purposive, and symbolic benefits to its followers and hope for the future, but these were no longer sufficient inducements. Frazier and Roberts write,

> Birmingham marked the entry of the Negro poor into the protest movement ... [which] forced a reevaluation of the goals of the movement, as well as the means of attaining those ends. Poor people are, out of frustration, intolerant of moderation and at the same time, contemptuous of the doctrine of nonviolence.

> Nearly a decade after the court decision desegregating schools legally and in the wake of ... the Birmingham summer, Negroes began to look at the civil rights movement and realize that it was inadequate. It became obvious to many that its goals weren't relevant to the poor masses. Black people began to recognize that the movement had done little or nothing in the crucial areas of jobs, housing, and education. America was still maintaining a caste system with the black man trapped at the bottom.[48]

The emergence of today's militant Negro groups and the rallying slogan of "black power" are indicative of the unresolved frustrations of the Negro masses. The organizational vacuum left by the loss of support for the more moderate civil rights groups and the death of Martin Luther King in 1968 was filled by more radical organizations such as the paramilitary Black Panthers. They too follow tactics of direct action and are given wide publicity by the press much as the SCLC, CORE, and SNCC received in the previous decade. Perhaps the recent history of Negro civil rights organizations can best be described as a unidirectional unfolding process with at least two basic components. First, there is the element of their respective bases of support. In the early fifties the dominant groups—the NAACP and the Urban League—were elitist organizations actively supported by only a small percentage of Negroes and liberal whites. Then came the era of CORE, SNCC, and the SCLC. These groups attracted much broader support from the Negro community; however, they could not accurately be called mass organizations. Many of those who participated in the demonstrations of this period "were still relatively privileged in comparison to the black masses."[49] The trend toward greater inclusiveness has been further displayed in the post-Birmingham era in that the masses of urban Negroes have also become active. In retrospect it appears that each victory won, regardless of how symbolic, limited, or superficial its content, elevated the general level of Negro expectations. And as general expectations rose, more and more individual black Americans were drawn into active participation.

A second significant aspect of the historical development of civil rights organizations relates to the tactics employed by groups in pressing their demands. The trend here has been predominantly legalistic and lobby-oriented activities, to direct but nonviolent demonstrations, to violent protest. Each of these styles has been associated with a particular type of demand. The conservative tactics of the earliest period were used to gain de jure recognition of Negro rights. Nonviolent demonstrations were directed against specific discriminatory policies amenable to political solutions. The more active militance of recent years has accompanied demands for the full and equal inclusion of the Negro in American society. These changes in the tactical resources employed by civil rights interest groups have resulted in part from changes in the goals of the most active segments of the Negro community. During each of the three phases, the types of political exchange in which they have engaged and the resources they have used appear to be uniquely suited to the goals being sought by civil rights organizations. Moreover, the reluctance on the part of authorities to respond to realistic demands by providing meaningful reforms rather than mere symbolic benefits has helped to precipitate the acceleration of activism and violence. Nieburg, commenting on the violent protests of recent years, writes,

[T]he direction of the black power movement has been largely a result of the response by dominant white power groups to early low-risk tactics of nonviolence. The process by which radical militants achieved legitimacy and entered the mainstream of Negro leadership has been largely dependent on the tokenism, evasion, and resistance which discredited the legalistic approach of the NAACP and the nonviolent methods of Martin Luther King. To the shame of the white community and its leadership, riots and insurrectionary sniping are accomplishing breakthroughs that seemed impossible before the long hot summers of the early 1960s.[50]

IDEOLOGICAL GROUPS

Classification of interest groups is always a difficult task and is of necessity somewhat arbitrary. In Chapter 3 we introduced a number of typological schemes for categorizing groups according to the goods they provide their members. Not only could any one of the schemes be used to refute another, but a typology based on organizational structure could equally satisfy the need for standards of classification. By focusing here on "ideological groups" we do not intend to imply that these organizations could not be considered according to some other schema, or that some of the groups we have discussed under other headings might not as readily fit within the present one. Many voluntary associations display some degree of ideological orientation, either in their demands on the political system or in the benefits they provide their members. The distinguishing features of what we are calling "ideological groups" are their heavy reliance on purposive goods to bind their members together and their emphasis on fundamental aspects of the political culture.[51] This concern over basic values may be either one of opposition or one of support, but regardless of the qualitative nature of their orientation, the specific doctrine that each espouses takes on the character of dogma, deviation from which is considered to be heresy.[52]

Social scientists have recognized that interest group politics, as a conceptual device, does not require that we assume that all groups function to achieve some tangible interest of immediate benefit for its members. A certain type of interest group may advocate long-range goals, which, if the welfare of its participants is taken into account, have no relation to individual aspirations. Samuel Eldersveld, drawing on the ideas of Robert C. Angell, Ralph H. Turner, and Lewis M. Killian, suggests a contrast between the "ideological 'struggle group' " and the "expediency-oriented 'control movement' " based on the existence of interests whose objectives are directed toward societal improvement rather than subgroup gratification.[53]

It should be clear, however, that such a categorization does not attempt to distinguish among groups according to the existence, or lack of existence, of "self-interest." Obviously, the members of an ideological group perceive the group's particular struggle as one of crucial importance and are able to identify the successful culmination of the struggle in terms of personal satisfaction. This might be considered the attitude of the members of the Americans for Democratic Action, Committee for Constitutional Government, United World Federalists, or John Birch Society. Thus, an official of the Americans for Democratic Action, in drawing a distinction between his organization and those organizations speaking for "private or commercial interests," explained that "our competition is in the realm of ideas."[54]

But to say that members of an ideological group receive personal satisfaction from their participation in the group is clearly too general a statement for analysis. Moreover, given our present understanding of the dynamics by which groups are formed and sustained, the statement is little more than tautological. We must probe deeper and attempt to explicate the particular types of satisfaction ideological groups provide their members. Geertz, drawing from the earlier work of Sutton et al., provides an insight into the problem.

> There are currently two main approaches to the study of the social determinants of ideology: the interest theory and the strain theory. For the first, ideology is a mask and a weapon; for the second, a symptom and a remedy. In the interest theory, ideological pronouncements are seen against the background of a universal struggle for advantage; in the strain theory, against the background of a chronic effort to correct sociopsychological disequilibrium. In the one, men pursue power; in the other they flee anxiety.[55]

Geertz observes that while the interest theory approach to explaining ideological phenomena formerly was dominant among social scientists, it failed to account for "the complexity of the interaction among social, psychological, and cultural factors it itself uncovered."[56] As a result, he argues that the inclusion of the sociopsychological elements represented in strain theory is necessary for a more complete understanding of the determinants and functions of ideology. We share this conviction and would only add that whether one emphasizes the strain approach or the interest approach depends on whether one is focusing on the external exchanges of ideological groups or on their internal exchanges.

In their interactions with the political system or with other social entities, ideological groups operate much as the interest theory approach suggests; that is, they employ their ideology as a persuasive resource to back up their political demands. Since ideologies tend to carry with them a certain moral imperative stemming from their particular holistic view of reality, ideological arguments are potentially very forceful. The persuasive effects of ideological arguments in the pursuit of group demands, however, are not so much a function of their logical consistency as they are of the degree to which decision-makers share the theoretical premises on which they are based. For example, once one dogmatically adheres to the Marxist view that a capitalistic economic structure *necessarily* leads to undesirable social consequences, then arguments for socialistic economic reform can be very persuasive. The key to success, of course, is in convincing the other fellow that the world is as one's ideology says it is. Therein lies the reason for the conspicuous lack of success of radical ideological organizations in their exchanges with American political authorities, for our political elites have tended to be pragmatic and unmoved by the appeals of extremist ideologies. Why this has been the case can best be explained by turning our attention to the benefits that individuals receive by virtue of their commitment to ideological groups. In so doing we will be approaching our topic from the second of the two major theoretical traditions identified by Geertz—strain theory.

The strain to which the theory refers is both social and psychological, the former inducing the latter. Briefly, when social integration is less than complete, those sectors of society which remain unassimilated are sources of strain for the system as a whole. Since no integrating mechanism is sufficiently inclusive or flexible enough to cope with the continuity of social change, some degree of strain can be expected within any modern society. To the individual members of unassimilated social strata, the ambiguities of their status create psychological strain.

> What is viewed collectively as structural inconsistency is felt individually as personal insecurity, for it is in the experience of the social actor that the imperfections of society and contradictions of character meet and exacerbate one another. . . .
>
> Ideological thought is, then, regarded as (one sort of) response to this desperation. . . . It provides a "symbolic outlet" for emotional disturbances generated by social disequilibrium.[57]

Blau, among others, indicates that a chain effect is at work in extreme ideological phenomena.[58] He notes that when the lowest stratum of society adopts a leftist ideology in rebellion against its state of absolute deprivation, it frequently stimulates a reaction from those immediately above it in the social hierarchy, who feel their relative superiority threatened. Thus, when Negro groups in the South began to assert themselves and make demands for improvement in their position within society in the 1950s and 60s, there was the concurrent reactionary activity of the White Citizens Councils whose memberships were "usually composed of individuals from working class and lower middle class stations."[59] In short, then, the strain theory gives us an understanding of why individuals derive psychological satisfaction from membership in ideological associations. Ideology, in Erik Erikson's words, "make[s] facts amenable to ideas, and ideas to facts, in order to create a world image convincing enough to support the collective and the individual sense of identity."[60]

While the strain theory tells us that individuals seek purposive and solidary goods through associated activity and while rational models of collective behavior indicate that instrumental policies are the goals of groups, in practice we find the two frequently intertwined. As Hofstadter observes, "We have, at all times, two kinds of processes going on in inextricable connection with each other: *interest politics*, the clash of material aims and needs among various groups and blocs; and *status politics*, the class of various projective rationalizations arising from status aspirations and other personal motives."[61] Thus, ideological groups may find that the ideas they embrace fit nicely with the interests of more economically-oriented organizations. For instance, the dedication of the Committee for Constitutional Government to the goals of fighting "for economic freedom as against encroaching big government . . . for lower taxes, for reducing the number of federal employees by 600,000, for curbing the power of labor monopolies, and for restoring equality before the law to all citizens, and for ending confiscatory upper-bracket taxation, so that industry can obtain more capital to provide better tools, a higher scale of living, and more remunerative jobs for oncoming youth"[62] would make the organization a useful ally for the National Association of Manufacturers. Similarly, the Americans for Democratic Action, by advocating "the protection of civil liberties, enactment of FEPC, repeal of the Taft-Hartley Act, and a return to the Wagner Act . . . ," gains the support of labor and minority groups.[63]

THE AMERICAN RIGHT AND STATUS POLITICS

America has a long tradition of radical right-wing political activity.[64] From the nativistic Know-Nothing Party of the 1840s through the Populist Party, the Ku Klux Klan, and the McCarthyism of the 1950s to the current radical right, there is a fundamental similarity in the goals espoused, the styles of action adopted, and the psychic gratifications received by supporters. Essentially, while the scapegoat, or symbol toward which hostility is expressed, has varied, the conspiratorial outlook has remained intact. The Know-Nothings vented their frustrations on Catholics and immigrant groups, the Populists on "the 'plutocrat' millionaires" as well as recent immigrants, and the KKK on religious and racial minorities.[65] Since World War II, the scapegoats have tended to be "communist conspirators" and liberal intellectuals, although religious and racial targets have not entirely disappeared. The rapidity with which the United States has undergone fundamental social and economic changes has ensured the nearly continuous supply of threatened or displaced elements of society who seek in reactionary extremist groups relief from "a disappearing way of life, a vanishing power, a diminishing group prestige, a heart-sinking change of social scenery, a lost sense of comfort and belongingness."[66] It is interesting to observe, as Hofstadter does, that such status-oriented political activity traditionally occurs during periods of relative prosperity.[67] This is contrary to what we have seen to be the case with respect to materially-oriented groups such as labor unions, which have experienced their most rapid growth during periods of economic decline or depression. This suggests the hypothesis that severe economic conditions tend to produce corrective action which in turn results in restructured social alignments. Groups which perceive a loss in their relative status as a result of such dislocations consequently suffer the status anxiety that makes them receptive to right-wing ideological appeals. Support for Senator Joseph McCarthy, for instance, might be explained by such a theory. Immediate reaction to the growth in labor organizations, business corporations, and government following the Depression of the 1930s was delayed by World War II; however after the war, which had itself contributed in no mean way to social change, McCarthyism flourished. Trow found that support for McCarthy was positively correlated with fear of both large labor unions and giant corporations. He notes that McCarthy expressed for these people ". . . their fear and mistrust of bigness, and the slick and subversive ideas that come out of the cities and the big institutions to erode old ways and faiths."[68]

It would be foolish, however, to argue that all right-wing organizations grow directly out of the repercussions of economic declines. Other forces can just as readily lead to status strain. That the depression hypothesis is so obvious no doubt results from the prominent and pervasive effects of the economy on all aspects of life. When status strain accompanies severe economic conditions, as it does during depressions, frustrations tend to be directed against the material manifestations of the problem. The salience of economic institutions and practices makes them visible targets for protest, which tends to take the form of instrumental demands that conform to the nature of the targets. Social strain that occurs during times of prosperity, however, has no such manifest target. Hence, frustrations are vented against symbolic scapegoats and demands are articulated in terms of ideological values. The John Birch Society, founded in 1958, is an excellent example of a strain-induced right-wing ideological group which arose during a time of relative prosperity and was not formed in direct response to socioeconomic restructuring following a depression.

The Birch Society, in Westin's words, represents a "nihilistic plea for the repeal of industrialism and the abolition of international politics."[69] Its image of the surrounding environment is totally con-spiratorial—so conspiratorial that it is reluctant to trust any govern-ment institution, voluntary association, religious institution, the mass media, or the schools or courts to be free of communist infiltra-tion. According to the *Blue Book*, the official statement of the posture of the Society, the communists are "taking us over by a process so gradual and insidious that Soviet rule is slipped over so far on the American people, before they ever realize it is happening, that they can no longer resist the Communist conspiracy as free citizens, but can resist the Communist conspiracy only by themselves becoming conspirators against the established government."[70]

Since most of the institutions of society are not to be relied on, there is nothing to be achieved unless we contemplate a form of action more basic than the mere election to public office of indi-viduals sympathetic with the goals of the Society. The political sys-tem, and especially politicians, are of only ephemeral value. Robert Welch, founder of the John Birch Society, writes, "I am thoroughly convinced . . . that we cannot count on politicians, political leader-ship, or even political action except as part of something much deeper and broader, to save us."[71] In rejecting the normal "playing the political game," the Society operates under a more authoritarian structure than most of the interest groups whose goals are more limited. This is not to deny the role of the minority in all organiza-tions, or to deny that internal conflict is always present, but to suggest that, in the extremist organization, the role of the leader is more pronounced. The Society is described as an "organic entity" which is loyal to, and under the direction of, a "dynamic personal leader." Welch often speaks of the desirability of the "hardboiled, dictatorial, and dynamic boss"—the person who, although not neces-sarily desirous of undertaking the strenuous task of substantial revision, is placed in the position of being the most qualified candi-date for the job by reason of the seriousness of the circumstances: "It is the imminence and the horror of this danger which drives me to so desperate a course as to offer myself as a personal leader in this fight, and to ask you to follow that leadership. It is not because I want so frightening a responsibility. . . . It is simply that, under the pressures of time and the exigencies of our need, you have no other choice, and neither do I."[72] Thus, the founder of the John Birch Society describes himself in terms similar to the "Fascist agitators" examined by Lowenthal and Guterman. They write of this type of leader for whom ". . . forces stronger and more imperious than his own will push him to leadership."[73]

With its remote objectives likely to be achieved only by dedicated fanaticism, there is no room for dissenters. The Society is conceived to be a monolithic body which will operate under "completely authoritative control at all levels." Welch makes dedication fundamental by saying "those members who cease to feel the necessary degree of loyalty can either resign or will be put out before they build up any splintering following of their own inside the Society. . . . Whenever differences of opinion become translated into a lack of loyal support, we shall have short cuts for eliminating both without going through any congress of so-called democratic processes. *Otherwise, Communist infiltrators could bog us down in interminable disagreements, schisms, and feuds before we ever became seriously effective.*"[74] Such statements indicate the personalized, authoritarian leadership structures that extreme ideological groups tend to develop. The leader cannot afford to delegate power or permit competing centers of authority to develop within the organization for fear of sowing the seeds of infiltration and subversion.[75] So complete is the authority of the central office that when supporters apply for membership in the Society they "abjectly fill out a membership form that is a resignation signed in advance, agreeing when they join that the Society can drop them at any time and without any necessary explanation for doing so."[76] Welch has not hesitated to purge those "heretics" who have deviated from the official line.

Structurally, the flow of communication descends from the top to the bottom. Its local chapters are kept small, usually made up of from ten to twenty members, and each chapter is assigned a leader from the national headquarters in Belmont, Massachusetts. Above the chapter leaders are coordinators, who are also expected to keep "strict and careful control on what every chapter is doing, and even every member of every chapter so far as the work of the John Birch Society is concerned."[77] The content of the downward communications flow is concerned with the undertaking of specific activities by local chapters. In contrast, the upward flow of communications consists of "members' monthly memos," a device whereby each member reports to the national headquarters on his or her activities.[78] Thus, a careful eye is kept on the members of the organization in keeping with the authoritarian structure on which it was founded. In a sense, then, the participants in the Society are not typical of the members of a voluntary association in that their function is that of "agent." The agent is expected to perform in a manner satisfactory to his immediate superiors or be expelled.[79]

During the early and mid-1960s the Birch Society experienced rapid growth. In 1962 its membership stood at approximately 60,000 and its income was estimated in the neighborhood of $1,600,000. It supported a weekly staff payroll of $12,000.[80] By the end of 1965 membership was approaching 100,000 and an annual income of $6 million was supporting a vastly expanded staff which was paid about $40,000 per week.[81] One major stimulant to the rapid expansion of the Society's support base during 1964 and 1965 was the 1964 presidential election. The clear ideological appeal of Goldwater caused many previously dormant political conservatives to become active in support of his candidacy and of right-wing causes in general. Among such persons were a number of well-educated individuals to whom the evocative rhetoric and simplistic conspiracy theories normally associated with extreme ideological groups held little appeal. To attract these potential members, the Birch Society capitalized on the legitimacy it could win by associating itself with Goldwater's candidacy. Commenting on its newfound legitimacy Epstein and Forster write,

> At the Republican convention, the Birch Society covered itself with a kind of respectability. Birchers misused the campaign as a vehicle to spread their own political propaganda and to recruit new members.
>
> Many Americans were swept into the Birch ranks on the emotional tide of the campaign period. Many others joined after Election Day, when the frustration of defeat made them ripe for recruitment and when the Birch Society's post-election appeal to this group was summed up in the simple slogan: "*Now* Will You Join the John Birch Society?"[82]

The concern over respectability has had qualitative as well as quantitative effects on Birch Society membership. It has given the organization a character rather unique among right-wing ideological groups. Normally, as we have observed, such organizations appeal to lower-middle-class individuals who feel status strain as a result of challenges from those lower in the social structure. The Birch Society, however, has attracted supporters from relatively high social strata. Although reliable data are difficult to obtain, several studies of the social composition of the Birch Society membership have been made.[83] Grupp, for instance, reports that Birchers tend to have attained a higher level of education than the national average, are predominantly recruited from among the ranks of business and professional persons, and have appreciably higher incomes than the average white American families.[84] However, he also points out that although 64% of them have attended college, fully 62% of the college-educated Birch Society members attended low-quality institutions.[85] Moreover, there is a much higher rate of discrepancy between educational attainment and occupational status than exists in the population at large.[86] The rate of occupational status not being as high as educational attainment would indicate is twice as great among Birchers, providing some indication of the source of status frustration felt by some members.

Lipset and Raab provide additional insights into the nature of sociopsychological strain that leads to support for the Society. They point out that the principal occupations of members and of leaders are those that would place them in the upper-middle class. Many are executives of moderately large business and industrial corporations (frequently family-owned), physicians, and military officers (often retired).[87] Such persons would appear to feel little immediate threat to their status from those below them in the social hierarchy. Bell, however, argues that the changes currently occurring in American society—those that create strain for "the old middle class"—are not those that result in dislocations along class lines.

> The most pervasive changes are those involving the structural relations between class position and power. Clearly, today, political position rather than wealth, and technical skill rather than property have become the bases from which power is wielded.[88]

The evidence indicates that Birch Society members enjoy both property and class status. What they lack, however, is the power and autonomy that they have come to expect as a direct result of their socioeconomic position. Organized labor, larger corporations, and big government have usurped much of the decision-making power that once was held by the top executives of moderately large corporations. Moreover, within the corporation itself, technological and managerial experts provide much of the leadership that was previously exercised by only the highest executive officers. Commenting on persons who perceive their actual power to be less than what they think is commensurate with their station in life, Lipset and Raab write,

> ... they are among the out-groups in the larger national society. The federal government, the mass media, the major national churches, oppose much of what they believe. Most of them have been involved in efforts to change the direction of American politics, but without success. In a real sense, these are the leaders of the marginal provincial power structures of the nation. And they are willing to go along with, or completely accept the conspiratorial world outlook of the Birch Society. Through the Society, they hope to turn the clock back, to recreate a world in which the tendencies toward bureaucracy and centralization of power are reversed.[89]

Many physicians and high-ranking military officers likewise have cause to feel powerless to combat what they perceive to be undesirable national tendencies. Physicians are threatened by what they see to be a trend toward the imposition of socialized medicine, while military officers see internationalism and pacifism as direct threats to patriotism, undermining "the belief that military strength is the best way to deter war and to assure that national interests are maintained."[90]

Each of these occupational categories contains relatively wealthy, high-status persons whose values harken back to earlier days of laissez-faire conservatism. They see incongruities between their status and their power to implement policies dictated by their values. The frustrations that result make them uniquely susceptible to the benefits provided by ideological organizations such as the John Birch Society. There they find solidarity with other like-minded individuals, purpose in the symbolic rhetoric and cabalistic atmosphere of the organization, and psychological release for their frustrations against the "communist" scapegoats so readily provided by the organization. The outward manifestations of Birch-style extremism are similar to, albeit somewhat more refined than, those traditionally displayed by right-wing ideological groups in America. We would argue, however, that the Society represents a significant departure from its predecessors in that it is tailored to appeal to a disaffected upper class of society rather than a threatened lower class.

The future success of the John Birch Society, or of any similar organization, for that matter, will depend on the existence of politically frustrated members of the economic and social elites in America. If we can call the Birch-style group one which suffers from "power strain," then the traditional class-oriented rightist ideological group is one which suffers from "status strain." Status strain will exist as long as there are horizontal cleavages within the social structure, for just as surely as economic and technological changes will continue to take place, they will have their social ramifications. Until such time as de facto social equality exists, those ramifications will have a threatening, anxiety-producing effect on sectors of American society which suffer the relative deprivation that results.

NOTES

[1]Samuel J. Eldersveld, "American Interest Groups: A Survey of Research and Some Implications for Theory and Method," *Interest Groups on Four Continents*, ed. Henry W. Ehrmann (Pittsburgh: University of Pittsburgh Press, 1958), pp. 192–93; and Harry M. Scoble, *Ideology and Electoral Action: A Comparative Case Study of the National Committee for an Effective Congress* (San Francisco: Chandler Publishing Company, 1967), pp. 17–18.

[2]Nathan Glazer and Daniel Patrick Moynihan, *Beyond the Melting Pot* (Cambridge, Mass.: The MIT Press, 1963), p. 303.

[3]*Ibid.*, p. 313.

[4]Robert E. Lane, *Political Life* (New York: The Free Press, 1959), p. 235.

[5]Mary E. Goodman, *Race Awareness in Young Children* (Reading, Mass.: Addison-Wesley Publishing Co., Inc., 1952).

[6]Marian Radke Yarrow, "Personality Development and Minority Group Membership," in Marshall Sklare, ed., *The Jews* (New York: The Free Press, 1958), p. 455.

[7]Arnold and Caroline Rose, *America Divided* (New York: Alfred A. Knopf, Inc., 1949), p. 178.

[8]Gordon W. Allport, *The Nature of Prejudice* (Garden City, N.Y.: Doubleday & Company, Inc., 1958), p. 8.

[9]Louis Wirth, "The Present Position of Minorities in the United States," in Elizabeth Wirth Marvick and Albert J. Reiss, Jr., eds., *Community Life and Social Policy* (Chicago: University of Chicago Press, 1956), p. 228.

[10]Wirth, "The Problem of Minority Groups," *ibid.*, p. 243.

[11]Allport, *op. cit.*, pp. 220–22.

[12]Lane, *op. cit.*, p. 247.

[13]William I. Thomas and Florian Znaniecki, *The Polish Peasant in Europe and America* (Boston: Richard G. Badger, 1918), Vol. 5, p. 113. Cited in Lane, *op. cit.*, p. 247.

[14]Rose, *op. cit.*, pp. 201–4. See also Morton Grodzins, *The Loyal and Disloyal* (Chicago: University of Chicago Press, 1956).

[15]Harry S Truman, *Years of Trial and Hope* (Garden City, N.Y.: Doubleday & Company, Inc., 1956), Vol. 2, pp. 158, 160. See also Louis L. Gerson, "Immigrant Groups and Foreign Policy," in George L. Anderson, ed., *Issues and Conflicts: Studies in Twentieth Century American Diplomacy* (Lawrence: University of Kansas Press, 1959), pp. 171–92.

[16]Rose, *op. cit.*, p. 58.

[17]Richard E. Morgan, *The Politics of Religious Conflict* (New York: Western Publishing Co., Inc., 1968), p. 61.

[18]*Ibid.*, p. 62.

[19]Murray S. Stedman, Jr., *Religion and Politics in America* (New York: Harcourt, Brace & World, Inc., 1964), pp. 92–93.

[20]*Ibid.*, p. 92.

[21]Morgan, *op. cit.*, pp. 63–64.

[22]A. L. Severson, "Nationality and Religion in Newspaper Ads," *American Journal of Sociology*, XLIV (Jan. 1939), p. 545.

[23]Rose, *op. cit.*, p. 198.

[24]Will Maslow, "The Legal Defense of Religious Liberty—The Strategy and Tactics of the American Jewish Congress" (paper presented to the American Political Science Association Meeting, Sept. 1961), p. 1.

[25]Donald S. Strong, *Organized Anti-Semitism in America* (Washington, D.C.: American Council on Public Affairs, 1941), pp. 146–47.

[26]Maslow, *op. cit.*, p. 6.

[27]*Ibid.*, p. 6. See also Solomon Sutker, "The Role of Social Clubs in the Atlanta Jewish Community," in Sklare, *op. cit.*, pp. 262–70.

[28]Maslow, *op. cit.*, p. 6.

[29]Truman, *The Governmental Process*, p. 156.

[30]Robin M. Williams, Jr., *The Reduction of Intergroup Tensions* (New York: Social Science Research Council, 1947), p. 61.

[31]*Ibid.*

[32]Gunnar Myrdal, *An American Dilemma* (New York: Harper & Row, Publishers, 1944), pp. 720–35.

[33]Booker T. Washington, *Up From Slavery* (Garden City, N.Y.: Doubleday & Company, Inc., 1905).

[34]Myrdal, *op. cit.*, p. 720.

[35]Kurt Lewin, *Resolving Social Conflicts* (New York: Harper & Row, Publishers, 1948), pp. 195–96.

[36]Roy Wilkins, "The Role of the NAACP in the Desegregation Process," *Social Problems*, II (Apr. 1955), p. 201.

[37]Herbert Garfinkle, *When Negroes March* (New York: The Free Press, 1959).

[38]It has been reported that "ten years after *Brown v. Board of Education of Topeka*, only about 2 percent of the Negroes in the South had actually been integrated; the other 98 percent remained in segregated schools." (Thomas R. Dye and L. Harmon Zeigler, *The Irony of Democracy: An Uncommon Introduction to American Politics* [Belmont, Calif.: Wadsworth Publishing Company, Inc., 1970], p. 296.)

[39]Eric Lincoln, *The Black Muslims in America* (Boston: Beacon Press, 1961), p. 146.

[40]Kenneth B. Clark, "The Civil Rights Movement: Momentum and Organization," *The Negro American*, eds. Talcott Parsons and Kenneth B. Clark (Boston: Beacon Press, 1967), p. 608.

[41]Dye and Zeigler, *op. cit.*, p. 298.

[42]Michael Lipsky, "Protest as a Political Resource," *American Political Science Review*, LXII (Dec. 1968), p. 1149.

[43]Daniel Patrick Moynihan, "Employment, Income, and the Ordeal of the Negro Family," in Parsons and Clark, *op. cit.*, p. 134.

[44]See William Brink and Louis Harris, *Black and White* (New York: Simon and Schuster, 1966), pp. 20–23, and Charles E. Silberman, *Crisis in Black and White* (New York: Random House, 1964), pp. 140–44.

[45]Clark, *op. cit.*, p. 612.

[46]Dye and Zeigler, *op. cit.*, p. 289.

[47]Arthur Frazier and Virgil Roberts, "A Discourse on Black Nationalism," *American Behavioral Scientist*, XII (March–April 1969), p. 53.

[48]*Ibid.*

[49]Dye and Zeigler, *op. cit.*, p. 298.

[50]H. L. Nieburg, *Political Violence: The Behavioral Process* (New York: St. Martin's Press, Inc., 1969), p. 148.

[51]For excellent analyses of the various ways in which the concept of ideology has been employed by social scientists, see David W. Minar, "Ideology and Political Behavior," *Midwest Journal of Political Science*, V (Nov. 1961), pp. 317–31; David E. Apter, ed., *Ideology and Discontent* (New York: The Free Press, 1964); and

Giovanni Sartori, "Politics, Ideology, and Belief Systems," *American Political Science Review*, LXIII (June 1969), pp. 398–411.

[52]Peter Blau, *Exchange and Power in Social Life* (New York: John Wiley & Sons, Inc., 1964), p. 239, and Lewis Coser, *The Functions of Social Conflict* (New York: The Free Press, 1956), pp. 67–72, 111–19.

[53]Samuel J. Eldersveld, "American Interest Groups: A Survey of Research and Some Implications for Theory and Method," in Ehrmann, *op. cit.*, p. 181.

[54]House Select Committee on Lobbying Activities, *Hearings*, Americans for Democratic Action, 81st Cong., 2nd Sess., 1950 (Washington, D.C.: Government Printing Office, 1950), pp. 3, 4.

[55]Clifford Geertz, "Ideology as a Culture System," *Ideology and Discontent*, ed. David E. Apter (New York: The Free Press, 1964), p. 52, citing F. X. Sutton, S. E. Harris, C. Kayson, and J. Tobin, *The American Business Creed* (Cambridge, Mass.: Harvard University Press, 1956), pp. 11–12, 303–10.

[56]*Ibid.*, p. 53.

[57]*Ibid.*, p. 54.

[58]Blau, *op. cit.*, pp. 240–42.

[59]James W. Vander Zanden, "The Southern White Resistance Movement to Integration" (unpublished Ph.D. dissertation, Department of Sociology, University of North Carolina, 1958), p. 311, quoted in Seymour Martin Lipset and Earl Raab, *The Politics of Unreason: Right Wing Extremism in America, 1790–1970* (New York: Harper & Row, Publishers, 1970), p. 277.

[60]Erik H. Erikson, *Young Man Luther: A Study in Psychoanalysis and History* (New York: W. W. Norton & Company, Inc., 1958), p. 22.

[61]Richard Hofstadter, "The Pseudo-Conservative Revolt," *The Radical Right*, ed. Daniel Bell (Garden City, N.Y.: Doubleday & Company, Inc., 1963), p. 71.

[62]House Select Committee on Lobbying Activities, *Hearings*, Committee for Constitutional Government, 81st Cong., 2nd Sess., 1950 (Washington, D.C.: Government Printing Office, 1950), p. 63.

[63]House Select Committee on Lobbying Activities, *Hearings*, Americans for Democratic Action (Washington, D.C.: Government Printing Office, 1950), p. 5.

[64]Excellent examinations of rightist extremism are contained in Bell, *op. cit.*; Lipset and Raab, *op. cit.*; and Robert A. Schoenberger, ed., *The American Right Wing: Readings in Political Behavior* (New York: Holt, Rinehart and Winston, Inc., 1969).

[65]Lipset, "The Sources of the Radical Right," in Bell, *op. cit.*, pp. 261–62.

[66]Lipset and Raab, *op. cit.*, p. 429.

[67]Hofstadter, in Bell, *op. cit.*, p. 71. Lipset also makes this point in Bell, *op. cit.*, p. 263.

[68]Martin Trow, "Small Businessmen, Political Tolerance, and McCarthy," *American Journal of Sociology*, LVIV (Nov. 1958), p. 278.

[69]Alan Westin, "The John Birch Society: Fundamentalism on the Right," *Commentary*, XXXII (Aug. 1961), p. 95.

[70]*The Blue Book of the John Birch Society* (Fifth Printing, 1961), p. 29 (Belmont, Mass.: John Birch Society).

[71]*Ibid.*, p. 121.

[72]*Ibid.*, pp. 116, 117, 170.

[73]Leo Lowenthal and Norbert Guterman, "Self Portrait of the Fascist Agitator," in Alvin W. Gouldner, ed., *Studies in Leadership* (New York: Harper & Row, Publishers, 1950), p. 87.

[74]*The Blue Book of the John Birch Society*, pp. 161–62.

[75]Edward A. Shils, "Authoritarianism 'Right' and 'Left,'" *Introductory Readings in Political Behavior*, ed. S. Sidney Ulmer (Chicago: Rand McNally & Company, 1961), p. 30.

[76]Benjamin R. Epstein and Arnold Forster, *Report on the John Birch Society 1966* (New York: Vintage Books, 1966), p. 3.

[77]*The Blue Book of the John Birch Society*, p. 165.

[78]Westin, *op. cit.*, p. 99.

[79]See Philip Selznick, *The Organizational Weapon* (New York: McGraw-Hill Book Company, Inc., 1952) for a discussion of the role of the agent.

[80]Alan F. Westin, "The John Birch Society: 'Radical Right' and 'Extreme Left' in the Political Context of Post World War II," in Bell, *op. cit.*, p. 202.

[81]Epstein and Forster, *op. cit.*, pp. 1, 88.

[82]*Ibid.*, pp. 4–5.

[83]One of the more comprehensive studies of this type is reported in Fred W. Grupp, Jr., "The Political Perspectives of Birch Society Members," in Schoenberger, *op. cit.*, pp. 83–118. Also see Lipset and Raab, *op. cit.*, pp. 288–333.

[84]Grupp, *op. cit.*, pp. 93–97.

[85]*Ibid.*, p. 95.

[86]*Ibid.*

[87]Lipset and Raab, *op. cit.*, pp. 309–17. They also point out that only policemen constitute a sizable lower-middle-class constituency for the Birch Society.

[88]Bell, "The Dispossessed," in Bell, *op. cit.*, pp. 16–17.

[89]Lipset and Raab, *op. cit.*, p. 311.

[90]*Ibid.*, p. 315.

Index